COURT OFFICER

Senior Court Officer

Court Clerk

E.P. Steinberg

MACMILLAN • USA

Eighth Edition

Macmillan General Reference
A Simon & Schuster Macmillan Company
1633 Broadway
New York, NY 10019-6785

An Arco Book

MACMILLAN is a registered trademark of Macmillan, Inc.
ARCO is a registered trademark of Prentice-Hall, Inc.

Library of Congress Cataloging-in-Publication Data

Steinberg, Eve P.
    Court officer : senior court officer, court clerk / E.P.
Steinberg. -- 8th ed.
        p.   cm.
    At head of title: Arco.
    "An Arco book."
    ISBN 0-02-860012-6
    1. Courts--New York (State)--Officials and employees-
-Examinations, questions, etc. I. Title.
KFN5979.Z9S74 1995
347.747'016--dc20
[347.470716]   94-36241
                                                         CIP

Manufactured in the United States of America

10 9 8 7 6 5 4

CONTENTS

INTRODUCTION

There must be order in the court. Without order, witnesses cannot testify, attorneys cannot cross-examine, jurors cannot concentrate, and judges cannot deliberate. The title and additional duties of the person who keeps order in the court vary from system to system and from jurisdiction to jurisdiction. Whether the person is titled court officer, bailiff, court attendant, courtroom deputy, or U.S. Marshal, he or she serves a vital role in the American justice system. Court officers under the supervision of and alongside their superior officers, senior court officers, and court clerks, control the atmosphere and decorum of the courtroom, maintain the integrity of documents and exhibits, ensure the security of juries, and see that they have optimum conditions under which to deliberate, and generally respond to the wishes of the judge.

Since the work of court officers is so vital to the functioning of the court, the position is a very well paid one. In addition, because of the need for constant coverage while one officer may be on an errand, court officers always serve in pairs or even in groups of more than two. Thus, the position offers less potential for physical danger than most other law enforcement work. The position of court officer is highly competitive. A passing score on the qualifying examination is not enough. A high score is essential to earn appointment as a court officer. Likewise, high scores are mandatory on the promotional exams for advancement to the titles of senior court officer and court clerk. This book is geared to help you earn those high scores.

The book begins with job descriptions and with official job announcements. Read these first. Find out what the jobs entail and how the court system itself defines the job qualifications and the nature of the exams. Then go on to our suggestions for successful test-taking.

Part One is devoted to the court officer exam. This part begins with help on specific test topics. Your court officer exam will most surely test, in some way, your powers of observation and memory. It will also undoubtedly measure your reading comprehension and interpretation and your ability to apply information gained from that reading to actual scenarios. There may be questions that test your attention to details and your facility in working with tabular information and numbers. Some court officer exams may include questions on grammar and writing ability.

Subject areas such as grammar and arithmetic cannot be taught over a short period of time, so your knowledge in these areas depends upon years of cumulative learning. However, there are some basic guidelines that, with practice, can help you answer certain kinds of questions with greater skill and confidence. For instance, even if you are a detail-minded person, a systematic method of comparing names and numbers can assist you in answering the clerical checking questions that appear on many court officer exams. Then, there are special ways of looking at pictures or of reading descriptions of events that can help you notice details on which you are likely to be tested. And, you can learn how to approach reading passages so as to ferret out the meaning, interpret the writer's point of view, and relate the content of the passage to facts and situations. The three chapters How to Answer Clerical Checking Questions, Observation and Memory, and How to Answer Reading Questions will give you valuable training in these three areas. Study these chapters before you attempt any of the model court officer exams and return to them as needed.

The four model exams are not actual exams. They are closely patterned on recent actual exams, exposing you to the kinds of questions asked and helping you learn to pace yourself and build confidence. Many of the questions have appeared on previous exams. Take each model exam under "battle conditions," as if you were taking the actual exam. Take the model exams in a quiet place, free from distraction, making sure to time each exam accurately. Do not look at the answers until you have completed the exam. When you finish, check your answers against the correct answers and score your exam. Note the areas in which you made the most errors. Were you careless? Do you need to devote more time to developing skill in observation and memory or in reading? Read the explanations of the answers to the questions you got wrong. Learn the reasons for your errors and think about how you might avoid similar errors on subsequent model exams and on the actual exam. Then read the explanations of the answers to the questions you got right. You might pick up new information and may gain further insight into the reasoning that goes into the questions.

Part Two deals with the promotional titles of senior court officer and court clerk. This part offers definitions of terms that you must master for the promotional exams. It also includes selected large portions of the laws from which promotional questions are drawn. The book concludes with questions taken from previous promotional exams and with explanations of all correct answers.

JOB DESCRIPTIONS

COURT OFFICER (Bailiff, Court Attendant)

Court officers are responsible for maintaining courtroom security and protecting the judge, jury, and other participants during hearings and trials. Under the supervision of a judge or court administrator, court officers take charge of and escort juries, transfer prisoners, deliver case files, and perform various related services.

The work of a court officer involves providing general services in the operation of a court. It includes maintaining order, calling defendants and witnesses to the stand, and notifying attorneys and other interested parties during trial. Some of their time is spent in delivering court minutes, law books, supplies, forms, and similar items necessary for use by the judge and court staff. They also perform other errands inside and outside the court and generally attend to the personal needs of the judge. When not attending court sessions, they may perform incidental clerical tasks such as filling out forms and operating a copying machine to duplicate court calendars.

Court officers start the day by inspecting the courtroom for cleanliness, orderliness, and proper heat, light, and ventilation. Court sessions are opened by announcing the entrance of the judge. Order in the court is maintained, and jurors, witnesses, attorneys, news reporters, and spectators are seated in specific areas of the courtroom. Persons disturbing the court's proceedings are ejected.

When necessary, food, lodging, and transportation are arranged for jurors, errands are run, and personal needs of jurors are taken care of when a jury is held overnight or longer. A court officer is responsible for the security of the jury during deliberations and, when they extend overnight, prevents jurors' having outside communication, thus avoiding a mistrial. Court officers escort jurors in and out of the courtroom before, after, and during trials; they not only accompany jurors to all meals but remain during the meal.

Job Requirements

To become a court officer, graduation from high school, or the equivalent, is required by the courts. In most states, appointment depends on passing a written and physical examination. The duties of these workers require the ability to understand and follow written instructions and to express themselves clearly and concisely, both orally and in writing. Tact and courtesy are also needed to deal effectively with the public, attorneys, witnesses, prisoners, and jurors. In addition, it is important to have knowledge of, or be experienced in, office practices, court procedures, and legal terminology and forms. In some courts, Court Officers are also expected to be skilled in the use of firearms.

Opportunities

Courts are expanding to keep pace with the need for their services, owing to the rising number of offenders and the desire of the courts and the public to speed up the handling of cases. The size and number of courts have also increased over the past few years, and this growth is expected to continue.

Opportunities for court officers exist in the local, state, and federal courts, and employment is expected to increase as fast as the court system expands. Court officers employed in the larger courts may advance to supervisory positions, such as Senior Court Officer or Court Clerk.

COURT CLERK

Court clerks serve as clerical assistants to circuit and other court judges, as supervisors of court clerks, and often as court administrators. They attend sessions of the court and enter information in the records about court proceedings, including witnesses' names, requests for rulings, verdicts reached, and other important facts. All documents brought to the court, including complaints, answers, attachments, executions, garnishments, orders to show cause, and restraining orders are received by the court clerk who makes sure that all requests affecting the progress of a case are properly handled.

The court clerk assists in preparation of the docket or calendar of cases to be called depending on type of crime, priorities, or direction of the judge. All legal documents submitted to the court are examined for adherence to regulations. Case folders are prepared, legal documents concerned with the operation of the court are posted, filed, or routed elsewhere. Sometimes names of prospective jurors are picked, the oath administered to witnesses and jurors, and subpoenas and court orders are issued. The duties of court clerks also include explaining procedures about forms to parties in a case, contacting witnesses and attorneys to obtain information for the court, and instructing individuals about dates to appear in court. Case disposition, court orders, and judge's rulings are recorded and payment of fees arranged, and sometimes collected.

Documents are checked not only for completeness of information but to determine general case category and to assign a docket number. The need for signatures on documents is determined, action is taken to obtain signatures, and documents are stamped with the official court seal.

Other job duties include recording, by hand, typewriter, or computer, case-identification data, and receipt of documents or court records. The clerks file cards, documents, and records according to date received, or to alphabetical or numerical filing systems. In smaller courts, the court clerks type jury lists, prepare and mail jury notices and assist in other functions concerned with receipts and expenditures.

Job Requirements

High school graduation or the equivalent, and 2 years of court officer or other court system experience is required. All court clerks must have knowledge of court procedures and policies, as well as of legal documents and laws. Some knowledge of court organization, its operations, functions, and scope of authority is also necessary. It is important that these workers have a good command of English and be able to deal effectively with legal personnel and the public.

Opportunities

Opportunities for court clerks exist in the local, state, and federal courts. Because of the rising number of offenders, courts are increasing both in number and size to keep pace not only with the need for services but to speed up handling of cases. This growth is expected to continue.

Court clerks, especially in the larger courts, may advance to the position of Chief Court Clerk.

ANNOUNCEMENTS

Career Opportunities in the New York State Unified Court System

Court Officer

THE OFFICE OF COURT ADMINISTRATION ANNOUNCES AN OPEN-COMPETITIVE EXAMINATION

TITLE

Court Officer   Exam Number: 45-612

Applicants Please Note: At the present time, there are approximately 950 Court Officer positions. All these positions are currently filled on a permanent basis. We expect to appoint approximately 150 Court Officers per year during the anticipated 4-year life of the eligible list.

LOCATION OF POSITIONS

The Court Officer title exists in the Civil, Criminal, Family, and Surrogate's Courts in New York City and the District, Family, and Surrogate's Courts in Nassau, Suffolk, and Westchester counties.

LOCATION OF TEST CENTERS

This examination will be held exclusively in New York City, Albany, Binghamton, Brentwood, Buffalo, Hicksville, Riverhead, Rochester, Syracuse, and White Plains.

STARTING SALARY

This title is graded at JG-16. Appointees may receive additional annual location pay.

MINIMUM QUALIFICATIONS

At the time of appointment, a Court Officer candidate must be at least 18 years old and possess a high school diploma or its equivalent. Candidates must be legally eligible to carry firearms. An unpardoned felon is ineligible to carry firearms under federal law. 18 U.S.C. section 1202 (A) (1). No candidate will be eligible for appointment if he or she has ever been convicted of a felony.

APPLICATION FEE

A $10 money order filing fee must accompany your application.

CITIZENSHIP

Candidates must be citizens of the United States at the time of appointment.

RESIDENCE

Candidates must be residents of New York State for one year prior to the date of the examination as well as at the time of appointment.

DISTINGUISHING FEATURES OF WORK

Court Officers are responsible for maintaining order and providing security in court facilities. They work under the direct supervision of security supervisors and court clerks. Court Officers are peace officers, required to wear uniforms, and may be authorized to carry firearms. They perform clerical duties while handling court documents and forms, may coordinate the activities of other court security personnel, and perform related duties.

SCOPE OF WRITTEN MEDICAL, PHYSICAL ABILITY, AND PSYCHOLOGICAL EXAMINATIONS

Candidates who are successful on the written portion of the examination will be called, in order of their rank on the eligible list, to qualify on the medical, physical ability, and psychological examinations and undergo a background investigation.

WRITTEN EXAMINATION

The written examination will be multiple-choice and will assess a candidate's ability to:

1. *Read, Understand, and Interpret Written Material*—Candidates will be presented with brief reading selections followed by questions relating to the selections. All of the information required to answer the questions will be provided in the selections; candidates will not be required to have any special knowledge relating to the content area covered in the selections.

2. *Remember Facts and Information*—Candidates will be provided with a series of pictures and/or a description of an event or incident. After a brief period of time to review and study the description and/or pictures, the description and/or pictures will be removed from the candidates. Candidates will later be asked questions about the facts involved in the event or incident.

3. *Apply Facts and Information to Given Situations*—Candidates will be provided with facts and information and will be asked questions that require the application of these facts and information to specific actions that should be taken in a given situation.

4. *Recognize and Size Up Written Information*—Candidates will be presented with written information designed to assess skills and abilities necessary to quickly and accurately recognize and size up verbal and numerical materials, to perceive differences in small details, and to classify and code information presented under timed conditions. Candidates will not be required to have any special knowledge of the content of the material presented.

MEDICAL EXAMINATION

Each candidate is required to be free of any medical impairment that would jeopardize his or her safety, health, or ability to carry out effectively the duties of the position. Candidates are required to meet the medical requirements both at the time of the medical examination and at the time of appointment. A partial list of the medical standards is shown below:

1. *Hearing*—Each candidate must be able to pass an audiometric test of hearing acuity in both ears. The average hearing loss in the voice frequency ranges of 500, 1,000, 2,000, and 3,000 Hz should not be greater than 30 decibels. Also, for the frequency ranges of 4,000, 6,000, and 8,000 Hz, the average hearing loss should not be greater than 35 decibels.

2. *Vision*—Each candidate must have at least 20/40 vision in each eye and have at least 20/30 vision using both eyes (corrective lenses or glasses are permitted). However, each candidate must have at least 20/70 vision using both eyes without correction. The visual fields must not be less than 145, and color vision is also required. Both near and far vision are tested. Vision will be tested with and without corrective lenses, including contacts.

3. *Cardiovascular System*—Candidates must be free of impairment due to organic heart disease resulting from failure of myocardial function and impairment of coronary circulatory function. Candidates are examined for hypertensive vascular disease and for vascular diseases affecting the extremities. Blood pressure should not exceed 146/90. Candidates will be evaluated on an individual basis relevant to the physical demands of the job.

4. *Alcohol or Drug Abuse*—Candidates must not be dependent on or abuse alcohol or drugs. Candidates are required to submit to a comprehensive drug-screening evaluation.

PHYSICAL EXAMINATION

Each candidate will be required to qualify on a series of physical tests designed to assess a candidate's ability to perform the physically demanding tasks required by the job. Minimum qualifying scores are required for each of the following five categories: strength/muscular endurance, coordination/equilibrium, arm–hand steadiness, flexibility, and stamina/aerobic fitness.

PSYCHOLOGICAL EXAMINATION

Each candidate will be required to undergo a psychological assessment designed to test for emotional or psychological problems that might interfere with effectively carrying out the duties of the position.

BACKGROUND INVESTIGATION

Each candidate will be investigated with respect to employment history, educational qualifications, military service record, arrest and summons record, and other pertinent factors deemed important to the performance of required job duties.

Important Information to All Candidates

APPLICATION FORMS

HOW TO FILE FOR THE EXAMINATION

A $10.00 application fee is being charged to file for this examination. The application must be accompanied by a money order made payable to N.Y.S. Office of Court Administration. Neither checks nor cash will be accepted. The applications must be post-marked no later than the close of filing and mailed to:

> State of New York, Unified Court System
> Office of Court Administration
> P.O. Box 1879
> Albany, New York 12201

Applications and fees not submitted in accordance with the above requirements will be returned unprocessed.

HOW TO OBTAIN AN APPLICATION PACKAGE

By Mail—To obtain an application by mail, you must submit a self-addressed, 9" × 12" envelope with $1.45 postage (five 29-cent stamps) to:

> State of New York
> Office of Court Administration
> P.O. Box 2951
> Church Street Station
> New York, New York 10008

Only one (1) application package will be sent for each self-addressed stamped envelope received. Requests for application packages which do not have the correct amount of postage and/or are received less than ten days before the close of filing cannot be processed.

EEO DATA COLLECTION FORM

Please complete the buff-color EEO data collection sheet in addition to the special Court Officer application form.

ADMISSION TO EXAMINATION

All candidates will receive a notice to appear for the examination. Contact the Office of Court Administration if you have not received your notice three days before the examination. You may not be admitted to the examination room without an official notice. Notice to appear for the test constitutes only conditional approval of your application. Your eligibility for a Court Officer position will be determined at the time you are considered for appointment. If you have not received your admission card 3 days before the examination, contact the Office of Court Administration at (212) 417-5891 or the Department of Civil Service at (518) 457-7020.

VETERANS

Disabled and nondisabled veterans who are eligible for extra credit will have 10 or 5 points, respectively, added to their scores if they are otherwise successful in the examination. They should claim these credits when they file their application. If granted, candidates will have an option to waive the Veteran's credits any time prior to appointment. If Veteran's credits are claimed, the Office of Court Administration will send forms to establish eligibility for such credits after the written examination. Veteran's credits will not be granted if they have previously been used for permanent or contingent permanent appointment from an eligible list in New York State or any of its political subdivisions since January 1, 1951.

RATINGS

The passing score for this examination will be determined at a date following the administration of the examination.

VERIFICATION OF QUALIFICATIONS

Candidates will be investigated or called for an interview to determine whether they are qualified for appointment. In addition to meeting specific requirements, candidates must be of good moral character.

RELIGIOUS OBSERVANCE

If, because of religious belief, you are unable to attend and take the examination on its scheduled date, special arrangements can be made to permit you to take this examination on another day without fee or penalty. Please indicate your needs on the application form.

HANDICAPPED INDIVIDUALS

Arrangements will be made for handicapped individuals who require special assistance on the date of the written examination. Please indicate your needs on the application form.

FINGERPRINTING FEE

A fingerprint fee of $44 will be charged to all candidates who are successful on the written portion of the examination and whose ranks are reached for further medical, physical, and other screening tests.

PROBATIONARY PERIOD

All appointees will be required to successfully complete a probationary period subsequent to their appointment. They will also be required to complete a training program during their probationary period.

SENIOR COURT OFFICER

THE OFFICE OF COURT ADMINISTRATION ANNOUNCES A PROMOTION EXAMINATION

TITLE

Senior Court Officer   Exam Number: 55-570

The promotion examination for Senior Court Officer is limited to qualified employees of the unified court system. There will be *no* open-competitive Senior Court Officer examination held in conjunction with this examination.

LOCATION OF POSITIONS

The Senior Court Officer title exists in the Supreme and Surrogate's Courts in New York City and the County, Supreme, and Surrogate's Courts in Nassau, Suffolk, and Westchester counties.

LOCATION OF TEST CENTERS

This examination will be held exclusively in New York City, Brentwood, and White Plains.

STARTING SALARY

This title is graded at JG-18. Appointees may receive additional annual location pay.

MINIMUM QUALIFICATIONS FOR TAKING EXAMINATION

To be eligible *to compete* in this examination, candidates must, by the examination date, have current, permanent competitive class status in the title of Court Officer. (Applicants please note: All individuals with permanent competitive class status in the title of Court Officer as of the date of the examination will be prefiled by this office. Therefore, they need not submit an application for this examination. Prior to the examination date, all permanent Court Officers will receive admission cards to examination sites based upon their work location.)

MINIMUM QUALIFICATIONS FOR APPOINTMENT

To be eligible for *appointment* from the resultant eligible list, candidates must have, at the time of appointment, one year of current, permanent competitive class service in the title of Court Officer.

CITIZENSHIP

Candidates must be citizens of the United States at the time of appointment.

DISTINGUISHING FEATURES OF WORK

Senior Court Officers are responsible for maintaining order and providing security in court facilities. They work under the direct supervision of security supervisors and court clerks. Senior Court Officers are peace officers, required to wear uniforms, and may be authorized to carry firearms. They are responsible for jury escort and security, perform clerical duties while handling court documents and forms, may coordinate the activities of other court security personnel, and perform related duties.

SCOPE OF EXAMINATION

The written examination will be multiple-choice and will assess a candidate's knowledge of the laws, rules, regulations, procedures, techniques, and practices relating to the duties and responsibilities of a Senior Court Officer including, but not necessarily limited to knowledge of the following topical areas shown below (in alphabetical order):

Arrest	Handling emergencies
Bail	Handling prisoners
Courthouse/courtroom security	Hostage situations
Court terminology, documents, and forms	Jury sequestration and tampering
	Operation and use of security
Crowd control and evacuation	equipment
Evidence	Search
Firearms and firearms licensing	Self-defense
First-aid and CPR	Use of physical force
	Warrants

Sources for these knowledge questions will be the Criminal Procedure Law, the Penal Law, and the various documents given to Court Officers during formal training and on the job.

Important Information to Senior Court Officer Promotion Candidates

ADMISSION TO EXAMINATION

All individuals with permanent status in the title of Court Officer as of the examination date will be prefiled and will receive a notice to appear for the examination. They are to contact the Office of Court Administration if they have not received their notice five days before the examination. They may not be admitted to the examination room without an official notice.

VETERANS

Disabled and nondisabled veterans who are eligible for extra credit will have 5 or 2.5 points, respectively, added to their scores if they are otherwise successful in the examination. Forms for claiming these credits will be available on the day of the examination. If granted, candidates will have an option to waive the Veteran's credits any time prior to appointment. If Veteran's credits are claimed, the Office of Court Administration will send forms to establish eligibility for such credits after the written examination. Veteran's credits will not be granted if they have previously been used for permanent or contingent permanent appointment from an eligible list in New York State or any of its political subdivisions since January 1, 1951.

RATINGS

The passing score for this examination will be determined at a date following the administration of the examination.

RELIGIOUS OBSERVANCE

If, because of religious belief, candidates are unable to attend and take the examination on its scheduled date, special arrangements can be made to permit them to take this examination on another day. They are to indicate their needs in a letter to the Examination Unit, Office of Court Administration, at least 12 weeks before the date of the examination.

Court Clerk

THE OFFICE OF COURT ADMINISTRATION ANNOUNCES A PROMOTION EXAMINATION

TITLE

Court Clerk   Exam Number: 55-581

THIS PROMOTION EXAMINATION IS LIMITED TO QUALIFIED EMPLOYEES OF THE UNIFIED COURT SYSTEM. [An examination for the title of Senior Court Clerk (55-582) will also be held on the same date. Candidates may apply for both examinations through the filing of separate applications. Please refer to the announcement for the Senior Court Clerk examination for further information.]

STARTING SALARY

The title of Court Clerk is graded at JG-18. In addition, employees in Rockland county may receive additional annual location pay.

ELIGIBLE LISTS

The eligible lists established as a result of this examination will be used to fill appropriate positions in the Unified Court System in New York State.

At present, the title of Court Clerk exists throughout most of New York State with the exception of New York City, Nassau, Suffolk, and Westchester counties.

Separate promotion unit eligible lists will be established for the Third through Ninth (except for Westchester County) Judicial Districts. If appropriate, separate promotion unit eligible lists may be established for other promotion units as well. In addition, a statewide general promotion list will be established but will not be used until the appropriate promotion unit list is exhausted.

MINIMUM QUALIFICATIONS TO COMPETE

To be eligible to compete in this examination, candidates must, by the close of filing, have current, permanent* competitive class status in any competitive title in the Unified Court System.

MINIMUM QUALIFICATIONS FOR APPOINTMENT

To be eligible for appointment from the resultant eligible list, successful candidates must have at the time of appointment two years of current, permanent* competitive class status in any competitive title in the Unified Court System.

*Under Section 25.15(h) of the Rules of the Chief Judge, includes: (1) Employees of the Unified Court System who are holding or who have held positions in the Noncompetitive, Exempt or Labor Class if said employees in the past have held qualifying competitive class positions on a permanent basis, and (2) Employees with Noncompetitive status in qualifying titles by virtue of the Handicapped Set Aside Program (HSAP).

CITIZENSHIP

Candidates must be citizens of the United States at the time of appointment.

DISTINGUISHING FEATURES OF WORK

Court Clerks work in the Court of Claims; Supreme and County Courts in counties with two or more full-time County Court Judges or one full-time County Court Judge and combined annual filings of indictments and Supreme Court civil actions exceeding 650; Family Courts with two or more full-time Judges; and city and district level courts with six or more full-time Judges. Court Clerks serve as part clerks swearing witnesses, polling jurors, maintaining custody of exhibits, and keeping court minutes in individual assignment system and other parts. Court Clerks also work in court offices where they supervise Court Assistants and other court personnel engaged in processing prisoner correspondence, reviewing calendaring decisions, motions for sufficiency and preference, and orders for conformance with decisions. Court Clerks may also supervise a full-time branch office of a court staffed by Court Assistants and may be designated to act in the absence of the Chief Clerk or Commissioner of Jurors and perform other related duties.

SUBJECT OF EXAMINATION

The written examination will be multiple-choice and designed to assess the following:

1. *Knowledge of Court Procedures and Legal Terminology*:

   Shall include but not be limited to topical areas such as jurisdiction, venue, service of process, service of papers, parties, motions, subpoenas, oaths, affirmations, calendar practice, trials in general, trials by jury, judgments, warrants, indictments, and pleas, as set forth in:

   a) Civil Practice Laws and Rules including but not limited to Articles 1, 3, 4, 5, 6, 10, 12, 21, 22, 23, 26, 30, 34, 40, 41, 42, 44, and 63.

   b) Criminal Procedure Law including but not limited to Articles 1, 10, 30, 120, 180, 190, 195, 200, 210, 220, 255, 260, 270, 300, 310, 320, 330, 350, 360, 380, 390, 410, 420, 430, 500, 720, 725, 730.

   c) Family Court Act including but not limited to Articles 1 (Parts 1, 5, 7), 3 (Parts 1, 2, 4, 5, 6), 4, 5, 6 (Parts 1, 3, 4, 5), 7 (Parts 2, 3, 4, 5, 7), 8, 10 (Parts 2, 3, 5), and 11.

2. *Ability to Understand, Interpret, and Apply Written Material (Reading Comprehension)*:

   Candidates will be presented with brief reading selections followed by questions that require the interpretation and/or application of the information presented in the reading selections to given situations. All of the information required to answer the questions will be provided in the selections. Candidates will not be required to have any special knowledge relating to the content area covered in the selections.

NOTES

Handicapped persons seeking special arrangements for testing are required to indicate their needs on the application form.

Please complete the beige EEO data collection sheet in addition to the green application form.

The passing score for this exam will be determined at a date following the administration of the examination.

INFORMATION FOR CANDIDATES (PROMOTION)—PLEASE READ CAREFULLY

ELIGIBILITY FOR EXAMINATION: To be eligible to compete in this examination you must be presently employed in the competitive class in a court or court agency of the Unified Court System specified on this announcement and must have been continuously employed on a permanent (or contingent permanent) basis in specified title(s) and/or grades(s) for the required length of time. You may not compete in a test for a title if you are permanently employed in that title or in a higher title in the direct promotion line. In the following instances you may take the examination if you meet the requirements detailed in this announcement:

  (a) You have been separated from service and permanently re-employed within one year or reinstated in the same or a higher grade position.

  (b) Your name is on a preferred eligible list.

APPLICATION FORMS: These forms may be obtained from your administrative office. If you want to submit additional information or make any change in your application after it has been filed, write to the Office of Court Administration.

VETERANS: Disabled and non-disabled veterans who are eligible for extra credit, will have 5 and $2^{1/2}$ points, respectively, added to their earned scores, if they are otherwise successful in the examination. You should claim these credits when you file your application and, if they are granted, you have an option to waive them any time prior to appointment. If you claim additional credits as a veteran, the Office of Court Administration will send forms to you for establishing your eligibility for such credits. If you do not receive these forms by the examination date, write to the Office of Court Administration (see mailing instructions below). Veteran's credits will not be granted if they have previously been used for permanent or contingent permanent appointment from an eligible list in New York State or any of its political subdivisions since January 1, 1951.

ADMISSION TO EXAMINATION: Notice to appear for the test does not constitute approval of your application by the Office of Court Administration. Review of application for minimum requirements may be made after the written test. CONTACT THE OFFICE OF COURT ADMINISTRATION IF YOU HAVE NOT RECEIVED YOUR NOTICE THREE DAYS BEFORE THE EXAMINATION.

TIME REQUIRED FOR WRITTEN TEST: The written tests usually will not exceed one session of four hours unless otherwise indicated on your admission notice.

RATINGS REQUIRED: Tests usually are rated on a scale of 100 with the passing mark at 70. Test instructions may further divide the tests into parts and set minimum standards for each part.

SENIORITY: Rating of seniority is based upon the length of your continuous permanent competitive service in the Unified Court System or predecessor courts or court agencies. Rating of seniority for this test shall be for service up to 20 years with 0.2 credits added per year of service for persons who are otherwise successful on the examination.

VERIFICATION OF QUALIFICATIONS: Candidates may be investigated or called for an interview to determine whether they are qualified for appointment. In addition to meeting specific requirements, candidates must be of good moral character and habits.

MEDICAL EXAMINATION: You may be required to take a medical examination as part of the qualifying process for the position(s) in the announcement.

RELIGIOUS OBSERVANCE: If, because of religious belief, you are unable to attend and take this examination on its scheduled date, special arrangements can be made to permit you to take the examination on another day without any additional fee or penalty. Please indicate your needs on the application form.

When writing to the Office of Court Administration concerning an examination, enter: Attention: EXAMINATION directly above the address. Include in your correspondence the number and title of the examination you are applying for.

IF YOU FILE AN APPLICATION FOR THIS EXAMINATION, RETAIN A COPY OF THIS ANNOUNCEMENT.

TEST-TAKING TECHNIQUES

Your last-minute preparations for any exam are based strictly on common sense. They include getting a good night's sleep and leaving home early enough so that you do not need to rush or worry. It is a good idea to wear a watch to your exam so that you can keep track of your own time and pace yourself. Also, bring along two sharpened #2 pencils with good, clean erasers. And do *not* forget to bring your official notice to appear for examination.

Once all examinees are seated in the examination room, the test administrator will hand out forms and will give instructions as to how to fill them out. Listen carefully and follow all instructions. Ask questions if necessary. The administrator will tell you of the procedure that will be followed when the exam begins. He or she will tell you how to recognize the *start* and *stop* signals, what to do if all your pencils break, or if a page seems to be missing from your test booklet. The instructions will be step-by-step and should be very clear, but if you are uncertain about anything, do not hesitate to ask.

When the exam begins, the key word is READ. READ every word of every question. Be alert for exclusionary words that might affect your answer—words like "not," "most," "all," "every," "except."

READ all the choices before you mark your answer. It is statistically true that most errors are made when the correct answer is the last choice. Too many people mark the first answer that seems correct, without reading through all the choices to find out which answer is *best*.

The following list consists of important suggestions for taking your exam. Read the suggestions right now, before you continue. Read them again before you attempt the model exams. Read them once more the evening before you take your exam.

1. Blacken your answer space firmly and completely. ● is the only correct way to mark the answer sheet. ◑, ⊗, ⊘, and ∅ are all unacceptable. The machine might not read them at all.

2. Mark only one answer for each question. If you mark more than one answer, you will be considered wrong even if one of the answers is correct.

3. If you change your mind, you must erase your mark. Attempting to cross out an incorrect answer like this ▨ will not work. You must erase any incorrect answer completely. An incomplete erasure might be read as a second answer.

4. All your answering should be in the form of blackened spaces. The machine cannot read English. Do not write any notes in the margins.

5. MOST IMPORTANT: Answer each question in the right place. Question 1 must be answered in space 1; question 52 in space 52. If you should skip an answer space and mark a series of answers in the wrong places, you must erase all those answers and do the questions over, marking your answers in the proper places. You cannot afford to use the limited time in this way. Therefore, as you answer *each* question, look at its number and check that you are marking your answer in the space with the same number.

6. Try to answer every question. If you are unsure of an answer you mark, put a check next to the question in the question booklet. Then, if you have time, you can quickly spot those questions to which you would like to give some extra thought.

7. Guess if you must. If you do not know the answer to a question, eliminate the answers that you know are wrong and guess from among those remaining. Most civil service examination scores are based only on those questions that are answered correctly. That is, there is no penalty for a wrong answer. This means that even a wild guess is better than a blank space. A wild guess gives you a 20% or 25% chance to be right, depending on the number of choices. If the space is blank, you have no chance at all. Ask the test administrator if there is a guessing penalty or if only right answers count. If the answer is "rights only," then guess.

8. If yours is the unusual civil service exam that has a guessing penalty, ignore this advice. Otherwise, if you notice that time is about to run out and you have not completed all the questions, mark all the remaining questions with the same answer. Some will probably be correct. In doing this, choose an answer other than (A). (A) is generally the correct answer less often than the other choices.

9. Stay alert. Concentrate. Be sure to mark the letter you mean.

10. If you finish before time is up, check to be sure that each question is answered in the right space and that there is only one answer for each question. Return to the difficult questions and rethink them.

Part One

The Court Officer Exam

HOW TO ANSWER CLERICAL CHECKING QUESTIONS

The court officer handles many forms and documents during the course of each working day. It is imperative that the information on each piece of paper be read accurately and that the information be processed correctly. The court officer must be able to read quickly *and* note errors or discrepancies. Clerical checking questions are designed to measure this skill.

Each clerical checking question presents three sets of basically the same information in three columns. Sometimes the items are in the same order and sometimes in a different order in each set. There may or may not be some slight variations in the information from one set to another. The directions tell the test taker to:

Mark (A) if *ALL THREE* sets are exactly alike
Mark (B) if only the *FIRST* and *THIRD* sets are exactly alike
Mark (C) if only the *FIRST* and *SECOND* sets are exactly alike
Mark (D) if *NONE* of the sets are exactly alike

These directions are very specific. They refer to the slightest of differences—even variations in spacing after colons, spelling of abbreviations, capitalization of prepositions in titles, etc.—as well as to the more obvious, real differences. Furthermore, any difference in presentation in any single item of information from one set to the next constitutes a difference between the sets. This narrows your task considerably. Once you have found any difference in any item from one set to the next, you need not compare any further items in those two sets.

In general, you should begin with the "easy" comparisons. If names have first or middle initials, check these first. Then go on to Jr., Sr., II, M.D., and the like, noting the presence or absence of punctuation as well as its placement. Another common area of easy-to-see difference is in prefixes like Mc, Mac, Van, von, de, D', etc. If there are no differences among the easy comparisons, you must focus on the names themselves. Be on the lookout for added or dropped e's or s's in particular. Look for the true identity of people's names. (Marie and Maria are two different people.) Check for spelling, double letters, letter reversals, and letters dropped into the middle of names. For numbers, check actual number of digits, groupings, spacings, and punctuation as well as digit reversals and digit substitutions.

There is a strategy for making comparisons quickly and accurately. It is more efficient to work through one item at a time rather than one set at a time. So, start with the first item in the first set. Compare it with the same item in the second set. If the two items are on the same line, this is quite easy. If they are not on the same line, you must engage in some visual gymnastics. If the item is identical in the first and second sets, compare the item in the second set with its counterpart in the third set. If the first and second are alike and the second and third are alike, then all three are alike. You do not need to compare the first with the third. If the first and second are alike, but the second and third are different, then the first and third are different and you do not need to compare the first with the third. If, on the other hand, the first and second are different, then you must make the visual leap and compare the item in the first and third sets. Each time you find an item which differs in any way from the item in the first set, draw a line through that item. Any set with any line drawn through it drops out of the comparisons for that question. The following simple comparisons illustrate this principle and the economy it represents.

1. Cyriac Aleyamma   Cyriac Aleyamma   Cyriac Aleyamma
   Eric O. Hartman   Eric O. Hartman   ~~Eric O. Harpman~~
   4726840   ~~4728640~~   4726840

-- STOP HERE

   Jaime Chiquimia   Jaime Chiquimia   Jaime Chiquimia
   7621489   7624189   7621849   Ⓐ Ⓑ Ⓒ ●

The first item is identical in all three sets, so you must move to the second item. The second item is identical in the first two sets, but in the third set, the last name is spelled differently. Draw a line through the item that shows a difference and move on to the third item in the first set. Comparing the third item in the first set with its counterpart in the second set, we find a digit reversal in the second set. Draw a line through that item and stop. We already know that the answer is **(D)**. None of the three sets are exactly alike. There is no need to look at any further items in question 1. Mark **(D)** and move on immediately.

2. Roy L. Gildesgame   ~~Roy L. Gildegame~~   Roy L. Gildesgame
   4243275   4243275   4243275
   3245270   3245270   3245270
   Susan B. Vizoski   Suzan B. Vizoski   Susan B. Vizoski
   M.R. von Weisenseel   M.R. von Weisensteel   M.R. von Weisenseel   Ⓐ ● Ⓒ Ⓓ

With the very first item, the second set is eliminated from further comparisons. Draw a line through the entry that differs. Then lightly X out the remainder of the second set. The correct answer to question 2 cannot be (A) or (C), but you must continue comparing the first and third sets to determine whether the answer is (B) or (D). Since the first and third sets are exactly alike, the correct answer is **(B).**

The procedure is similar, though somewhat more difficult, when the items are not on the same lines in each set.

3. Cornelius Detwiler   Rose T. Waldhofer   1768232
   1768232   1065407   9673035
   9673035   Cornelius Detwiler   ~~Rose T. Walderhofer~~
   Rose T. Waldhofer   1768232   1065047
   1065407   9673035   Cornelius Detwiler   Ⓐ Ⓑ ● Ⓓ

Our system is of limited usefulness in this question. The first three items are exactly the same in all three sets. The fourth item is the same in the first two sets, but different in the third. Cross it out. You must still consider the fifth item because it might introduce a difference into the second set. In this instance it does not. The first and second sets are exactly alike, and the answer is **(C)**. There is already a difference in the third set, so the last item need not be compared there.

4. 2312793   Frima V. Spiner, MD   6219354
   Stricklund Kanedy   7692138   2312793
   6219354   2312793   Frima V. Spiner, MD
   Frima V. Spiner, MD   Stricklund Kanedy   7692138
   7692138   6219354   Stricklund Kanedy   ● Ⓑ Ⓒ Ⓓ

This is perhaps the most difficult type of question of all. Since you have found no differences, you must make all of the comparisons. This is time consuming. Then, you must trust yourself. Do NOT go back and check again for differences. If you have found no differences in one round of comparison, mark **(A)** and go on. There are questions in which all three sets are exactly alike.

Now try your new-found skill with this system on a number of questions that are similar in style and difficulty to questions on a recent exam.

DIRECTIONS: Each question consists of three sets of information appearing in three columns. In some of the questions, the same information appears on the same line in all three sets. In other questions, the information appears on a different line in each set. The position of the information is irrelevant. You are to compare the information in the three sets, searching for any differences in the information presented. Any difference at all makes the sets different. Mark your answer sheet as follows:

Mark (A) if *ALL THREE* sets are exactly alike
Mark (B) if only the *FIRST* and *THIRD* sets are exactly alike
Mark (C) if only the *FIRST* and *SECOND* sets are exactly alike
Mark (D) if *NONE* of the sets are exactly alike

1. Kanganis Bros.   Kanganis Bros.   Kanganis Bros.
   Epstein, Newman & Lubitz   Epstein, Newman & Lubitz   Epstein, Newman, & Lubitz
   733-5400.294X   733-5400.294X   733-5400.294X
   Insight Burma/Myanmar   Insight Burma/Myanmar   Insight Burma/Myanmar
   ISBN 0-13-466913-4   ISBN 0-13-466913-4   ISBN 0-13-466913-4

2. Carotenuto J & Sons   Carotenuto J & Sons   Carotenuto J & Sons
   KF368.H982143   KF368.H982143   KF368.H982143
   Inspectamerica Engineering   InspectAmerica Engineering   InspectAmerica Engineering
   8527-2511.6019E   8527-2511.6019E   8527-2511.6019E
   Hsin Tai Hwa Chinese Rest.   Hsin Tai Hwa Chinese Rest.   Hsin Tai Hwa Chinese Rest.

3. ISBN 0-316-48889-5   ISBN 0-316-48889-5   ISBN 0-316-48889-5
   Glossbrenner's Guide   Glossbrenner's Guide   Glossbrenner's Guide
   Fax (212) 397-4572   Fax (212) 397-4572   Fax (212) 397-4572
   34-3-220-85-65   34-3-220-85-65   34-3-220-85-65
   Kol Zagreda Realty   Kol Zagreda Realty   Kol Zagreda Realty

4. Local Law 73 of 1959   Local Law 73 of 1959   Local Law 73 of 1959
   GBC Wilson-Jones-IT   GBC Wilson-Jonas-IT   GBC Wilson-Jones-IT
   ISBN 0-671-95493-8   ISBN 0-671-95493-8   ISBN 0-671-95493-8
   Internetworking with OSI   Internetworking with OSI   Internetworking with OSI
   KG781.L93846.2   KG781.L93846.2   KG781.L93846.2

5. Kramer, Dillor, Tessel   Kramer, Dillor, Tessel   Kramer,Dillor,Tessel
   113-82-6128 BS   113-82-6128 BS   113-82-6128 BS
   Maritime Regulation 3.2   Maritime Regulation 3.2   Maritime Regulation 3.2
   690.05-690.55(a)(i)   690.05-690.55(a)(i)   690.05-690.55(a)(i)
   Houghton Mifflin/Lawrence   Houghton Mifflin/Laurence   Houghton Mifflin/Lawrence

6. Tirana Roofing Corp.   907-889-8736/5804   ISBN 0-87364-650-9
   La Revancha Social Club   Tieger S L Harbert, Inc.   907-889-8736/5804
   907-889-8736/5804   Tirana Roofing Corp.   La Revancha Social Club
   Tieger S L Harbert, Inc.   ISBN 0-87634-650-9   Tirana Roofing Corp.
   ISBN 0-87634-650-9   La Revancha Social Club   Tieger S L Harbert, Inc.

7. 9-1-683-4214x3828 Kingsbridge Locksmiths PC section 434a-7.0
 Kingsbridge Locksmiths PC 9-1-683-4214x3828   Salomon Jones & Bros.
 section 434a-7.0   FS786.90832G3-4   9-1-683-4214x3828
 Salomon Jones & Bros. section 434a-7.0   Knightsbridge Locksmiths PC
 FS786.90832G3-4   Salomon Jones & Bros. FS786.90832G3-4

8. Stephen J. Phillips & Assoc. 548-5699-542-1245   Hullaballoons Plus
 548-5699-542-1245 FX673029/38402PT   Stephen J. Phillips & Assoc.
 1672E,233-324.8748 Hullaballoons Plus   FX673029/38402PT
 FX673029/38402PT Stephen J. Phillips & Assoc. 548-5699-542-1245
 Hullaballoons Plus   1672E,233-324.8748 1672E,233-324.8748

9. Tillotson, Lurting & Catano GK3783729/10458.iv ISBN 0-1-85367-093-6
 GK3783729/10458.iv El Pabellon de Oro Chinese Tillotson, Lurting & Catano
 718-894-9025-x.8611/2 ISBN 0-1-85367-093-6 GK3873729/10458.iv
 El Pabellon de Oro Chinese Tillotson, Lurtine & Catano 718-894-9025-x.8611/2
 ISBN 0-1-85367-093-6 718-894-9025-x.8611/2 El Pabellon de Oro Chinese

10. Recognizance and Bail Alcofoam Thermofiber 470.45(iii)-473.05(v)(d)
 KF1093.H087165   S 83604-7211 TS   Recognizance and Bail
 470.45(iii)-473.05(v)(d) KF1093.H087165   Alcofoam Thermafiber
 S 83604-7211 TS   Recognizance and Bail KF1093.H087165
 Alcofoam Thermafiber 470.45(iii)-473.05(v)(d) S 83604-7211 TS

Answer Strip

1 Ⓐ Ⓑ Ⓒ Ⓓ   3 Ⓐ Ⓑ Ⓒ Ⓓ   5 Ⓐ Ⓑ Ⓒ Ⓓ   7 Ⓐ Ⓑ Ⓒ Ⓓ   9 Ⓐ Ⓑ Ⓒ Ⓓ

2 Ⓐ Ⓑ Ⓒ Ⓓ   4 Ⓐ Ⓑ Ⓒ Ⓓ   6 Ⓐ Ⓑ Ⓒ Ⓓ   8 Ⓐ Ⓑ Ⓒ Ⓓ   10 Ⓐ Ⓑ Ⓒ Ⓓ

Correct Answers

1. **(C)** The first two sets are exactly alike. In the third set, a comma has been inserted after the name "Newman."

2. **(D)** The second and third sets are exactly alike, but both are different from the first set, making (D) the only possible answer. The difference lies in the capitalizing of Inspectamerica in the first set and InspectAmerica in the second and third sets.

3. **(A)** All three sets are exactly alike.

4. **(B)** The first and third sets are exactly alike. In the second set, the name "Jones" is misspelled as "Jonas."

5. **(D)** None of the sets are alike. In the third set, the spaces have been omitted after the commas in the first name. In the second set, the name "Lawrence" is spelled "Laurence."

6. **(C)** The first two sets are exactly alike. In the third set, there is a digit reversal in the ISBN.

7. **(C)** The first two sets are exactly alike. In the third set, "Kingsbridge" becomes "Knightsbridge."

8. **(A)** All three sets are exactly alike.

9. **(D)** None of the sets are alike. In the second set, the name "Lurting" is misspelled as "Lurtine." In the third set, there is a digit reversal in the entry beginning with "GK."

10. **(B)** The first and third sets are exactly alike. In the second set, the word "Thermafiber" is misspelled "Thermofiber."

OBSERVATION AND MEMORY

Memory is a very individualized skill. Some people remember details of what they see and hear, others remember only the most obvious facts. Some people memorize easily, others find memorizing very difficult. Some people remember forever, others forget in a short time. Some people can memorize in a systematic manner, others are haphazard in their methods or have no method at all.

We really cannot tell you how to memorize. We can, however, teach you how to observe, show you how to look at photographs, and point out the details on which you should concentrate. The systematic observation of photographs transfers very readily to the systematic study of narrative description of events. The Memory questions on your court officer exam may be based on pictures, narrative, or both.

Photograph for Exercise 1—**The Auto Body Shop**

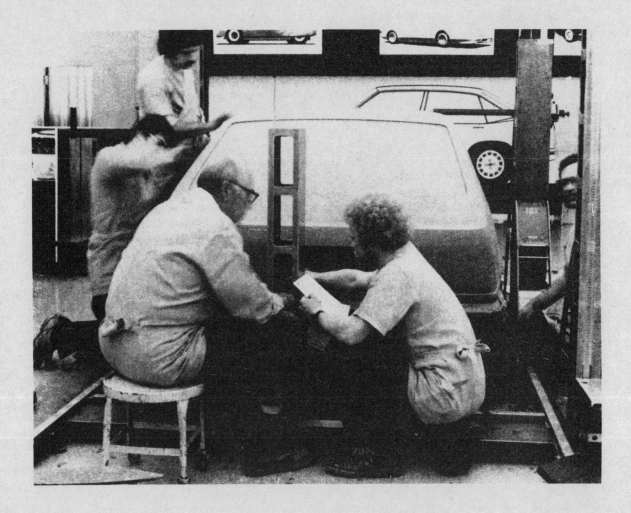

(Photograph courtesy of General Motors)

EXERCISE 1

Let us begin by looking together at the photograph of the Auto Body Shop. Start with the people:

1. How many people are in the photograph?

2. How many men? How many women?

3. What do the people appear to be doing?

4. Are the people all working together? If not, how many are working alone? How many together? is the man on the right working?

5. Note the clothing. Dark pants, dark socks, light shirts crossed across the chest and tied in back. The two men in the foreground have on the same shoes, but the other visible pair of shoes is different.

6. Note glasses. Which men wear them?

7. Note hair. Which men have dark hair? Which light? Can you describe the hairstyles of the light-haired men?

8. One man is sitting on a stool. Which man? How many legs does the stool have? Of what does the stool appear to be made? Does it move on casters?

9. Which of the men have beards? Mustaches?

10. Is anyone wearing a watch? Who?

Observe the action:

11. What does the man in the right foreground have in his hand? What is he probably doing?

12. What does the man who is standing appear to be doing? What about the man kneeling beside him?

13. What might be the relationship of the older man to the younger ones?

Note the background:

14. There are pictures of cars on the walls. Parts of how many cars are visible? How many tires are shown?

15. What else can be seen on the walls? Telephone? Calendar? Bookcase?

16. Is the car on which the men are working up on a lift?

17. How many levels of floor are visible? Is the floor clean?

18. There is a number on one piece of equipment. Did you notice the number? Remember it!

In looking at a photograph, focus first on the people. Notice their clothing, physical features, and activities. Count, but also make note of which person or persons are wearing what, doing what, interacting with whom, and so on. Then notice the prominent objects. Next, turn your attention to the background, floors, walls, and so forth. Finally, start at the left side of the photograph and move your eyes very slowly to the right, noticing special details such as numbers, calibrations, dirt spots, and unidentified objects. If you work very hard at noticing, you are likely to remember what you noticed, at least for the duration of the exam.

Photograph for Exercise 2—**Time Out for Refreshments**

(Photograph courtesy of The Coleman Company, Inc.)

EXERCISE 2

Let us look at the photograph called "Time Out for Refreshments."

1. The people in the picture are . . . number, sex, age.

2. The people are wearing . . . notice the boy's belt, label on jeans (even if you cannot read it, you should notice that it is there), long-sleeved plaid shirts.

3. Notice hair color, type (curly or straight), and length.

4. Note that no shoes are visible; neither person wears glasses, a watch, or a hat.

5. What is the boy doing? What is the girl doing?

6. Who is standing? Who sitting? On what?

7. On what is the soda can resting? On what is the cooler resting?

8. What else is on the table? Notice lantern, covered pot, box, and coffeepot.

9. How many slats make up the table? The bench?

10. What is on the ground? Snow? Sand? Gravel? Lawn? Rocks? Flowers? Wild grasses?

11. The day is . . . cold? warm? rainy? cloudy? sunny? Where is the sun in the picture?

12. In the background are (is) . . . mountains? trees? water? boats? tents? more grass? other people? animals?

13. What can you see in the sky? What is on or in the water? What else is there on the land?

14. Does the cooler have a handle on top. Where? Is it all one color? How many colors? Describe the design of the cooler.

15. Where is the fill valve on the lantern?

16. Does the coffeepot have a handle?

17. Does the tent have a visible window?

18. Describe the end of the bench? Squared off? Rounded? Other?

How did you do with this photograph? Are you developing skill at noticing everything?

Narrative Description for Exercise 3

On October 30, the Belton First National Bank discovered that the $3,000 it had received that morning from the Greenville First National Bank was in counterfeit $10, $20, and $50 bills. The genuine $3,000 had been counted by Greenville First National Bank clerk, Iris Stewart, the preceding afternoon. They were packed in eight black leather satchels and stored in the bank vault overnight. Greenville First National clerk, Brian Caruthers, accompanied armor carriers James Clark and Howard O'Keefe to Belton in an armored truck. Belton First National clerk, Cynthia Randall, discovered the counterfeit bills when she examined the serial numbers of the bills.

During the course of the investigation, the following statements were made:

1. Gerald Hathaway, clerk of the Greenville bank, told investigators that he had found the bank office open when he arrived to work on the morning of October 30. The only articles which appeared to be missing were eight black leather satchels of the type used to transport large sums of money.

2. Jon Perkins, head teller, told investigators that he did not check the contents of the black leather satchels after locking them in the vault around 4:30 p.m. on October 29.

3. Henry Green, janitor, said that he noticed Jon Perkins leaving the bank office around 5:30 p.m., one-half hour after the bank closed on October 29. He said that Perkins locked the door.

4. A scrap of cloth identical to the material of the armor carriers' uniforms was found caught in the seal of one of the black leather satchels delivered to Belton.

5. Brian Caruthers, clerk, said he saw James Clark and Howard O'Keefe talking in a secretive manner in the armored truck.

6. Thomas Stillman, bank executive, identified the eight black leather satchels containing the counterfeit money that arrived at the Belton First National Bank as the eight satchels that had disappeared from the bank office. He had noticed a slight difference in the linings of the satchels.

EXERCISE 3

Approach the story in the same way that you approached the photographs.

Who are the people?

Iris Stewart—clerk, Greenville First National Bank
Brian Caruthers—clerk, Greenville First National Bank
James Clark—armor carrier
Howard O'Keefe—armor carrier
Cynthia Randall—clerk, Belton First National Bank
Gerald Hathaway—clerk, Greenville First National Bank
Jon Perkins—head teller, Greenville First National Bank
Henry Green—janitor, Greenville First National Bank
Thomas Stillman—bank executive, Greenville First National Bank

What is the chronology?

Money counted and packed afternoon of October 29
Satchels locked into vault at 4:30 p.m., October 29
Bank closed at 5:00 p.m.
Jon Perkins left and locked bank office 5:30 p.m., October 29
Satchels delivered morning of October 30
Counterfeit discovered October 30

Other details?

The total sum was $3000
Money was in $10, $20, and $50 bills
Money was packed in eight black leather satchels
Counterfeit discovered by Cynthia Randall examining serial numbers of bills
Apparent theft and switching of black satchels
Scrap of armor carrier uniform cloth caught in seal on one satchel
Money transported from Greenville First National Bank to Belton First National Bank

Who did what?

Iris Stewart counted the genuine $3,000.
Jon Perkins locked the vault.
Henry Green saw Jon Perkins lock the bank.
James Clark and Howard O'Keefe delivered the satchels.
Brian Caruthers accompanied the armor carriers in the armored truck and noticed them whispering.
Gerald Hathaway found the Greenville bank open in the morning and noticed that eight satchels were missing.
Cynthia Randall discovered that the money was counterfeit.
Thomas Stillman noticed a slight difference in linings of satchels and was able to identify the ones that had arrived at Belton as the ones missing from Greenville.

Obviously, there are a great many details on which you might be questioned. Read carefully. Organize people, events, and facts in some logical order. Remember as much as you can in the best way you know how. The questions immediately follow the memorizing time, so you will not need to remember for long.

HOW TO ANSWER READING QUESTIONS

The key to success with reading questions is not speed but comprehension. Civil service exams are not, as a rule, heavily speeded. There is ample time in which to complete the exam, provided that you do not spend excessive time struggling with one or two "impossible" questions. If you are reading with comprehension, your mind will not wander, and your speed will be adequate.

Between now and the test day, you must work to improve your reading concentration and comprehension. Your daily newspaper provides excellent material to improve your reading. Make a point of reading all the way through any article that you begin. Do not be satisfied with the first paragraph or two. Read with a pencil in hand. Underscore details and ideas that seem to be crucial to the meaning of the article. Notice points of view, arguments, and supporting information. When you have finished the article, summarize it for yourself. Do you know the purpose of the article? The main idea presented? The attitude of the writer? The points over which there is controversy? Did you find certain information lacking? As you answer these questions, skim back over your underlinings. Did you focus on important words and ideas? Did you read with comprehension?

As you repeat this process day after day, you will find that your reading will become more efficient. You will read with greater understanding and will "get more" from your newspaper.

One aspect of your daily reading that deserves special attention is vocabulary building. The most effective reader has a rich, extensive vocabulary. As you read, make a list of unfamiliar words. Include in your list words that you understand within the context of the article but that you cannot really define. In addition, mark words that you do not understand at all. When you put aside your newspaper, go to the dictionary and look up *every* new and unfamiliar word. Write the word and its definition in a special notebook. Writing the words and their definitions helps seal them in your memory far better than just reading them, and the notebook serves as a handy reference for your own use. A sensitivity to the meanings of words and an understanding of more words will make reading easier and more enjoyable even if none of the words you learn in this way crops up on your exam. In fact, the habit of vocabulary building is a good lifetime habit to develop.

Success with reading questions depends on more than reading comprehension. You must also know how to draw the answers from the reading selection and be able to distinguish the *best* answer from a number of answers that all seem to be good ones, or from a number of answers that all seem to be wrong.

Strange as it may seem, it's a good idea to approach reading comprehension questions by reading the questions—not the answer choices, just the questions themselves—before you read the selection. The questions will alert you to look for certain details, ideas and points of view. Use your pencil. Underscore key words in the questions. These will help you direct your attention as you read.

Next skim the selection very rapidly to get an idea of its subject matter and its organization. If key words or ideas pop out at you, underline them, but do not consciously search out details in the preliminary skimming.

Now read the selection carefully with comprehension as your main goal. Underscore the important words as you have been doing in your newspaper reading.

Finally, return to the questions. Read each question carefully. Be sure you know what it asks. Misreading of questions is a major cause of error on reading comprehension questions. Read *all* the answer choices. Eliminate the obviously incorrect answers. You may be left with only one possible answer. If you find yourself with more than one possible answer, reread the question. Then skim the passage once more, focusing on the underlined segments. By now you should be able to conclude which answer is *best*.

Reading comprehension questions may take a number of different forms. In general, some of the most common forms are as follows:

1. **Question of fact or detail.** You may have to mentally rephrase or rearrange, but you should find the answer stated in the body of the selection.

2. **Best title or main idea.** The answer may be obvious, but the incorrect choices to the "main idea" question are often half-truths that are easily confused with the main idea. They may misstate the idea, omit part of the idea, or even offer a supporting idea quoted directly from the text. The correct answer is the one that covers the largest part of the selection.

3. **Interpretation.** This type of question asks you what the passage *means*, not just what it says.

4. **Inference.** This is the most difficult type of reading comprehension question. It asks you to go beyond what the selection says, and to predict what might happen next. Your answer must be based upon the information in the selection and your own common sense, but not upon any other information you may have about the subject. A variation of the inference question might be stated as, "The author would expect that. . . ." To answer this question, you must understand the author's point of view, and then make an inference from that viewpoint based upon the information in the selection.

5. **Vocabulary.** Some civil service reading sections, directly or indirectly, ask the meanings of certain words as used in the selection.

Let's now work together on some typical reading comprehension selections and questions.

SELECTION FOR QUESTIONS 1 TO 4

The recipient gains an impression of a typewritten letter before beginning to read the message. Factors that give a good first impression include margins and spacing that are visually pleasing, formal parts of the letter that are correctly placed according to the style of the letter, copy that is free of obvious erasures and overstrikes, and transcript that is even and clear. The problem for the typist is how to produce that first, positive impression of her work.

There are several general rules that a typist can follow when she wishes to prepare a properly spaced letter on a sheet of letterhead. The width of a letter should ordinarily not be less than 4 inches nor more than 6 inches. The side margins should also have a desirable relation to the bottom margin, as well as the space between the letterhead and the body of the letter. Usually the most appealing arrangement is when the side margins are even, and the bottom margin is slightly wider than the side margins. In some offices, however, a standard line length is used for all business letters; the secretary then varies the spacing between the date line and the inside address according to the length of the letter.

1. The best title for the preceding paragraphs is   1. ⒶⒷⒸⒹ

    (A) "Writing Office Letters"
    (B) "Making Good First Impressions"
    (C) "Judging Well-Typed Letters"
    (D) "Good Placing and Spacing for Office Letters"

2. According to the preceding paragraphs, which of the following might be   2. ⒶⒷⒸⒹ
considered the way that people quickly judge the quality of work that has
been typed?

    (A) by measuring the margins to see if they are correct
    (B) by looking at the spacing and cleanliness of the typescript
    (C) by scanning the body of the letter for meaning
    (D) by reading the date line and address for errors

3. According to the preceding paragraphs, what would be definitely undesir-   3. ⒶⒷⒸⒹ
able as the average line length of a typed letter?

    (A) 4″
    (B) 5″
    (C) 6″
    (D) 7″

4. According to the preceding paragraphs, when the line length is kept stan-   4. ⒶⒷⒸⒹ
dard, the secretary

    (A) does not have to vary the spacing at all because this also is standard
    (B) adjusts the spacing between the date line and inside address for differ-
        ent lengths of letters
    (C) uses the longest line as a guideline for spacing between the date line and
        inside address
    (D) varies the number of spaces between the lines

      Begin by skimming the questions and underscoring key words. Your underscored ques-
tions should look more or less like this:

    1. What is the <u>best title</u> for the preceding paragraphs?

    2. According to the preceding paragraphs, which of the following might be considered
       the way that people <u>quickly judge the quality</u> of work that has been typed?

    3. According to the preceding paragraphs, what would be definitely <u>undesirable</u> as the
       <u>average line length</u> of a typed letter?

    4. According to the preceding paragraphs, <u>when the line length is kept standard</u>, the
       secretary

      Now skim the selection. This quick reading should give you an idea of the structure of
the selection and of its overall meaning.
      Next read the selection carefully and underscore words that seem important or that you
think hold keys to the question answers. Your underscored selection should look something like this:

    The recipient gains an impression of a typewritten letter before he begins to read the
    message. <u>Factors that give a good first impression</u> include <u>margins and spacing that
    are visually pleasing</u>, formal parts of the letter that are <u>correctly placed</u> according to
    the style of the letter, copy that is <u>free of obvious erasures and overstrikes</u>, and tran-

script that is <u>even and clear</u>. The problem for the typist is how to produce that first, positive impression of her work.

There are several general rules that a typist can follow when she wishes to prepare a properly spaced letter on a sheet of letterhead. The width of a letter should ordinarily <u>not be less than 4 inches, nor more than 6 inches</u>. The side margins should also have a desirable relation to the bottom margin as well as the space between the letterhead and the body of the letter. Usually the most appealing arrangement is when the <u>side margins are even</u>, and the <u>bottom margin is slightly wider</u> than the side margins. In some offices, however, a <u>standard line length is used for all business letters</u>, and the secretary then <u>varies the spacing between the date line and the inside address</u> according to the length of the letter.

Finally, read the questions and answer choices, and try to choose the correct answer for each question.

The correct answers are: 1. **(D)**, 2. **(B)**, 3. **(D)**, 4. **(B)**. Did you get them all right? Whether you made any errors or not, read these explanations.

1. **(D)** The best title for any selection is the one that takes in all the ideas presented without being too broad or too narrow. Choice (D) provides the most inclusive title for this passage. A look at the other choices shows you why. Choice (A) can be eliminated because the passage discusses typing a letter, not writing one. Although the first paragraph states that a letter should make a good first impression, the passage is clearly devoted to the letter, not the first impression, so choice (B) can be eliminated. Choice (C) places the emphasis on the wrong aspect of the typewritten letter. The passage concerns how to type a properly spaced letter, not how to judge one.

2. **(B)** Both spacing and cleanliness are mentioned in paragraph 1 as ways to judge the quality of a typed letter. The first paragraph states that the margins should be "visually pleasing" in relationship to the body of the letter, but that does not imply margins of a particular measure, so choice (A) is incorrect. Meaning is not discussed in the passage, only the look of the finished letter, so choice (C) is incorrect. The passage makes no mention of errors, only the avoidance of erasures and overstrikes, so (D) is incorrect.

3. **(D)** This answer comes from the information provided in paragraph 2, that the width of a letter "should not be less than 4 inches nor more than 6 inches." According to this rule, 7 inches is an undesirable line length.

4. **(B)** The answer to this question is stated in the last sentence of the reading passage. When a standard line length is used, the secretary "varies the spacing between the date line and the inside address according to the length of the letter." The passage offers no support for any other choice.

Let us try another together.

SELECTION FOR QUESTIONS 5 TO 9

Cotton fabrics treated with the XYZ process have features that make them far superior to any previously known flame-retardant-treated cotton fabrics. XYZ process-treated fabrics are <u>durable</u> to repeated laundering and dry cleaning; are glow resistant as well as <u>flame resistant</u>; when exposed to flames or intense heat form tough, pliable, and protective chars; are inert physiologically to persons handling or exposed to the fabric; are only slightly heavier than untreated fabrics; and are susceptible to further wet and dry finishing treatments. In addition, the treated fabrics exhibit little or no adverse change in feel, texture, and appearance and are shrink, rot, and mildew resistant. The treatment <u>reduces strength</u> only slightly. Finished fabrics have "easy care" properties in that they are <u>wrinkle resistant</u> and <u>dry rapidly</u>.

5. It is most accurate to state that the author in the preceding selection presents   5. Ⓐ Ⓑ Ⓒ Ⓓ

    (A) facts but reaches no conclusion concerning the value of the process
    (B) a conclusion concerning the value of the process and facts to support that conclusion
    (C) a conclusion concerning the value of the process unsupported by facts
    (D) neither facts nor conclusions, but merely describes the process

6. The one of the following articles for which the XYZ process would be most suitable is   6. Ⓐ Ⓑ Ⓒ Ⓓ

    (A) nylon stockings
    (B) woolen shirt
    (C) silk tie
    (D) cotton bedsheet

7. The one of the following aspects of the XYZ process that is *not* discussed in the preceding selection is its effects on   7. Ⓐ Ⓑ Ⓒ Ⓓ

    (A) costs
    (B) washability
    (C) wearability
    (D) the human body

8. The main reason for treating a fabric with the XYZ process is to   8. Ⓐ Ⓑ Ⓒ Ⓓ

    (A) prepare the fabric for other wet and dry finishing treatment
    (B) render it shrink, rot, and mildew resistant
    (C) increase its weight and strength
    (D) reduce the chance that it will catch fire

9. The one of the following that would be considered a minor drawback of the XYZ process is that it   9. Ⓐ Ⓑ Ⓒ Ⓓ

    (A) forms chars when exposed to flame
    (B) makes fabrics mildew resistant
    (C) adds to the weight of fabrics
    (D) is compatible with other finishing treatments

    Skim the questions and underscore the words that you consider to be key. The questions should look something like this:

    5. It is most accurate to state that the <u>author</u>, in the preceding selection, <u>presents</u>

    6. The one of the following articles for which the <u>XYZ process</u> would be <u>most suitable</u> is

    7. The one of the following <u>aspects</u> of the XYZ process that is <u>*not* discussed</u> in the preceding selection is its effect on

    8. The <u>main reason for treating</u> a fabric with the XYZ process is to

    9. The one of the following which would be considered a <u>minor drawback</u> of the XYZ process is that it

Skim the reading selection to get an idea of its subject matter and organization. Then read the selection carefully and underscore the words which you think are especially important. This fact-filled selection might be underlined like this:

Cotton fabrics treated with the XYZ process have features that make them far superior to any previously known flame-retardant-treated cotton fabrics. XYZ process-treated fabrics are durable to repeated laundering and dry cleaning; are glow resistant as well as flame resistant; when exposed to flames or intense heat form tough, pliable, and protective chars; are inert physiologically to persons handling or exposed to the fabric; are only slightly heavier than untreated fabrics; and are susceptible to further wet and dry finishing treatments. In addition, the treated fabrics exhibit little or no adverse change in feel, texture, and appearance, and are shrink, rot, and mildew resistant. The treatment reduces strength only slightly. Finished fabrics have "easy care" properties in that they are wrinkle resistant and dry rapidly.

Now read each question and all its answer choices, and try to choose the correct answer for each question.

The correct answers are: 5. **(B)**, 6. **(D)**, 7. **(A)**, 8. **(D)**, 9. **(C)**. How did you do on these? Read the explanantions.

5. **(B)** This is a combination main idea and interpretation question. If you cannot answer this question readily, reread the selection. The author clearly thinks that the XYZ process is terrific and says so in the first sentence. The rest of the selection presents a wealth of facts to support the initial claim.

6. **(D)** At first glance, you might think that this is an inference question requiring you to make a judgment on the basis of the few drawbacks of the process. Closer reading, however, shows you that there is no contest for correct answer here. This is a simple question of fact. The XYZ process is a treatment for *cotton* fabrics.

7. **(A)** Your underlinings should help you with this question of fact. Cost is not mentioned; all other aspects of the XYZ process are. If you are having trouble finding mention of the effect of the XYZ process on the human body, add to your vocabulary list "inert" and "physiologically."

8. **(D)** This is a main idea question. You must distinguish between the main idea and the supporting and incidental facts.

9. **(C)** Obviously a drawback is a negative feature. The selection mentions only two negative features. The treatment reduces strength slightly, and it makes fabrics slightly heavier than untreated fabrics. Only one of these negative features is offered among the answer choices.

You should be getting better at reading and at answering questions. Try this next selection on your own. Read and underline the questions. Skim the selection. Read and underline the selection. Read questions and answer choices and mark your answers. Then check your answers against the answers and explanations that follow the selection.

SELECTION FOR QUESTIONS 10 TO 12

Language performs an essentially social function: It helps us get along together, communicate, and achieve a great measure of concerted action. Words are signs that have significance by convention, and those people who do not adopt the conventions simply fail to communicate. They do not "get along," and a social force arises that encourages them to achieve the correct associations. By "correct" is meant as used by other members of the social group. Some of the vital points about language are brought home to an English visitor to America, and vice versa, because our vocabularies are nearly the same—but not quite.

10. As defined in the preceding selection, usage of a word is "correct" when it is as

    (A) defined in standard dictionaries
    (B) used by the majority of persons throughout the world who speak the same language.
    (C) used by the majority of educated persons who speak the same language
    (D) used by other persons with whom we are associating

10. Ⓐ Ⓑ Ⓒ Ⓓ

11. In the preceding selection, the author is concerned primarily with the

    (A) meaning of words
    (B) pronunciation of words
    (C) structure of sentences
    (D) origin and development of language

11. Ⓐ Ⓑ Ⓒ Ⓓ

12. According to the preceding selection, the main language problem of an English visitor to America stems from the fact that an English person

    (A) uses some words that have different meanings for Americans
    (B) has different social values than the Americans
    (C) has had more exposure to non-English-speaking persons than Americans have had
    (D) pronounces words differently than Americans do

12. Ⓐ Ⓑ Ⓒ Ⓓ

The correct answers are: 10. **(D)**, 11. **(A)**, 12. **(A)**.

10. **(D)** The answer to this question is stated in the next to last sentence of the selection.

11. **(A)** This main idea question is an easy one to answer. You should have readily eliminated all the wrong choices.

12. **(A)** This is a question of fact. The phrasing of the question is quite different from the phrasing of the last sentence, but the meaning is the same. You may have found this reading selection more difficult to absorb than some of the others, but you should have had no difficulty answering this question by eliminating the wrong answers.

Here is one more reading selection and its questions. Once more explanations follow the correct answers. Follow the procedure you have learned, and be sure to read the explanations even if you have a perfect score.

SELECTION FOR QUESTIONS 13 TO 18

Since almost every office has some contact with data-processed records, a senior stenographer should have some understanding of the basic operations of data processing. Data processing systems now handle about one third of all office paper work. On punched cards, magnetic tape, or on other mediums, data are recorded before being fed into the computer for processing. A machine such as the key punch is used to convert the data written on the source document into the coded symbols on punched cards or tapes. After data have been converted, they must be verified to guarantee absolute accuracy of conversion. In this manner data become a permanent record that can be read by electronic computers that compare, store, compute, and otherwise process data at high speeds.

One key person in a computer installation is a programmer, the person who puts business and scientific problems into special symbolic languages that can be read by the computer. Jobs done by the computer range all the way from payroll operations to chemical process control, but most computer applications are directed toward management data. About half the programmers employed by business come to their positions with college degrees; the remaining half are promoted to their positions, without regard to education, from within the organization on the basis of demonstrated ability.

13. Of the following, the best title for the preceding selection is   13. Ⓐ Ⓑ Ⓒ Ⓓ

    (A) "The Stenographer as Data Processor"
    (B) "The Relationship of Key Punching to Stenography"
    (C) "Understanding Data Processing"
    (D) "Permanent Office Records"

14. According to the preceding selection, a senior stenographer should understand the basic operations of data processing because   14. Ⓐ Ⓑ Ⓒ Ⓓ

    (A) almost every office today has contact with data processed by computer
    (B) any office worker may be asked to verify the accuracy of data
    (C) most offices are involved in the production of permanent records
    (D) data may be converted into computer language by typing on a key punch

15. According to the preceding selection, the data that the computer understands is most often expressed   15. Ⓐ Ⓑ Ⓒ Ⓓ

    (A) as a scientific programming language
    (B) as records or symbols punched on tape, cards, or other mediums
    (C) as records on cards
    (D) as records on tape

16. According to the preceding selection, computers are used most often to handle   16. Ⓐ Ⓑ Ⓒ Ⓓ

    (A) management data
    (B) problems of higher education
    (C) the control of chemical processes
    (D) payroll operations

17. Computer programming is taught in many colleges and business schools. 17. ⒶⒷⒸⒹ
The preceding selection implies that programmers in industry

   (A) must have professional training
   (B) need professional training to advance
   (C) must have at least a college education to do adequate programming
       tasks
   (D) do not need college education to do programming work

18. According to the preceding selection, data to be processed by computer 18. ⒶⒷⒸⒹ
should be

   (A) recent
   (B) complete
   (C) basic
   (D) verified

   The correct answers are: 13. **(C)**, 14. **(A)**, 15. **(B)**, 16. **(A)**, 17. **(D)**, 18. **(D)**.

13. **(C)** Choosing the best title for this selection is not easy. Although the senior stenographer is mentioned in the first sentence, the selection is really not concerned with stenographers or with their relationship to key punching. Eliminate choices (A) and (B). Permanent office records are mentioned in the selection, but only along with other equally important uses for data processing. Eliminate choice (D). When in doubt, the most general title is usually correct.

14. **(A)** This is a question of fact. Any one of the answer choices could be correct, but the answer is given almost verbatim in the first sentence. Take advantage of answers that are handed to you in this way.

15. **(B)** This is a question of fact, but it is a tricky one. The program language is a symbolic language, not a scientific one. Reread carefully and eliminate choice (A). (B) includes more of the information in the selection than either (C) or (D), and so is the best answer.

16. **(A)** This is a question of fact. The answer is stated in the next to the last sentence.

17. **(D)** Remember that you are answering the questions on the basis of the information given in the selection. In spite of any information you may have to the contrary, the last sentence of the selection states that half the programmers employed in business achieved their positions by moving up from the ranks without regard to education.

18. **(D)** Judicious underlining proves very helpful to you in finding the correct answer to this question buried in the middle of the selection. Since any one of the answers might be correct, the way to deal with this question is to skim the underlined words in the selection, eliminate those that are not mentioned, and choose the appropriate answer.

   Before you begin the model exams, review this list of hints for scoring high on reading comprehension tests.

   1. Read the questions and underline key words.

   2. Skim the selection to get a general idea of the subject matter, the point that is being made, and organization of the material.

   3. Reread the selection giving attention to details and point of view. Underscore key words and phrases.

4. If the author has quoted material from another source, be sure that you understand the purpose of the quote. Does the author agree or disagree?

5. Carefully read each question or incomplete statement. Determine exactly what is being asked. Watch for negatives or all-inclusive words, such as *always, never, all, only, every, absolutely, completely, none, entirely, no.*

6. Read all the answer choices. Eliminate those choices that are obviously incorrect. Reread the remaining choices and refer to the selection, if necessary, to determine the *best* answer.

7. Avoid inserting your own judgments into your answers. Even if you disagree with the author or even if you spot a factual error in the selection, you must answer on the basis of what is stated or implied in the selection.

8. Do not allow yourself to spend too much time on any one question. If looking back at the selection does not help you to find or figure out the answer, choose from among the answers, mark the question in the test booklet, and go on. If you have time at the end of the exam or exam portion, reread the selection and the question. Often a fresh look provides new insights.

Model Court Officer Exam I
Answer Sheet

1 Ⓐ Ⓑ Ⓒ Ⓓ	21 Ⓐ Ⓑ Ⓒ Ⓓ	41 Ⓐ Ⓑ Ⓒ Ⓓ	61 Ⓐ Ⓑ Ⓒ Ⓓ	81 Ⓐ Ⓑ Ⓒ Ⓓ
2 Ⓐ Ⓑ Ⓒ Ⓓ	22 Ⓐ Ⓑ Ⓒ Ⓓ	42 Ⓐ Ⓑ Ⓒ Ⓓ	62 Ⓐ Ⓑ Ⓒ Ⓓ	82 Ⓐ Ⓑ Ⓒ Ⓓ
3 Ⓐ Ⓑ Ⓒ Ⓓ	23 Ⓐ Ⓑ Ⓒ Ⓓ	43 Ⓐ Ⓑ Ⓒ Ⓓ	63 Ⓐ Ⓑ Ⓒ Ⓓ	83 Ⓐ Ⓑ Ⓒ Ⓓ
4 Ⓐ Ⓑ Ⓒ Ⓓ	24 Ⓐ Ⓑ Ⓒ Ⓓ	44 Ⓐ Ⓑ Ⓒ Ⓓ	64 Ⓐ Ⓑ Ⓒ Ⓓ	84 Ⓐ Ⓑ Ⓒ Ⓓ
5 Ⓐ Ⓑ Ⓒ Ⓓ	25 Ⓐ Ⓑ Ⓒ Ⓓ	45 Ⓐ Ⓑ Ⓒ Ⓓ	65 Ⓐ Ⓑ Ⓒ Ⓓ	85 Ⓐ Ⓑ Ⓒ Ⓓ
6 Ⓐ Ⓑ Ⓒ Ⓓ	26 Ⓐ Ⓑ Ⓒ Ⓓ	46 Ⓐ Ⓑ Ⓒ Ⓓ	66 Ⓐ Ⓑ Ⓒ Ⓓ	86 Ⓐ Ⓑ Ⓒ Ⓓ
7 Ⓐ Ⓑ Ⓒ Ⓓ	27 Ⓐ Ⓑ Ⓒ Ⓓ	47 Ⓐ Ⓑ Ⓒ Ⓓ	67 Ⓐ Ⓑ Ⓒ Ⓓ	87 Ⓐ Ⓑ Ⓒ Ⓓ
8 Ⓐ Ⓑ Ⓒ Ⓓ	28 Ⓐ Ⓑ Ⓒ Ⓓ	48 Ⓐ Ⓑ Ⓒ Ⓓ	68 Ⓐ Ⓑ Ⓒ Ⓓ	88 Ⓐ Ⓑ Ⓒ Ⓓ
9 Ⓐ Ⓑ Ⓒ Ⓓ	29 Ⓐ Ⓑ Ⓒ Ⓓ	49 Ⓐ Ⓑ Ⓒ Ⓓ	69 Ⓐ Ⓑ Ⓒ Ⓓ	89 Ⓐ Ⓑ Ⓒ Ⓓ
10 Ⓐ Ⓑ Ⓒ Ⓓ	30 Ⓐ Ⓑ Ⓒ Ⓓ	50 Ⓐ Ⓑ Ⓒ Ⓓ	70 Ⓐ Ⓑ Ⓒ Ⓓ	90 Ⓐ Ⓑ Ⓒ Ⓓ
11 Ⓐ Ⓑ Ⓒ Ⓓ	31 Ⓐ Ⓑ Ⓒ Ⓓ	51 Ⓐ Ⓑ Ⓒ Ⓓ	71 Ⓐ Ⓑ Ⓒ Ⓓ	91 Ⓐ Ⓑ Ⓒ Ⓓ
12 Ⓐ Ⓑ Ⓒ Ⓓ	32 Ⓐ Ⓑ Ⓒ Ⓓ	52 Ⓐ Ⓑ Ⓒ Ⓓ	72 Ⓐ Ⓑ Ⓒ Ⓓ	92 Ⓐ Ⓑ Ⓒ Ⓓ
13 Ⓐ Ⓑ Ⓒ Ⓓ	33 Ⓐ Ⓑ Ⓒ Ⓓ	53 Ⓐ Ⓑ Ⓒ Ⓓ	73 Ⓐ Ⓑ Ⓒ Ⓓ	93 Ⓐ Ⓑ Ⓒ Ⓓ
14 Ⓐ Ⓑ Ⓒ Ⓓ	34 Ⓐ Ⓑ Ⓒ Ⓓ	54 Ⓐ Ⓑ Ⓒ Ⓓ	74 Ⓐ Ⓑ Ⓒ Ⓓ	94 Ⓐ Ⓑ Ⓒ Ⓓ
15 Ⓐ Ⓑ Ⓒ Ⓓ	35 Ⓐ Ⓑ Ⓒ Ⓓ	55 Ⓐ Ⓑ Ⓒ Ⓓ	75 Ⓐ Ⓑ Ⓒ Ⓓ	95 Ⓐ Ⓑ Ⓒ Ⓓ
16 Ⓐ Ⓑ Ⓒ Ⓓ	36 Ⓐ Ⓑ Ⓒ Ⓓ	56 Ⓐ Ⓑ Ⓒ Ⓓ	76 Ⓐ Ⓑ Ⓒ Ⓓ	96 Ⓐ Ⓑ Ⓒ Ⓓ
17 Ⓐ Ⓑ Ⓒ Ⓓ	37 Ⓐ Ⓑ Ⓒ Ⓓ	57 Ⓐ Ⓑ Ⓒ Ⓓ	77 Ⓐ Ⓑ Ⓒ Ⓓ	97 Ⓐ Ⓑ Ⓒ Ⓓ
18 Ⓐ Ⓑ Ⓒ Ⓓ	38 Ⓐ Ⓑ Ⓒ Ⓓ	58 Ⓐ Ⓑ Ⓒ Ⓓ	78 Ⓐ Ⓑ Ⓒ Ⓓ	98 Ⓐ Ⓑ Ⓒ Ⓓ
19 Ⓐ Ⓑ Ⓒ Ⓓ	39 Ⓐ Ⓑ Ⓒ Ⓓ	59 Ⓐ Ⓑ Ⓒ Ⓓ	79 Ⓐ Ⓑ Ⓒ Ⓓ	99 Ⓐ Ⓑ Ⓒ Ⓓ
20 Ⓐ Ⓑ Ⓒ Ⓓ	40 Ⓐ Ⓑ Ⓒ Ⓓ	60 Ⓐ Ⓑ Ⓒ Ⓓ	80 Ⓐ Ⓑ Ⓒ Ⓓ	100 Ⓐ Ⓑ Ⓒ Ⓓ

TEAR HERE

MODEL COURT OFFICER EXAM I

TIME ALLOWED FOR ENTIRE EXAMINATION—3 HOURS.

DIRECTIONS: Each question has four suggested answers, lettered A, B, C, and D. Decide which one is the best answer and, on your answer sheet, darken the space for that letter.

Memory Section

Questions 1 to 15 are to be answered on the basis of the incident described below. You will have 10 minutes to read and study the description of the incident. Then you will have to answer the 15 questions about the incident without referring back to the description of the incident.

Police Officers Brown and Reid are on patrol in a radio car on a Saturday afternoon in the fall. They receive a radio message that a burglary is in progress on the fifth floor of a seven-floor building on the corner of 7th Street and Main. They immediately proceed to that location to investigate and take appropriate action.

The police officers are familiar with the location and they know that the Fine Jewelry Company occupies the entire fifth floor of the building. They are also aware that the owner, who is not in the office on weekends, often leaves large amounts of gold in his office safe. Upon arrival at the scene, the officers lock their radio car and proceed to look for the building superintendent in order to get into the building. The superintendent states that he has not heard or seen anything unusual, although admitting he did leave the premises for approximately 1 hour to have lunch. The officers start for the fifth floor, using the main elevator. As they reach that floor and open the door, they hear noises followed by the sound of the freight elevator door in the rear of the building closing and the elevator descending. They quickly run through the open door of the Fine Jewelry Company and observe that the office safe is open and empty. The officers then proceed to the rear of the building and use the rear staircase to reach the ground floor. They open the rear door and go out onto the street, where they observe four individuals running up the street, crossing at the corner. At that point, the police officers get a clear view of the suspects. They are three males and one female. One of the males appears to be white, one is obviously Hispanic, and the other male is black. The female is white.

The white male is bearded. He is dressed in jeans and white sneakers and a red and blue jacket. He is carrying a white duffel bag on his shoulder. The Hispanic male limps slightly and he has a large dark moustache. He is wearing brown slacks, a green shirt, and brown shoes. He is carrying a blue duffel bag on his shoulder. The black male is clean shaven, is wearing black pants, a white shirt, a green cap, and black shoes. He is carrying what appears to be a tool box. The white female is carrying a sawed off shotgun, has long brown hair, and is wearing white jeans, a blue blouse, and blue sneakers. She has a red kerchief around her neck.

45

The officers chase the suspects for two blocks without being able to catch them. At that point, the suspects separate. The white and black males quickly get into a black 1973 Chevrolet station wagon with Connecticut license plates with the letters AWK on it and drive away. The Hispanic male and the white female get away in an old light blue Dodge van. The van has a prominent CB antenna on top and large yellow streaks running along the doors on both sides. There is a large dent on the right rear fender, and the van bears New Jersey license plates which the officers are unable to read.

The station wagon turns left and enters the expressway headed towards Connecticut. The van makes a right turn and proceeds in the direction of the tunnel headed for New Jersey.

The officers quickly return to their radio car to report what has happened.

1. The officers were able to read the following letters from the license plates on the station wagon

    (A) WAX
    (B) EWK
    (C) AUK
    (D) AWK

2. The van used by the suspects had a dented

    (A) left front fender
    (B) right front fender
    (C) right rear fender
    (D) left rear fender

3. The officers observed that the van was headed in the direction of

    (A) Long Island
    (B) Pennsylvania
    (C) New Jersey
    (D) Connecticut

4. The best description of the female suspect's hair is

    (A) short and light in color
    (B) long and light in color
    (C) short and dark in color
    (D) long and dark in color

5. The suspect who was wearing a white shirt is the

    (A) white male
    (B) Hispanic male
    (C) black male
    (D) white female

6. The suspect who wore white jeans is the

    (A) white male
    (B) Hispanic male
    (C) black male
    (D) white female

7. The Hispanic male suspect carried a duffel bag of what color?

   (A) yellow
   (B) red
   (C) blue
   (D) brown

8. Of the following, the best description of the shoes worn by the Hispanic suspect is

   (A) white sneakers
   (B) black shoes
   (C) black boots
   (D) brown shoes

9. The suspect who was carrying the white duffel bag was the

   (A) white female
   (B) black male
   (C) Hispanic male
   (D) white male

10. The suspect who was carrying the shotgun was the

    (A) white female
    (B) black male
    (C) Hispanic male
    (D) white male

11. The green cap was worn by the

    (A) white female
    (B) black male
    (C) Hispanic male
    (D) white male

12. The suspect who limped when he or she ran was the

    (A) white female
    (B) black male
    (C) Hispanic male
    (D) white male

13. Of the following, the best description of the station wagon used by the suspects is a

    (A) 1973 black Chevrolet station wagon
    (B) 1971 blue Ford
    (C) 1971 green Dodge
    (D) 1976 red Ford

14. The best description of the suspects who used the station wagon to depart is

    (A) a black male and a white female
    (B) a black male and a white male
    (C) a white female and a Hispanic male
    (D) a black male and a Hispanic male

15. The van's license plate was from which of the following states?

   (A) New York
   (B) Delaware
   (C) New Jersey
   (D) Connecticut

16. "Physical and mental health are essential to the peace officer." According to this statement, the peace officer must be

   (A) wise as well as strong
   (B) smarter than most people
   (C) sound in mind and body
   (D) smarter than the average criminal

17. "Since a court officer is paid from city funds, a court officer who refuses to waive immunity from prosecution when called on to testify in court automatically terminates employment." From this statement only, it may be best inferred that

   (A) a court officer who refuses to waive immunity will be dismissed
   (B) all city employees are court officers
   (C) city employees may be fired only for malfeasance
   (D) court officers who waive immunity may not be prosecuted

18. "Teamwork is the basis of successful law enforcement." The factor stressed by this statement is

   (A) cooperation
   (B) determination
   (C) initiative
   (D) pride

19. "Legal procedure is a means, not an end. Its function is merely to accomplish the enforcement of legal rights. A litigant has no vested interest in the observance of the rules of the procedure as such. All that he or she should be entitled to demand is an opportunity for a fair and impartial trial of his or her case. The litigant should not be permitted to invoke the aid of technical rules merely to embarrass an adversary." According to this paragraph, it is most correct to state that

   (A) observance of the rules of procedure guarantees a fair trial
   (B) embarrassment of an adversary through technical rules does not make for a fair trial
   (C) a litigant is not interested in the observance of rules of procedure
   (D) technical rules must not be used in a trial

Your answers to questions 20 through 23 are to be based only on the information given in the following paragraph.

A court officer shall give reasonable aid to a sick or injured person. He or she shall summon an ambulance, if necessary, by telephoning the Police Department, which shall notify the hospital concerned. He or she shall wait in a place where the arriving ambulance can see him or her, if possible, so as to direct the ambulance doctor or attendant to the patient. If the ambulance does not arrive within a half-hour, the court officers should call a second time, telling the department that this is a second call. However, if the injured person is conscious, the court officer should ask whether such person is willing to go to a hospital before calling for an ambulance.

20. According to the preceding paragraph, the court officer who wishes to summon an ambulance should telephone the

   (A) nearest hospital
   (B) Department of Hospitals
   (C) Police Department
   (D) nearest police precinct

21. According to the preceding paragraph, if an ambulance doesn't arrive within half an hour, the court officer should

   (A) ask the person injured if he or she wants to go to the hospital in a cab
   (B) call the Police Department
   (C) call the nearest police precinct
   (D) call the nearest hospital

22. According to the preceding paragraph, a court officer who is called to help a person who has fallen on the courthouse steps and apparently has a broken leg should

   (A) put the leg in traction so that the doctor will have no difficulty setting it
   (B) ask the person, if he or she is conscious, whether he or she wishes to go to a hospital
   (C) attempt to get the story behind the injury to determine if the city is involved
   (D) put in a call for an ambulance at once

23. According to the preceding paragraph, a court officer who is present when a witness becomes ill while waiting to testify should

   (A) wait in front of the room until the ambulance arrives
   (B) send a bystander to the courtroom to page a doctor
   (C) ask the witness if he or she wishes to go to a hospital
   (D) call the court clerk for instructions

Answer questions 24 through 26 on the basis of the following paragraph.

Accident-proneness is a subject that deserves much more objective and competent study than it has received to date. In discussing accident proneness, it is important to differentiate between the employee who is a "repeater" and one who is truly accident-prone. It is obvious that any person assigned to work without thorough training in safe practice is liable to injury until he or she does learn the "how" of it. Few workers left to their own devices develop adequate safe practices, and therefore they must be trained. Only those who fail to respond to proper training should be regarded as accident-prone. The repeater whose accident record can be explained by a correctible physical defect, by correctible plant or machine hazards, or by assignment to work for which he or she is not suited because of physical deficiencies or special abilities cannot be fairly called accident-prone.

24. According to the preceding paragraph, people are considered accident-prone if

(A) they have accidents regardless of the fact that they have been properly trained
(B) they have many accidents
(C) it is possible for them to have accidents
(D) they work at a job where accidents are possible

25. According to the preceding paragraph

(A) workers learn the safe way of doing things if left to their own intelligence
(B) most workers must be trained to be safe
(C) a worker who has had more than one accident has not been properly trained
(D) intelligent workers are always safe

26. According to the preceding paragraph, a person would not be called accident-prone if the cause of the accident was

(A) a lack of interest in the job
(B) recklessness
(C) high-speed machinery
(D) eyeglasses that don't fit properly

27. "A sufficient quantity of material supplied as evidence enables the laboratory expert to determine the true nature of the substance, whereas an extremely limited specimen may be an abnormal sample containing foreign matter not indicative of the true nature of the material." On the basis of this statement alone, it may be concluded that a reason for giving an adequate sample of material for evidence to a laboratory expert is that

(A) a limited specimen spoils more quickly than a larger sample
(B) a small sample may not truly represent the evidence
(C) he or she cannot analyze a small sample correctly
(D) he or she must have enough material to keep a part of it untouched to show in court

28. "Upon retirement from service a member shall receive a retirement allowance that shall consist of an annuity that shall be the actuarial equivalent of his accumulated deductions at the time of his retirement; a pension in addition to this annuity that shall be equal to one service-fraction of his final compensation, multiplied by the number of years of City service since he last became a member credited to him; and a pension that is the actuarial equivalent of the reserve-for-increased-take-home-pay to which he may then be entitled, if any." According to this selection, a retirement allowance shall consist of

(A) an annuity plus a pension plus an actuarial equivalent
(B) an annuity plus a pension reserve-for-increased-take-home-pay, if any
(C) an annuity plus reserve-for-increased-take-home-pay, if any, plus final compensation
(D) a pension plus reserve-for-increased-take-home-pay, if any, plus accumulated deductions

Answer questions 29 to 31 on the basis of the following paragraph.

What is required is a program that will protect our citizens and their property from criminal and antisocial acts, will effectively restrain and reform juvenile deliquents, and will prevent the further development of antisocial behavior. Discipline and punishment of offenders must necessarily play an important part in any such program. Serious offenders cannot be mollycoddled merely because they are under 21. Restraint and punishment necessarily follow serious antisocial acts. But punishment, if it is to be effective, must be a planned part of a more comprehensive program of treating delinquency.

29. The one of the following goals not included among those listed in the paragraph is to

   (A) stop young people from defacing public property
   (B) keep homes from being broken into
   (C) develop an intra-city boys' baseball league
   (D) change juvenile deliquents into useful citizens

30. According to the preceding paragraph, punishment is

   (A) not satisfactory in any program dealing with juvenile deliquents
   (B) the most effective means by which young vandals and hooligans can be reformed
   (C) not used sufficiently when dealing with serious offenders who are under 21
   (D) of value in reducing juvenile deliquency only if it is part of a complete program

31. With respect to serious offenders who are under 21 years of age, the paragraph suggests that they

   (A) be mollycoddled
   (B) be dealt with as part of a comprehensive program to punish mature criminals
   (C) should be punished
   (D) be prevented, by brute force if necessary, from performing antisocial acts

Answer questions 32 to 34 on the basis of the following paragraph.

A number of crimes, such a robbery, assault, rape, and certain forms of theft and burglary, are high visibility crimes in that it is apparent to all concerned that they are criminal acts prior to or at the time they are committed. In contrast to these, check forgeries, especially those committed by first offenders, have low visibility. Little in the criminal act or in the interaction between the check passer and the person cashing the check identifies it as a crime. Closely related to this special quality of a forgery is the fact that, while it is formally defined and treated as a felonious or infamous crime, it is informally held by the legally untrained public to be a relatively harmless form of crime.

32. According to the preceding paragraph, crimes of "high visibility"

   (A) are immediately recognized as crimes by the victims
   (B) take place in public view
   (C) always involve violence or the threat of violence
   (D) usually are committed after dark

33. According to the preceding paragraph,

   (A) the public regards check forgery as a minor crime
   (B) the law regards check forgery as a minor crime
   (C) the law distinguishes between check forgery and other forgery
   (D) it is easier to spot inexperienced check forgers than other criminals

34. As used in this paragraph, an "infamous" crime is

    (A) more serious than a felony
    (B) less serious than a felony
    (C) more or less serious than a felony, depending on circumstances
    (D) the same as a felony

35. "The housing authority not only faces every problem of the private developer, it must also assume responsibilities of which a private building is free. The authority must account to the community; it must conform to federal regulations and it must overcome the prejudices of contractors, bankers, and prospective tenants against public operations. These authorities are being watched by antihousing enthusiasts for the first error of judgment or the first evidence of high costs that can be torn to bits before a congressional committee." On the basis of this selection, which statement would be most correct?

    (A) Private builders do not have the opposition of contractors, bankers, and prospective tenants.
    (B) Congressional committees impede the progress of public housing by petty investigations.
    (C) A housing authority must deal with all the difficulties encountered by the private builder.
    (D) Housing authorities are no more immune to errors in judgment than private developers.

36. "If you are in doubt as to whether any matter is properly mailable, you should ask the postmaster. Even though the Post Office has not expressly declared any matter to be nonmailable, the sender of such matter may be held fully liable for violation of law if he does actually send nonmailable matter through the mails." Of the following, the most accurate statement made concerning this selection is:

    (A) nonmailable matter is not always clearly defined
    (B) ignorance of what constitutes nonmailable matter relieves the sender of all responsibility
    (C) though doubt may exist about the mailability of any matter, the sender is fully liable for law violation if such matter should be nonmailable
    (D) the Post Office Department is not explicit in its position on the violation of the nonmailable matter law

37. "Statistics tell us that heart disease kills more people than any other illness, and the death rate continues to rise. People over 30 have a 50–50 chance of escaping, for heart disease is chiefly an illness of people in late middle age and advanced years. Since more people in this age group are living today than were some years ago, heart disease is able to find more victims." On the basis of this selection, the one of the following statements which is most nearly correct is that

    (A) half of the people over 30 years of age have heart disease today
    (B) more people die of heart disease than of all other diseases combined
    (C) older people are the chief victims of heart disease
    (D) the rising birth rate has increased the possibility that the average person will die of heart disease

Answer questions 38 to 40 on the basis of the following paragraph.

Discontent of some citizens with the practices and policies of local government leads here and there to the creation of those American institutions, the local civic associations. Completely outside of government, manned by a few devoted volunteers, understaffed, and with pitifully few dues-paying members, they attempt to arouse widespread public opinion on selected issues by presenting facts and ideas. The findings of these civic associations are widely trusted by press and public, and amidst the records of rebuffs received are found more than enough achievements to justify what little their activities cost. Civic associations can, by use of the initiative, get constructive measures placed on the ballot; the influence of these associations is substantial when brought to bear on a referendum question. Civic associations are politically nonpartisan. Hence their vitality is drawn from true political independents who in most communities are a trifling minority. Except in a few large cities, civic associations are seldom affluent enough to maintain an office or to afford even a small paid staff.

38. It can be inferred from the preceding paragraph that the main reason for the formation of civic associations is to

    (A) provide independent candidates for local public office with an opportunity to be heard
    (B) bring about changes in the activities of local government
    (C) allow persons who are politically nonpartisan to express themselves on local public issues
    (D) permit the small minority of true political independents to supply leadership for nonpartisan causes

39. According to the preceding paragraph, the statements that civic associations make on issues of general interest are

    (A) accepted by large segments of the public
    (B) taken at face value only by the few people who are true political independents
    (C) questioned as to their accuracy by most newspapers
    (D) expressed as a result of aroused widespread public opinion

40. On the basis of the information concerning civic associations contained in the preceding paragraph, it is most accurate to conclude that since

    (A) they deal with many public issues, the cost of their efforts on each issue is small
    (B) their attempts to attain their objectives often fail, little money is contributed to civic associations
    (C) they spend little money in their efforts, they are ineffective when they become involved in major issues
    (D) their achievements outweigh the small cost of their efforts, civic associations are considered worthwhile

41. Assume that a court officer is allowed 17¹/₂¢ a mile for the use of her automobile for the purpose of conducting defendants to and from court sessions. The first month she drove 416 miles; the second month 328 miles; the third month 2012 miles; the fourth month 187 miles; the fifth month 713 miles; the sixth month 1608 miles. Her expenditures for gasoline averaged 90¢ a gallon and her general average of miles per gallon was 16; she used 32 quarts of oil @ $1.25 quart and spent $351.20 on care and general

upkeep of her car for the 6 months. Without considering the depreciation in value of her car, she would have received above her expenditures

(A) $233.90
(B) $296.10
(C) $40.00
(D) $263.20

42. Assume that you borrowed $2,000 on November 1, 1985, for the use of which you were required to pay simple interest semiannually at 7% a year. By May 1, 1991, you would have paid interest amounting to

(A) $140.00
(B) $700.00
(C) $770.00
(D) $280.00

Answer questions 43 to 45 on the basis of the following table. Data for certain categories have been omitted from the table. You are to calculate the missing numbers, if needed, to answer the questions.

	1988	1989	Numerical Increase
Clerical staff	1,226	1,347	
Court officers	495	529	34
Deputy sheriffs	38	40	
Supervisors	_____	464	_____
Totals	2,180	2,414	

43. The number in the "supervisors" group in 1988 was most nearly

(A) 500
(B) 475
(C) 450
(D) 425

44. The largest percentage increase from 1988 to 1989 was in the group of

(A) clerical staff
(B) court officers
(C) deputy sheriffs
(D) supervisors

45. In 1989, the ratio of the number of clerical staff to the total of the other three categories of employees was most nearly

(A) 1:1
(B) 2:1
(C) 3:1
(D) 4:1

46. A courtroom contains 72 persons, which is two fifths of its capacity. The number of persons that the courtroom can hold is

(A) 28
(B) 180
(C) 129
(D) greater than 200 and less than 300

47. The total cost of 30 pencils at 18¢ a dozen, 12 paper pads at 27½¢ each, and 8 boxes of paper clips at 5¼¢ a box is

(A) more than $10
(B) $1.50
(C) $4.17
(D) $1.52

48. A worked 5 days on overhauling an old car. Then B worked 4 days to finish the job. After the sale of the car, the net profit was $243. They wanted to divide the profit on the basis of the time spent by each. A's share of the profit was

(A) $108
(B) $135
(C) $127
(D) $143

49. A clock that loses 4 minutes every 24 hours was set at 6 a.m. on October 1. What time was indicated by the clock when the *correct* time was 12:00 noon on October 6?

(A) 11:36 a.m.
(B) 11:38 a.m.
(C) 11:39 a.m.
(D) 11:40 a.m.

50. A secretary is entitled to 1⅓ days of sick leave for every 32 days of work. How many days of work must the secretary have to her credit in order to be entitled to 12 days of sick leave?

(A) 272
(B) 288
(C) 290
(D) 512

DIRECTIONS for questions 51 to 60: Each question lists four names or numbers. The names or numbers may or may not be exactly the same. Compare the four names or numbers in each question, and mark your answer as follows:

Mark (A) if all four names or numbers are *DIFFERENT*
Mark (B) if *TWO* of the names or numbers are exactly the same
Mark (C) if *THREE* of the names or numbers are exactly the same
Mark (D) if all *FOUR* of the names or numbers are exactly the same

51. W.E. Johnston
W.E. Johnson
W.E. Johnson
W.B. Johnson

52. Vergil L. Muller
Vergil L. Muller
Vergil L. Muller
Vergil L. Muller

53. 5261383
    5263183
    5263183
    5623183

54. Atherton R. Warde
    Asheton R. Warde
    Atherton P. Warde
    Athertin P. Warde

55. 8125690
    8126690
    8125609
    8125609

56. E. Owens McVey
    E. Owen McVey
    E. Owen McVay
    E. Owen McVey

57. Emily Neal Rouse
    Emily Neal Rowse
    Emily Neal Roose
    Emily Neal Rowse

58. Francis Ramsdell
    Francis Ransdell
    Francis Ramsdell
    Francis Ramsdell

59. 2395890
    2395890
    2395890
    2395890

60. 1926341
    1962341
    1963241
    1926341

DIRECTIONS for questions 61 to 70: Each of the following questions contains four sentences. You are to select that sentence in each question that is **best** with respect to grammar and good usage. On your answer sheet, mark the letter preceding your sentence choice.

61. (A) One of us have to make the reply before tomorrow.
    (B) Making the reply before tomorrow will have to be done by one of us.
    (C) One of us has to reply before tomorrow.
    (D) Anyone has to reply before tomorrow.

62. (A) There is several ways to organize a good report.
    (B) Several ways exist in organizing a good report.
    (C) To organize a good report, several ways exist.
    (D) There are several ways to organize a good report.

63. (A) All employees whose record of service ranged between 51 down to 40 years were retired.
    (B) All employees who had served from 40 to 51 years were retired.
    (C) All employees serving 40 to 51 years were retired.
    (D) Those retired were employees serving 40 to 51 years.

64. (A) Of all the employees, he spends the most time at the office.
    (B) He spends more time at the office than that of his employees.
    (C) His working hours are longer or at least equal to those of the other employees.
    (D) He devotes as much, if not more, time to his work than the rest of the employees.

65. (A) She made lots of errors in her typed report, and which caused her to be reprimanded.
    (B) The supervisor reprimanded the typist, whom she believed had made careless errors.
    (C) Many errors were found in the report which she typed and could not disregard them.
    (D) The errors in the typed report were so numerous that they could hardly be overlooked.

66. (A) He suspects that the service is not so satisfactory as it should be.
    (B) He believes that we should try and find whether the service is satisfactory.
    (C) He believes that the service that we are giving is unsatisfactory.
    (D) He believes that the quality of our services are poor. —— *Error in Subject/Verb agreement*

67. (A) Most of these statements have been supported by persons who are reliable and can be depended on.
    (B) The persons which have guaranteed these statements are reliable. *unacceptable*
    (C) Reliable persons guarantee the facts with regards to the truth of these statements.
    (D) These statements can be depended on, for their truth has been guaranteed by reliable persons.

68. (A) The personnel office has charge of employment, dismissals, and employee's welfare.
    (B) The personnel office is responsible for the employment, dismissal, and welfare of employees.
    (C) Employment, together with dismissals and employee's welfare, are handled by the personnel department.
    (D) The personnel office takes care of employment, dismissals, and etc.

69. (A) This kind of pen is some better than that kind.
    (B) I prefer having these pens than any other.
    (C) This kind of pen is the most satisfactory for my use.
    (D) In comparison with that kind of pen, this kind is more preferable.

70. (A) We often come across people to whom we disagree.
    (B) We often come across people in whom we disagree.
    (C) We often come across people in regard for whom we disagree.
    (D) We often come across people with whom we disagree.

DIRECTIONS for questions 71 to 80: The numbers on each line of each question should correspond with the code letters on the same line in accordance with the table below:

Code Letter	R	D	F	G	K	Z	E	P	A	T
Number	0	1	2	3	4	5	6	7	8	9

In some of the lines below, an error exists in the coding. Compare the numbers and letters in each question very carefully. Mark your answers according to how many lines in each question contain errors.

Mark (A) if only *ONE* line contains an error or errors
Mark (B) if *TWO* lines contain errors
Mark (C) if all *THREE* lines contain errors
Mark (D) if *NONE* of the lines contains an error

71. KDEPAPT   4167879   73. PFDRKTE   7210496
     AGFKZEP   8324567   DETZFKA   1695248
     RGDKTEZ   0314965   AKDFEPR   8512670

72. KFPEZT   427659   74. GDFPKZE   3226456
     FETGEZ   269365   KGPTAFG   4379823
     ZKDEFP   546127   AEGPTRD   6837910

75.	KDPZETG	4175693	78.	PEZKTGE	7654936
	GREKTZE	3065956		GEPEKDF	3676421
	PGARFDG	7380123		DFPTAGZ	1399835

76.	ZPGKRGT	5734039	79.	KDRTEZ	410965
	TFKGPRD	9234710		GAZFET	385269
	KDAPEKZ	4187644		DPETGA	179948

77.	PZKFGET	7452369	80.	KTEFRAT	4962098
	RDPEKGF	0176432		PGKDEGP	7314637
	KDFPTAZ	4172983		ZEPEGKF	5676432

Questions 81 to 85 are based on the following enumeration of the duties of a court officer.

Throughout the session of the court, the officer must see that proper order and decorum are maintained in the courtroom. Above everything else, silence must be constantly observed, and every possible distraction must be eliminated so as not to delay the most efficient functioning of the court.

The officer must carry out such duties as may be required by the court and clerk. Examples of such duties are directing witnesses to the witness stand and assisting the court clerk and counsel in the handling of exhibits. At times, the officer must act as a messenger in procuring any books from the court library that are required by the attorneys and ordered by the court clerk.

The enforcement of the rules of the court requires courteous behavior on the part of the court officer, although firmness and strictness are necessary when the occasion requires such an attitude.

81. Testimony has been given, the witnesses have been cross-examined, and the attorneys have given their summations. Now the judge is charging the jury. A court officer has been stationed outside the courtroom door to prevent anyone from entering during the charge. The president of the City Council arrives, accompanied by a woman, and attempts to enter the courtroom. The court officer should

(A) apologize and explain why they cannot be permitted to enter
(B) permit the man to enter, since he is the president of the City Council, but exclude the woman
(C) permit them to enter because surely the judge would make an exception for such important people
(D) send a note in to the judge to ask whether they may be permitted to enter

82. A witness who is waiting to be called to the stand appears to be very nervous. He wiggles and squirms, stands and stretches, looks over his shoulder at the courtroom door, and waves to spectators and television cameras. The court officer should

(A) tell the witness to leave the courtroom at once
(B) handcuff the witness
(C) ask the witness to please sit still and try to restrain himself
(D) suggest to the judge that he call this witness next

83. During the course of cross-examination, a defendant frequently refers to a book that she claims has had a great influence on her life and that she claims justifies her behavior in the instance for which she is charged. In the jury box, two jurors begin a lively

discussion of whether the defendant is quoting accurately. The best action for the court officer is to

(A) ask the court clerk for permission to go to the library to get the book
(B) send a messenger to get the book
(C) assure the jurors that the book is being accurately quoted and that only the interpretation is in question
(D) remind the jurors that they are not to converse in the courtroom

84. A group of spectators, friends of the plaintiff, is seated near the rear of the courtroom. As the trial progresses, they raise inoffensive but loud shouts of encouragement, such as "Right on" and "Way to go." Stern looks mute their enthusiasm for only a moment or two, and then they continue with their verbal support. In this case, the court officer should

(A) warn them that they are prejudicing their friend's case
(B) ask the group to leave the courtroom
(C) take each member by the hand and forcibly eject him or her from the courtroom
(D) call a police officer to arrest the noisy spectators

85. The judge has asked the court clerk to hand her Exhibit B, a document that she identifies by its title as well as by its Exhibit B designation. The court clerk requests that the court officer transmit the document to the judge. The court officer goes to the exhibit table and discovers that Exhibit B is an entirely different document and that the document that the judge has requested is really Exhibit F. The court officer should

(A) bring the judge Exhibit B
(B) bring the judge Exhibit F
(C) bring both Exhibits B and F
(D) tell the judge of her error and ask which document she really wants

Answer questions 86 through 95 on the basis of the following legal definitions.

Burglary is committed when a person enters a building to commit a crime therein.

Larceny is committed when a person wrongfully takes, obtains, or withholds the property of another.

Robbery is the forcible stealing of property. If a person, while committing a larceny, uses or threatens the *immediate* use of force, the crime changes from larceny to robbery.

Sexual abuse is committed when a person subjects another person to sexual contact without the second person's consent or when a person has sexual contact with another person less than 17 years of age. (A person less than 17 years of age cannot legally consent to any sexual conduct.) "Sexual contact" may be defined as touching the sexual or other intimate parts of a person to achieve sexual gratification.

Sexual misconduct is committed when a male has sexual intercourse with a consenting female who is at least 13 years of age but less than 17 years of age.

Harassment is committed when a person intends to harass, annoy, or alarm another person and does so by striking, shoving, kicking, or otherwise subjecting the other person to physical contact.

Assault is committed when a person unlawfully causes a physical injury to another person.

86. James Kelly enters the home of Mary Smith with the intention of taking Mary's portable TV set. While Kelly is in the apartment, Mary wakes up and attempts to retrieve her TV set from Kelly. Kelly punches Mary in the face and flees with the TV set. Kelly can be charged with

    (A) burglary and larceny
    (B) burglary only
    (C) robbery and larceny
    (D) burglary and robbery

87. John Brown enters a department store with the intention of doing some shopping. Brown has a .38 caliber revolver in his coat pocket and also has a criminal conviction for armed robbery. As he passes the jewelry counter, he notices an expensive watch lying on the showcase. He checks to see whether anyone is watching him and, when he feels that he is not being observed, he slips the watch into his pocket and leaves the store. Brown could be charged with

    (A) larceny
    (B) burglary and larceny
    (C) burglary and robbery
    (D) robbery

88. Tom Murphy enters a crowded subway car. He positions himself behind a woman and starts to touch her buttocks with his hand. The woman becomes very annoyed and starts to move away. As she does so, Murphy reaches into her pocketbook and removes $10. He then exits the train at the next station. Murphy could be charged with

    (A) robbery, larceny, and sexual misconduct
    (B) burglary, robbery, and sexual abuse
    (C) burglary, larceny, and sexual misconduct
    (D) larceny and sexual abuse

89. Ed Saunders entered into the apartment of Jane Robers with the intent to sexually abuse her. However, Robers was not at home and Saunders left the apartment. Saunders could be charged with

    (A) sexual abuse
    (B) sexual misconduct
    (C) burglary
    (D) none of the above, as a crime did not take place because Robers was not at home

90. Frank Taylor entered the apartment of his 16-year-old girlfriend, Doris, to have sexual intercourse with her. Doris consented to this sexual conduct and they engaged in intercouse. Taylor could be charged with

    (A) burglary
    (B) sexual misconduct
    (C) both burglary and sexual misconduct
    (D) no crime, as Doris consented to the activity

91. Brian Jones asks his 17-year-old girlfriend, Mary, if she would like to go to a motel and have sexual intercourse. She agrees and they go to the motel. Jones could be charged with

    (A) burglary
    (B) sexual misconduct
    (C) both burglary and sexual misconduct
    (D) no crime, as she consented to the activity

92. Bill is at a party at Joan's house. An argument ensues between several of the guests. Bill overhears Helen make a derogatory comment about him. He walks up to Helen and demands she "apologize or else." Helen refuses to apologize; Bill slaps her in the face and then rushes from the apartment. Bill could be charged with

    (A) assault
    (B) burglary and assault
    (C) harassment
    (D) burglary and harassment

93. Joe is on his way to work. He is in a very bad mood. As he enters the warehouse where he works, he slips and falls to the floor. This only escalates his foul mood. As he is getting up, he sees a fellow worker who had made some unkind remarks to him two days before. Joe picks up a piece of board that is lying on the floor, walks up to the other worker, and hits him across the arm. This causes the other worker to suffer a broken arm. Joe could be charged with

    (A) assault
    (B) burglary and assault
    (C) harassment
    (D) none of the above, as Joe was emotionally upset

94. Jim enters a school through a rear window at 2:00 a.m. He wants to take a movie projector that he knows is kept in a specific room. He enters the room, takes the projector, and starts to leave when he is confronted by a security guard. The guard attempts to grab Jim; however Jim slips away. As the guard again attempts to apprehend him, Jim swings the projector, striking the guard in the face. The guard falls to the floor unconscious and suffers a broken nose. Jim could be charged with

    (A) burglary, larceny, and robbery
    (B) robbery, larceny, and assault
    (C) burglary, larceny, and assault
    (D) burglary, robbery, and assault

95. Sue invites Tom to her apartment for dinner. After dinner, Tom decides that he would like to have a sexual encounter with Sue. She attempts to discourage his advances. Tom then proceeds to hold her down on the couch and to fondle her breasts and touch her private parts. When Sue starts to scream, Tom rushes from the apartment. Tom could be charged with

    (A) burglary and sexual abuse
    (B) burglary and sexual misconduct
    (C) sexual abuse
    (D) no crime, as Sue invited him to her apartment

Base your answers to questions 96 to 98 on the following paragraph, describing responsibilities of a court officer.

The jurors may go to dinner only with the permission of the judge. If permission is granted, the court officer must accompany the jury and make certain that it does not separate. Under no circumstances may the court officer allow any person to communicate with the jury without official permission or allow anybody to molest them. The jury must be returned to the jury room as soon as the members have finished eating.

96. It is a beautiful spring evening, and the jury has just finished dinner. It is really too nice to go in. The court officers in charge of this jury should

    (A) accompany the entire jury on a brisk walk along the waterfront, then return to the courthouse
    (B) return directly to the courthouse
    (C) allow those jurors who request some exercise to jog once around the park accompanied by one of the court officers while the other officer stands by with the remaining jurors
    (D) allow the jurors to deliberate for a while in a quiet section of the park

97. The judge has given permission for the jury to go out to dinner. The jurors and alternates comprise a truly diverse group; they constitute an ideal jury. However, they have very different tastes in food. Three would like to go to a Chinese restaurant, seven want Italian food, and five have their hearts set on a well-known delicatessen. The court officers should

    (A) require that each juror choose one of the more popular restaurants—Italian or delicatessen—then divide into two groups, each accompanied by a court officer.
    (B) ask the court clerk to join the jury for dinner so as to have a court officer accompanying each group
    (C) refuse to take the jury out for dinner and send out for sandwiches
    (D) ask for a vote between the two most popular cuisines, then take everyone to the winner

98. The jury is about to go to dinner. A large group of day care workers is picketing outside the courthouse. The day care workers are carrying signs and are demanding that they be included in the city's pension plan. The pickets are orderly but are very intense and vocal. Their concerns are in no way related to the case that the jury is deliberating. The court officers should

    (A) tell the jurors to walk straight ahead, looking neither to the right nor the left and paying no attention to the pickets
    (B) step outside before the jurors and ask the pickets for total silence until the jury passes
    (C) ask a police officer to silence the pickets and to have them lay their signs on the ground as the jury passes
    (D) take the jurors out through another exit

Answer questions 99 and 100 on the basis of the following paragraph.

Certain inmate types are generally found in prisons. These types are called gorillas, toughs, hipsters, and merchants. Gorillas deliberately use violence to intimidate fearful inmates into providing favors. Toughs are swift to explode into violence against prisoners, because of real or imagined insult. Exploitation of others is not their major goal. Hipsters are bullies who choose victims with caution in order to win acceptance among inmates by demonstrating physical bravery. Their bravery, however, is false. Merchants exploit other inmates through manipulation in sharp trading of goods stolen from prison supplies or in trickery in gambling.

99. Martins frequently beats up Smith and Brooks. Smith and Brooks provide Martins with extra cigarettes and coffee. Martins is a

    (A) tough
    (B) gorilla
    (C) merchant
    (D) hipster

100. White and Miller are in the same cell block and are often assigned to be in the same place at the same time. They are scheduled for the same kitchen duty and the same exercise group. White is cross-eyed. It is often difficult to determine exactly where he is looking, and it often appears that he is directing his gaze in one direction. One day, Miller trips White and beats him about the head with a board. Miller is a

    (A) tough
    (B) gorilla
    (C) merchant
    (D) hipster

End of Exam

Correct Answers for Model Court Officer
Exam I

1. D	21. B	41. A	61. C	81. A
2. C	22. B	42. C	62. D	82. C
3. C	23. C	43. D	63. B	83. D
4. D	24. A	44. D	64. A	84. B
5. C	25. B	45. A	65. D	85. C
6. D	26. D	46. B	66. C	86. D
7. C	27. B	47. C	67. D	87. A
8. D	28. B	48. B	68. B	88. D
9. D	29. C	49. C	69. C	89. C
10. A	30. D	50. B	70. D	90. C
11. B	31. C	51. B	71. D	91. D
12. C	32. A	52. D	72. A	92. C
13. A	33. A	53. B	73. A	93. A
14. B	34. D	54. A	74. B	94. D
15. C	35. C	55. B	75. B	95. C
16. C	36. C	56. B	76. B	96. B
17. A	37. C	57. B	77. B	97. D
18. A	38. B	58. C	78. B	98. D
19. B	39. A	59. D	79. A	99. B
20. C	40. D	60. B	80. C	100. A

Explanations of Correct Answers

If you made any errors in answering questions 1 to 15, reread the description of the event and the questions. Confirm the correctness of the given answer.

16. **(C)** Physical and mental health constitute soundness of mind and body.

17. **(A)** The words "automatically terminates" serve as your clue that a court officer who refuses to waive immunity will be dismissed.

18. **(A)** Teamwork is cooperation.

19. **(B)** The last sentence makes this statement.

20. **(C)** The court officer must telephone the Police Department, which, in turn, will notify a hospital to send an ambulance.

21. **(B)** The court officer must wait patiently for half an hour and then call the Police Department again.

22. **(B)** The last sentence says that the court officer should ask a conscious person if he or she is willing to go to a hospital.

23. **(C)** Assuming that the ill witness is conscious, the witness must be asked whether he or she wishes to go to the hospital before any further action is taken.

24. **(A)** Accident-proneness is defined as susceptibility to frequent accidents despite proper training.

25. **(B)** Since few workers develop adequate safe practices on their own, most must be trained to be safe.

26. **(D)** The fitting of eyeglasses is a correctible situation. The person whose accidents are eliminated by the refitting of eyeglasses is not accident-prone.

27. **(B)** "... a limited specimen may be an abnormal sample ... not indicative of the true nature of the material."

28. **(B)** The three components of the retirement allowance are separated by semicolons. They are an annuity, a pension, and a pension that is the actuarial equivalent of the reserve-for-increased-take-home pay.

29. **(C)** While participation in sports may help to turn youths from antisocial behavior, the paragraph specifically addresses crime, punishment, and reform.

30. **(D)** The last sentence makes this point very clearly.

31. **(C)** The paragraph states that serious young offenders should be punished and should not be mollycoddled because of their age. It does not suggest treating them as mature criminals.

32. **(A)** Without a doubt, victims of robbery, assault, rape, theft, and burglary immediately recognize that they have been victims of crimes.

33. **(A)** The law considers check forgery to be a felony, but the layman considers forgery to be relatively minor, probably because it is nonviolent.

34. **(D)** This definition is given in the last sentence.

35. **(C)** See the first sentence.

36. **(C)** The sender of nonmailable material is fully liable for violation of the law even though he or she may not have known that the material was not mailable. In other words, ignorance of the law is no excuse. When in doubt, ask.

37. **(C)** "... heart disease is chiefly an illness of people in late middle age and advanced years."

38. **(B)** See the first sentence.

39. **(A)** The findings of civic associations are widely trusted by press and public.

40. **(D)** "more than enough achievements to justify what little their activities cost."

41. **(A)** First add the monthly mileages to determine how many miles the court officer drove in the 6 months.
$416 + 328 + 2012 + 187 + 713 + 1608 = 5,264$ miles
She was reinbursed $5,264 \times \$.175 = \$921.20$
She used $5,264 \div 16 = 329$ gallons of gasoline at 90¢ a gallon, for a cost of $329 \times \$.90 = \$296.10$
Oil cost her $32 \times \$1.25 = \$40$ and general upkeep $351.20.
Total expenses were $\$296.10 + \$40.00 + \$351.20 = \$687.30$.
$\$921.20 - \$687.30 = \$233.90$

42. **(C)** November 1, 1985 to May 1, 1991 is $5\frac{1}{2}$ years.
$\$2,000 \times 7\% = \$140 \times 5.5 = \$770$.

43. **(D)** You will need almost all the figures to calculate answers to the three questions, so begin by completing the table.

	1988	1989	Numerical Increase
Clerical staff	1,226	1,347	121
Court officers	495	529	34
Deputy sheriffs	38	40	2
Supervisors	421	498	77
Totals	2,180	2,414	234

44. **(D)** To find percentage increase, divide the numerical increase by the original number. The approximate percentage increases are: clerical staff 10%; court officers 7%; deputy sheriffs 5%; supervisors 18%.

45. **(A)** The total of employees other than clerical staff in 1989 was 1,067. The ratio of others to clerical staff was closest to 1:1.

46. **(B)** If $2/5 = 72$, then $1/5 = 36$ and $5/5$ or a full courtroom $= 180$.

47. **(C)** 30 pencils $= 2^1/_2$ dozen $\times$ \$.18 doz. $=$ \$ .45
12 pads $\times$ \$.275 $=$ 3.30
8 boxes paper clips $\times$ \$.0525 $= +$ .42
\$4.17

48. **(B)** Altogether A and B worked 9 days on the car.
\$243 $\div$ 9 $=$ \$27 profit per day. A's 5 days were worth \$27 $\times$ 5 $=$ \$135.

49. **(C)** From 6 a.m. October 1 to noon on October 5 is $5^1/_4$ days.
$4 \times 5.25 = 21$ 21 minutes were lost; noon minus 21 $=$ 11:39 a.m.

50. **(B)** The secretary gets $1^1/_3$ days of sick leave for 32 days of work.
She therefore gets 1 day of sick leave for 24 days' work.
$24 \times 12 = 288$ days of work for 12 days' sick leave.

51. **(B)** The second and third names are the same.

52. **(D)** All four names are the same.

53. **(B)** The second and third numbers are the same.

54. **(A)** All four last names are the same, but only the first and third first names are the same, and those two have different middle initials.

55. **(B)** The third and fourth numbers are the same.

56. **(B)** The second and fourth names are exactly the same.

57. **(B)** The second and fourth names are the same.

58. **(C)** The first, third, and fourth names are the same.

59. **(D)** All four numbers are exactly the same.

60. **(B)** The first and fourth numbers are the same.

61. **(C)** Choice (A) incorrectly uses the plural verb form *have* with the singular subject *one*. (B) is awkward and wordy. (D) incorrectly changes the subject from *one of us to anyone*.

62. **(D)** Choice (A) incorrectly uses the singular verb form *is* with the plural subject *ways*. In (B) *in organizing* should be *to organize*. The inverted construction in sentence (C) is not as direct or as clear as the expression in sentence (D).

63. **(B)** This sentence is most specific and therefore best.

64. **(A)** Answer choices (B) and (D) contain faulty comparisons; the working hours must be compared with the those of any *other* employee. (C) requires the phrase *longer than or equal to.*

65. **(D)** Answer choices (A), (B), and (C) all contain glaring grammatical errors.

66. **(C)** In (A) *suspicion* is incorrectly used as a verb. (B) incorrectly uses *try and find* for *try to find out*. (D) has an error in subject–verb agreement *(quality are).*   NO

67. **(D)** Answer choice (A) contains the unacceptable expression *most all*. (B) incorrectly uses *which* to refer to persons. (C) includes the unacceptable expression *with regards to.*

68. **(B)** Choice (A) is not parallel. (C) contains an error in agreement between subject and verb *(employment are)*. (D) uses the unacceptable combination *and etc.*

69. **(C)** Answer choices (A) and (D) use the unacceptable expressions *same better* [Some] and *more preferable*. (B) is awkward.

70. **(D)** The correct idiom is *to disagree with.*

71. **(D)** There are no errors in these three lines of code.

72. **(A)** The numbers of D and E are reversed in the third line.

73. **(A)** K is miscoded in the third line.

74. **(B)** D and P are miscoded in the first line. In the third line, there are code reversals for A and E and for R and D.

75. **(B)** K is miscoded in the second line. In the third line, the code numbers for F and D are reversed.

76. **(B)** In the second line, there are code reversals for K and G and for R and D. In the third line, Z is miscoded.

77. **(B)** In the first line, there is code reversal for K and F. In the third line, there is code reversal for F and P and miscoding of Z.

78. **(B)** In the second line, there is code reversal of D and F. In the third line, P and T are both miscoded.

79. **(A)** In the third line, E and G are miscoded.

80. **(C)** In the first line, there is code reversal for A and T. In the second line, there is code reversal for K and D. In the third line, there is code reversal at G and K.

81. **(A)** If the court officer has been stationed outside the courtroom door to prevent anyone from entering, that is what the court officer must do. The court officer does not have the authority to make exceptions. Sending a note to the judge would be distracting and would impede efficient operation of that court.

82. **(C)** The duty of the court officer is to maintain order and decorum in the courtroom. Certainly the first step the officer should take is to advise the witness that his behavior is distracting and to request that the witness sit quietly. It is not the place of the court officer to make suggestions to the judge. If the witness continues to be distracting, the judge may ask the court officer to remove him, but the court officer may not make such a decision on his or her own.

83. **(D)** The court officer is charged with maintaining silence and order. He or she must admonish the jurors to keep silent. If the judge wants the book in the courtroom, he or she may order it.

84. **(B)** Since attending a trial is a privilege, not a right or a duty, noisy spectators must be asked to leave. Polite asking precedes forcible ejection.

85. **(C)** The court officer must follow directions yet must also be sensible and discreet. Exhibit B is the document requested by label, so it must be delivered. Exhibit F is the document requested by name; it also must be delivered. The court officer should do this in such a manner as not to embarrass the judge nor disrupt proceedings in any way.

86. **(D)** The situation fits both the definition of burglary (to enter a building to commit a crime) and of robbery (stealing by force—in this case, the punch in the face).

87. **(A)** John Brown can be charged with larceny only, as there was no intent to commit a crime when he entered the store, and there was no force used. Brown may also be open to a weapons charge, but that is beyond the scope of this question.

88. **(D)** The charges are sexual abuse (touching of the buttocks) and larceny (taking $10 from the pocketbook). No force was used to remove the money, thereby eliminating the charge of robbery.

89. **(C)** To charge a person with burglary, it must only be shown that the building was entered with the intention of committing a crime therein. (In this case, the crime was sexual abuse.) Despite the fact that Saunders was unsuccessful in committing the crime he intended, the intention was there.

90. **(C)** Taylor's intention for entering the apartment was to have sexual intercourse with his 16-year-old girlfriend, a crime because she is less than 17 years of age. He could be charged with burglary (intent to commit a crime) and sexual misconduct (sexual intercourse with a female less than 17 years of age).

91. **(D)** Mary is 17 years old and gave her consent.

92. **(C)** There was neither any intention to commit a crime when Bill entered the building nor was any injury incurred. For the charge to be assault, there must be some kind of injury.

93. **(A)** Joe had no intent to commit a crime before he entered the warehouse. He caused an injury to a fellow worker, a broken arm, by his actions; therefore, the charge of assault could be preferred. Emotional disturbance is not a valid excuse for such actions.

94. **(D)** The charges are burglary (entering the school with the intention of taking a movie projector), robbery (using force on the security guard to take the projector), and assault (causing an injury, the broken nose, to the security guard).

95. **(C)** Because Tom used force to touch Sue's private parts, he could be charged with sexual abuse. Since there was no intention to commit the crime prior to his entering her apartment, the possibility of a burglary charge is eliminated.

96. **(B)** The court officers have no discretion in this matter. They must return the jurors directly to the courthouse and jury room.

97. **(D)** The jury must not separate. It would be possible to bring in dinner instead, but a break is probably desirable and preferable. This is a democracy, so let the majority rule. Go to the restaurant that pleases the greatest number of jurors.

98. **(D)** No one may either communicate with or molest any juror in any way. The best way to avoid the possibility of communication or molestation is to avoid the people

who wish to communicate. Go out another door and avert any possibility of confrontation.

99. **(B)** Beating other inmates so as to extract cigarettes and coffee from them is using violence to intimidate and to gain favors, behavior typical of the gorilla.

100. **(A)** White is so cross-eyed that it is difficult to determine just where he is looking, but Miller imagines that White is staring and insulting him and so erupts into violence. Miller is a tough.

MODEL COURT OFFICER EXAM II

TIME ALLOWED FOR ENTIRE EXAMINATION—3 HOURS.

DIRECTIONS: Each question has four suggested answers lettered A, B, C, and D. Decide which one is the best answer and, on your answer sheet, darken the space for that letter.

Memory Section

DIRECTIONS: You will have 10 minutes to study the following three pictures, to note details, and to commit them to memory. Then you will have to answer 15 questions about the three pictures without looking back at them.

Picture for questions 1 to 5—At **The Bank**

*Picture for questions 6 to 10—*__The Meeting of the Board__

*Picture for questions 11 to 15—*__A Rap Session__

Answer questions 1 to 5 on the basis of the picture, "At The Bank."

1. The teller is

 (A) wearing a striped tie
 (B) wearing glasses
 (C) making change
 (D) left-handed

2. The man wearing a hat is also

 (A) handing money to the teller
 (B) wearing a bow tie
 (C) talking to another man in the line
 (D) smoking a pipe

3. The teller's name is

 (A) R. Smith
 (B) T. Jones
 (C) T. Smith
 (D) R. Jones

4. The woman in the striped dress is

 (A) carrying a handbag
 (B) wearing a pendant
 (C) holding gloves
 (D) third in line

5. The time of day is

 (A) early morning
 (B) lunchtime
 (C) mid-afternoon
 (D) late afternoon

Answer questions 6 to 10 on the basis of the picture, "The Meeting of the Board."

6. How many of the men at the table have glasses?

 (A) one
 (B) two
 (C) three
 (D) four

7. Which of the following items is NOT shown on the table?

 (A) a file box
 (B) a water pitcher
 (C) an ashtray
 (D) a glass of water

8. The man at the head of the table is

   (A) pointing to the map
   (B) reading the papers in front of him
   (C) looking at a man on his right
   (D) looking at a man on his left

9. The man with the mustache is

   (A) holding a pencil
   (B) wearing a striped tie
   (C) bald
   (D) wearing a dark suit

10. All of the following statements are true EXCEPT

    (A) There are seven men at the table.
    (B) The map is directly behind the man at the head of the table.
    (C) The man who is speaking has a glass of water in front of him.
    (D) One of the men is holding a pipe.

Answer questions 11 to 15 on the basis of the picture, **"A Rap Session."**

11. The number of people in this picture is

    (A) 5
    (B) 6
    (C) 7
    (D) 8

12. The person wearing boots

    (A) is lying down
    (B) has blond hair
    (C) has a mustache
    (D) is smoking a cigarette

13. The person wearing white socks

    (A) is commanding the attention of the rest of the group
    (B) is also wearing a leather jacket
    (C) wears glasses
    (D) none of these

14. The man who is reclining is

    (A) raising one hand for attention
    (B) leaning on his right elbow
    (C) leaning on his left elbow
    (D) taking notes

15. The man who is wearing sneakers is

    (A) looking at his watch
    (B) rubbing his left eye
    (C) speaking
    (D) cannot tell from this picture

16. "Ideally, a correctional system should include several types of institutions to provide different degrees of custody." On the basis of this statement, one could most reasonably say that

    (A) as the number of institutions in a correctional system increases, the efficiency of the system increases
    (B) the difference in degree of custody for the inmate depends on the types of institutions in a correctional system
    (C) the greater the variety of institutions, the stricter the degree of custody that can be maintained
    (D) the same type of correctional institution is not desirable for the custody of all prisoners

17. "The enforced idleness of a large percentage of adult men and women in our prisons is one of the direct causes of the tensions that burst forth in riot and disorder." On the basis of this statement, a good reason why inmates should perform daily work of some kind is that

    (A) better morale and discipline can be maintained when inmates are kept busy
    (B) daily work is an effective way of punishing inmates for the crimes they have committed
    (C) law-abiding citizens must work therefore labor should also be required of inmates
    (D) products of inmates' labor will in part pay the cost of their maintenance

18. "With industry invading rural areas, the use of the automobile, and the speed of modern communications and transportation, the problems of neglect and delinquency are no longer peculiar to cities but are an established feature of everyday life." This statement implies most directly that

    (A) delinquents are moving from cities to rural areas
    (B) delinquency and neglect are found in rural areas
    (C) delinquency is not as much of a problem in rural areas as in cities
    (D) rural areas now surpass cities in industry

19. "Young men from minority groups, if unable to find employment, become discouraged and hopeless because of their economic position and may finally resort to any means of supplying their wants." The most reasonable of the following conclusions that may be drawn from this statement only is that

    (A) discouragement sometimes leads to crime
    (B) in general, young men from minority groups are criminals
    (C) unemployment turns young men from crime
    (D) young men from minority groups are seldom employed

20. "To prevent crime, we must deal with the possible criminals long before they reach the prison. Our aim should be not merely to reform the law breakers but to strike at the roots of crime: neglectful parents, bad companions, unsatisfactory homes, selfishness, disregard for the rights of others, and bad social conditions." The above statement recommends

    (A) abolition of prisons
    (B) better reformatories
    (C) compulsory education
    (D) general social reform

21. "There is evidence that shows that comic books which glorify the criminal and criminal acts have a distinct influence in producing young criminals." According to this statement,

    (A) comic books affect the development of criminal careers
    (B) comic books specialize in reporting criminal acts
    (C) young criminals read comic books exclusively
    (D) young criminals should not be permitted to read comic books

22. A study shows that juvenile delinquents are equal in intelligence but up to three school grades behind juvenile nondelinquents. On the basis of this information only, it is most reasonable to say that

    (A) a delinquent usually progresses to the educational limit set by intelligence
    (B) educational achievement depends on intelligence only
    (C) educational achievement is closely associated with delinquency
    (D) lack of intelligence is closely associated with delinquency

23. "Prevention of crime is of greater value to the community than the punishment of crime." If this statement is accepted as true, greatest emphasis should be placed on

    (A) execution
    (B) medication
    (C) imprisonment
    (D) rehabilitation

Answer questions 24 to 27 on the basis of the following paragraph.

All automotive accidents, no matter how slight, are to be reported to the Safety Division by the employee involved on Accident Report Form S–23 in duplicate. When the accident is of such a nature that it requires the filling out of the State Motor Vehicle Report Form MV–104, this form is also prepared by the employee in duplicate, and sent to the Safety Division for comparison with the Form S–23. The Safety Division forwards both copies of Form MV–104 to the Corporation Counsel, which sends one copy to the State Bureau of Motor Vehicles. When the information on the Form S–23 indicates that the employee may be at fault, an investigation is made by the Safety Division. If this investigation shows that the employee was at fault, the employee's dispatcher is asked to file a complaint on Form D–11. The foreman of mechanics prepares a damage report on Form D–8 and an estimate of the cost of repairs on Form D–9. The dispatcher's complaint, the damage report, the repair estimate and the employee's previous accident record are sent to the Safety Division where they are studied together with the accident report. The Safety Division then recommends whether disciplinary action should be taken against the employee.

24. According to the preceding paragraph, the Safety Division should be notified whenever an automotive accident has occurred by means of

    (A) Form S–23
    (B) Forms S–23 and MV–104
    (C) Forms S–23, MV–104, D–8, D–9, and D–11
    (D) Forms S–23, MV–104, D–8, D–9, D–11, and employee's accident record

25. According to the preceding paragraph, the forwarding of the Form MV—104 to the State Bureau of Motor Vehicles is done by the

    (A) corporation counsel
    (B) dispatcher
    (C) employee involved in the accident
    (D) Safety Division

26. According to the preceding paragraph, the Safety Division investigates an automotive accident if the

    (A) accident is serious enough to be reported to the State Bureau of Motor Vehicles
    (B) dispatcher files a complaint
    (C) employee appears to have been at fault
    (D) employee's previous accident record is poor

27. Of the forms mentioned in the preceding paragraph, the dispatcher is responsible for preparing the

    (A) accident report form
    (B) damage report
    (C) complaint form
    (D) estimate of cost of repairs

28. A painter being instructed in his duties was told by his foreman, "Experience is the best teacher." The one of the following that most nearly expresses the meaning of this quotation is

    (A) a good teacher will make a hard job look easy
    (B) bad experience does more harm than good
    (C) lack of experience will make an easy job hard
    (D) the best way to learn to do a thing is by doing it

29. "Once the purposes or goals of an organization have been determined, they must be communicated to subordinate levels of supervisory staff." On the basis of this quotation, the most accurate of the following statements is that

    (A) supervisory personnel should participate in the formulation of the goals of an organization
    (B) the structure of an organization should be considered in determining the organization's goals
    (C) the goals that have been established for the different levels of an organization should be reviewed regularly
    (D) information about the goals of an organization should be distributed to supervisory personnel

30. "Close examination of traffic accident statistics reveals that traffic accidents are frequently the result of violations of traffic laws—and usually the violations are the result of illegal and dangerous driving behavior, rather than the result of mechanical defects or poor road conditions." According to this statement, the majority of dangerous traffic violations are caused by

    (A) poor driving
    (B) bad roads
    (C) unsafe cars
    (D) unwise traffic laws

Answer questions 31 to 33 on the basis of the following paragraph.

The supervisor gains the respect of his staff members, and increases his influence over them by controlling his temper and avoiding criticizing anyone publicly. When a mistake is made, the good supervisor will talk it over with the employee quietly and privately. The supervisor listens to the employee's story, suggests a better way to do the job, and offers help so the mistake won't happen again. Before closing the discussion, the supervisor should try to find something good to say about other aspects of the employee's work. Some praise and appreciation, along with instruction, is likely to encourage an employee to improve in those areas where he is weakest.

31. A good title that would show the meaning of this entire paragraph would be

    (A) How to Correct Employee Errors
    (B) How to Praise Employees
    (C) Mistakes are Preventable
    (D) The Weak Employee

32. According to the preceding paragraph, the work of an employee who has made a mistake is more likely to improve if the supervisor

    (A) avoids criticizing him
    (B) gives him a chance to suggest a better way of doing the work
    (C) listens to the employee's excuses to see if he is right
    (D) praises good work at the same time he corrects the mistake

33. According to the preceding paragraph, when a supervisor needs to correct an employee's mistake, it is important that he

    (A) allow some time to go by after the mistake is made
    (B) do so when other employees are not present
    (C) show his influence by his tone of voice
    (D) tell other employees to avoid the same mistake

34. "Determination of total, or even partial, guilt and responsibility as viewed by law cannot be made solely on the basis of a consideration of the external factors of the case, but rather should be made mainly in the light of the individual defendant's history and development." The above statement reflects a philosophy of law that requires that

    (A) the punishment fit the crime
    (B) the individual, rather than the crime, be considered first
    (C) motivations behind a crime are relatively unimportant
    (D) the individual's knowledge of right and wrong be the sole determinant of guilt

35. A city traffic regulation says, "No driver shall enter an intersection unless there is sufficient unobstructed space beyond the intersection to accommodate the vehicle he or she is operating, notwithstanding any traffic-control signal indication to the contrary." This regulation means that

    (A) a driver should not go through an intersection if there are no parking spaces available in the next block
    (B) a driver should not enter an intersection when the traffic light is red
    (C) a driver should not enter an intersection if traffic ahead is so badly backed up that he or she would not be able to go ahead and would block the intersection
    (D) a driver should ignore traffic signals completely whenever there are obstructions in the road ahead

Answer questions 36 to 40 on the basis of the following paragraph.

A large proportion of people behind bars are not convicted criminals, but people who have been arrested and are being held until their trial in court. Experts have often pointed out that this detention system does not operate fairly. For instance, a person who can afford to pay bail usually will not get locked up. The theory of the bail system is that the person will make sure to show up in court when he or she is supposed to; otherwise, bail will be forfeited—the person will lose the money that was put up. Sometimes a person who can show that he or she is a stable citizen with a job and a family will be released on "personal recognizance" (without bail). The result is that the well-to-do, the employed, and the family men can often avoid the detention system. The people who do wind up in detention tend to be the poor, the unemployed, the single, and the young.

36. According to the preceding passage, people who are put behind bars

    (A) are almost always dangerous criminals
    (B) include many innocent people who have been arrested by mistake
    (C) are often people who have been arrested but have not yet come to trial
    (D) are all poor people who tend to be young and single

37. The passage says that the detention system works unfairly against people who are

    (A) rich
    (B) old
    (C) married
    (D) unemployed

38. The passage uses the expression "bail will be forfeited." Even if you had not seen the word *forfeit* before, you could figure out from the way it is used in the passage that *forfeiting* probably means

    (A) losing track of something
    (B) finding something
    (C) giving up something
    (D) avoiding something

39. When someone is released on "personal recognizance," this means that

    (A) the judge knows that the person is innocent
    (B) he or she does not have to show up for a trial
    (C) he or she has a record of previous convictions
    (D) he or she does not have to pay bail

40. Suppose that two men were booked on the same charge at the same time and that the same bail was set for both of them. One man was able to put up bail, and he was released. The second man was not able to put up bail, and he was held in detention. The writer of the passage would most likely feel that this result is

    (A) unfair, because it does not have any relationship to guilt or innocence
    (B) unfair, because the first man deserves severe punishment
    (C) fair, because the first man is obviously innocent
    (D) fair, because the law should be tougher on the poor people than on the rich

41. If a peace officer's weekly salary is increased from $320.00 to $360.00, the percentage of increase is

    (A) 10%
    (B) 11 1/9%
    (C) 12 1/2%
    (D) 20%

42. Suppose that one half the peace officers in a department have served for more than 10 years and one third have served for more than 15 years. The fraction of peace officers in the department who have served between 10 and 15 years is

    (A) 1/3
    (B) 1/5
    (C) 1/6
    (D) 1/12

$$\frac{1}{3} \times \frac{1}{2} = \frac{1}{6}$$

43. Suppose that 10% of those who commit serious crimes are convicted and that 15 percent of those convicted are sentenced for more than 3 years. The percentage of those committing serious crimes who are sentenced for more than 3 years is

    (A) 15%
    (B) 1.5%
    (C) 0.15
    (D) 0.015%

44. Assume that there are 1,100 employees in a state agency. Of these, 15% are peace officers, 80% of whom are attorneys; of the attorneys, two fifths have been with the agency more than 5 years. The number of peace officers who are attorneys and have more than 5 years' experience with the agency is most nearly

    (A) 45
    (B) 53
    (C) 132
    (D) 165

1100 X .15 = 165 peace offi.
165 X .80 = 132 ATNY
2/5 X 132 = 52.8

45. An employee who has 500 cartons of supplies to pack can pack them at the rate of 50 an hour. After this employee has worked for a half-hour, he is joined by another employee, who can pack 45 cartons an hour. Assuming that both employees can maintain their respective rates of speed, then the total number of hours required to pack all the cartons is

475 aftr 1/2 hr
95 per hr 2 guys

    (A) 4 1/2
    (B) 5
    (C) 5 1/2
    (D) 6 1/2

475 ÷ 95 = 5.5

46. Thirty-six officers can complete an assignment in 22 days. Assuming that all officers work at the same rate of speed, the number of officers that would be needed to complete this assignment in 12 days is

proportion

    (A) 42
    (B) 54
    (C) 66
    (D) 72

36:22 = x:12   mult both sides
12x = (36 x 22) = 792 Div by 12 (both sides)
x = 66

Answer questions 47 to 50 using the information given in the table below.

Age Composition in the Labor Force in City A (1975–1985)

	Age Group	1975	1980	1985
Men	14–24	8,430	10,900	14,340
	25–44	22,200	22,350	26,065
	45 +	17,550	19,800	21,970
Women	14–24	4,450	6,915	7,680
	25–44	9,080	10,010	11,550
	45 +	7,325	9,470	13,180

47. The greatest increase in the number of people in the labor force between 1975 and 1980 occurred among

(A) men between the ages of 14 and 24
(B) men age 45 and over
(C) women between the ages of 14 and 24
(D) women age 45 and over

48. If the total number of women of all ages in the labor force increases from 1985 to 1990 by the same number as it did from 1980 to 1985, the total number of all women of all ages in the labor force in 1990 will be

(A) 27,425
(B) 29,675
(C) 37,525
(D) 38,425

49. The total increase in numbers of women in the labor force from 1975 to 1980 differs from the total increase of men in the same years by being

(A) 770 less than that of men
(B) 670 more than that of men
(C) 770 more than that of men
(D) 1,670 more than that of men

50. In 1975 the proportion of married women in each group was as follows: 1/5 of the women in the 14–24 age group, 1/4 of those in the 25–44 age group, and 2/5 of those 45 and over. How many married women were in the labor force in 1975?

(A) 4,625
(B) 5,990
(C) 6,090
(D) 7,910

DIRECTIONS for questions 51 to 60: Each question gives the name and identification number of an employee. You are to choose the *ONE* answer that has exactly the same identification number and name as those given in the question, and blacken its letter on your answer sheet.

51. 176823   Katherine Blau

 (A) 176823   Catherine Blau
 (B) 176283   Katherine Blau
 (C) 176823   Katherine Blau
 (D) 176823   Katherine Blaw

52. 673403   Boris T. Frame

 (A) 673403   Boris P. Frame
 (B) 673403   Boris T. Frame
 (C) 673403   Boris T. Fraim
 (D) 673430   Boris T. Frame

53. 498832   Hyman Ziebart

 (A) 498832   Hyman Zeibart
 (B) 498832   Hiram Ziebart
 (C) 498832   Hyman Ziebardt
 (D) 498832   Hyman Ziebart

54. 506745   Barbara O'Dey

 (A) 507645   Barbara O'Day
 (B) 506745   Barbara O'Day
 (C) 506475   Barbara O'Day
 (D) 506745   Barbara O'Dey

55. 344223   Morton Sklar

 (A) 344223   Morton Sklar
 (B) 344332   Norton Sklar
 (C) 344332   Morton Sklaar
 (D) 343322   Morton Sklar

56. 816040   Betsy B. Voight

 (A) 816404   Betsy B. Voight
 (B) 814060   Betsy B. Voight
 (C) 816040   Betsy B. Voight
 (D) 816040   Betsey B. Voight

57. 913576   Harold Howritz

 (A) 913576   Harold Horwitz
 (B) 913576   Harold Howritz
 (C) 913756   Harold Howritz
 (D) 913576   Harald Howritz

58. 621190   Jayne T. Downs

 (A) 621990   Janie T. Downs
 (B) 621190   Janie T. Downs
 (C) 622190   Janie T. Downs
 (D) 621190   Jayne T. Downs

59. 004620   George McBoyd

 (A) 006420   George McBoyd
 (B) 006420   George MacBoyd
 (C) 006420   George McBoid
 (D) 004620   George McBoyd

60. 723495   Alice Appleton

 (A) 723495   Alice Appleton
 (B) 723594   Alica Appleton
 (C) 723459   Alice Appleton
 (D) 732495   Alice Appleton

DIRECTIONS for questions 61 to 70: Each of the following questions contains four sentences. You are to select that sentence in each question that is **best** with respect to grammar and good usage. On your answer sheet, mark the letter preceding your sentence choice.

61. (A) You have got to get rid of some of these people if you expect to have the quality of the work improve.
 (B) The quality of the work would improve if they would leave fewer people do it.
 (C) I believe it would be desirable to have fewer persons doing this work.
 (D) If you had planned on employing fewer people than this to do the work, this situation would not have arose.

62. (A) This kind of worker achieves success through patience.
 (B) Success does not often come to men of this type except they who are patient.
 (C) Because they are patient, these sort of workers usually achieve success.
 (D) This worker has more patience than any man in his office.

63. (A) Nobody but you and your brother know the reason for my coming.
 (B) The reason for my coming is only known to you and your brother.
 (C) My reason for coming is known by nobody except you and your brother.
 (D) My reason for coming is known only by you and your brother.

64. (A) They are alike in this respect.
    (B) They are both alike in this respect.
    (C) He is alike to him in this respect.
    (D) They are alike to this respect.

65. (A) It is they.
    (B) It is them.
    (C) It is us.
    (D) It is me.

66. (A) Where is he at?
    (B) At where is he?
    (C) Where is he?
    (D) What place is he at now?

67. (A) I cannot believe but what he is guilty.
    (B) I cannot believe but where he is guilty.
    (C) I cannot believe but how he is guilty.
    (D) I cannot but believe that he is guilty.

68. (A) This data is correct.
    (B) Them data is correct.
    (C) These data are correct.
    (D) Those data is correct.

69. (A) The one is different with the other.
    (B) The one is different to the other.
    (C) The one is different from the other.
    (D) The one is different than the other.

70. (A) The draperies were not hanged well.
    (B) The draperies were not hanged good.
    (C) The draperies were not hung well.
    (D) The draperies were not hung good.

DIRECTIONS for questions 71 to 80: In this test of speed and accuracy you are asked to make the kind of code changes that are required when code words and numbers are changed. An office used the following to code cost prices secretly:

```
f i n d   b y   z e a l
1 2 3 4   5 6   7 8 9 0
```

The office then decided to switch the code to:

```
w r i t e s   a b l y
1 2 3 4 5 6   7 8 9 0
```

This entailed changing all the price tags. In the left-hand column you are given a list of tag prices in the old code marks. From among the choices in the right hand column you must choose the letters called for by the new code.

OLD CODE		NEW CODE		
71. dnb	(A) tie	(B) ris	(C) ati	(D) wit
72. nba	(A) eil	(B) bir	(C) iel	(D) ieb
73. blz	(A) tls	(B) bai	(C) elb	(D) eya
74. lzdy	(A) stay	(B) ybia	(C) yats	(D) lwab
75. ife	(A) wrb	(B) brw	(C) rbw	(D) rwb
76. fye	(A) wsb	(B) ral	(C) wbs	(D) iwb
77. alzd	(A) layt	(B) lyat	(C) layt	(D) bayt
78. nel	(A) tay	(B) rab	(C) ibl	(D) iby
79. ilza	(A) rial	(B) liar	(C) lair	(D) ryal
80. ndb	(A) rit	(B) ite	(C) tes	(D) rte

Questions 81 to 85 are based on the following enumeration of the duties of a court officer.

The court officer has important functions in connection with the control of the jury. He or she must confirm that every juror has the proper place in the box and must be constantly on watch to prevent any juror from leaving the jury box while the trial is in progress. Should a juror desire to leave the box while the case is going on, the court officer must first inform the judge of the juror's desire to determine whether the judge will grant or refuse the juror's wish. If the judge approves, the trial is stopped and the court officer is instructed to accompany the juror while he or she is out of the jury box. In order to prevent any stoppage or mistrial, the court officer must not allow the juror to get out of the range of sight or hearing. The officer must always bear in mind that the juror should be returned as quickly as possible, without any unnecessary delay. The juror must not enter into any conversation with anybody or read any matter that he or she may have or that may be given by another person.

The court officer must be particularly careful when placed in charge of a jury that has retired to deliberate. The court officer must conduct the jury to the jury room and see to it that no juror talks with anyone on the way. If a juror does talk with someone, the event may afford grounds for a mistrial.

81. A juror has requested and received permission to go to the men's room. As he approaches the door, he takes out a sports magazine he has brought from home as "bathroom literature." The court officer who has accompanied him should

(A) permit the juror to read his sports magazine
(B) check the magazine for papers that might be hidden between the pages, then let the juror read it
(C) offer the juror something of his own to read, something that the court officer knows will not influence the juror in any way
(D) tell the juror that reading in the men's room is not permitted

82. While leading a jury from the courtroom to the jury room, a court officer notices a person leaning against a corridor wall making active hand motions as a juror stares intently. The *first* thing for the court officer to do is to

(A) tell the juror to look straight ahead and keep walking
(B) step between the juror and the person making the hand motions so as to interrupt the juror's line of vision
(C) ask the juror what he is looking at
(D) call a police officer to arrest the person with the active hands

83. This question is based on the scenario described in question 82. A court officer ascertains that a message was being transmitted by an outside person to a juror. It would be best for the court officer to

(A) keep this information secret
(B) ask the juror what the message was all about
(C) deliver the jury to the jury room, then discuss the matter with the court clerk
(D) accompany the juror to the judge and tell the judge exactly what the court officer observed

84. During the course of testimony, a juror begins to cough uncontrollably. The coughing is loud and distressing. The court officer should

(A) summon a doctor at once
(B) lead the juror from the courtroom as quickly and as quietly as possible
(C) bring the juror a glass of water
(D) ask the judge what to do

85. On the third day of a trial, a court officer notices that an alternate is sitting in the front row in the seat of one of the regular jurors while the juror is sitting in the alternate's seat. When questioned, the alternate explains that he is very short and has trouble watching the action from his assigned seat, while the juror doesn't mind the back row. The court officer should

   (A) tell them that they are required to sit in their assigned seats at all times
   (B) permit the switch, since it harms no one
   (C) tell them that the switch of seats involves a change of status and that the alternate is now a juror and the juror an alternate
   (D) threaten to cite them for contempt of court if they do not immediately return to their assigned seats

Use the information in the paragraph below to answer questions 86 to 89.

The success or failure of a criminal prosecution usually depends on the evidence presented to the court. Evidence may be divided into three major classifications: direct evidence, circumstantial evidence, and real evidence. Evidence must also be admissible, that is, material and relevant. An eyewitness account of a criminal act is direct evidence. Where an eyewitness does not have immediate experience, but reasonably infers what happened, circumstantial evidence is offered. Real evidence comprises objects introduced at a trial to prove or disprove a fact. For example, a gun, fingerprints, or bloodstains are real evidence. Real evidence may be direct or circumstantial. Evidence is immaterial if it is unimportant to the trial. For example, if someone is being tried for larceny of a crate of oranges, it is immaterial that the oranges were yellow in color. Evidence is irrelevant or immaterial if it does not prove the truth of a fact at issue. For example, if a murder has been committed with a bow and arrow, it is irrelevant to show that the defendant was well acquainted with firearms.

86. Jones and Smith go into a room together and close the door. Richards stands outside the door and sees Jones and Smith go in. A shot is heard and Smith rushes out with a smoking gun in his hand. Richards rushes into the room and finds Jones lying on the floor, dead. Richards did not see Smith fire the shot. At Smith's trial for murdering Jones, Richards tells the court what he saw and heard. Richard's story is

   (A) inadmissible evidence
   (B) real evidence
   (C) irrelevant evidence
   (D) circumstantial evidence

87. In Smith's trial for murdering Jones, in the above case, Smith's attorney could prove that Smith was an excellent student of history in high school. Such evidence would most likely be classified as

   (A) real and material
   (B) direct and relevant
   (C) immaterial and irrelevant
   (D) circumstantial and admissible

88. As Smith's trial for murdering Jones proceeds, the prosecutor proves that Smith owned the gun that killed Jones. Of the following, such evidence is most likely

   (A) direct
   (B) inadmissible
   (C) irrelevant
   (D) material

89. As Smith's trial for murdering Jones continues, the prosecutor introduces a surprise witness, Rogers, who says that, from an apartment across the street, he looked into the window of the room Jones and Smith were in and actually saw Smith point a gun at Jones and shoot him, after which Jones fell to the floor, and Smith rushed out of the room. Rogers' story is best described as

   (A) real and circumstantial evidence
   (B) direct and relevant evidence
   (C) circumstantial and admissible evidence
   (D) relevant and real evidence

90. Prison Rule: A correction officer must be in control of all of his or her keys at all times.
   Prison Rule: Under no circumstances may a prisoner be unsupervised. A correction officer is escorting a prisoner to a dental appointment in another part of the prison. As he passes through a gate from one section to another, his key breaks in the lock. He is unable to remove the portion of the key from the lock. The correction officer should

   (A) continue with the prisoner, since the key is stuck and useless
   (B) stay with the key and send the prisoner along to the dental appointment
   (C) send the prisoner back to get another correction officer as escort
   (D) remain with the prisoner beside the gate until another correction officer appears to escort the prisoner and to send for the locksmith, even though it will make the prisoner late for the dentist.

The four paragraphs below are descriptions of four personality types often attributed to youthful offenders. Use these descriptions to answer questions 91 to 96.

"Personality W"   These offenders are lazy and show a general lack of interest in most things around them. Their actions are childish, and often we would consider them helpless. They are weak and, although they lose their tempers, they are not violent. Frequently they seem preoccupied and may give the impression of being 'out of it.'

"Personality X"   Offenders in this class feel very guilty and genuinely sorry for their actions, but they are quite likely to repeat the same thing tomorrow. Despite being very selective about their friendships, they usually are willing to talk about their problems. These individuals frequently have nervous or anxious ways. They may impress you as feeling sad or unhappy much of the time.

"Personality Y"   This type of offender is very hostile and aggressive, showing little, if any, concern for the welfare of others. These people have a high need to create excitement, since for them things quickly become too boring. Attempts to control them verbally are not very effective. They are frequently both verbally and physically aggressive. Without qualms, they will lie and manipulate others to gain their own ends.

"Personality Z"   These individuals have usually been involved in gang activities and demonstrate a high degree of loyalty to that peer group. They are relatively unconcerned about adults because their pleasure is obtained by going along with their friends. Except for their delinquent acts, these people appear quite normal. They are able to get along reasonably well in correctional institutions, but generally revert to their prior behavior after release.

91. A counselor described a young offender, Jack K., as follows: "Was nervous during our talk, bit his nails, looked sad and worried, although attentive. Last week he told me he felt 'real bad' about handing in his work report late, and I could see that he did. But the very next day, he was late again with his report." These comments best fit the description of Personality

   (A) W   (B) X   (C) Y   (D) Z

92. A counselor described a young offender, Edward F., as follows: "Prefers the company of his former gang members. This is his second time at the institution. He probably won't be able to steer clear of involvement when he gets out again. Gets along with fellow offenders, appears normal, but won't talk about his problems." These comments most nearly fit the description of Personality

   (A) W   (B) X   (C) Y   (D) Z

93. A counselor described a young offender, Arthur B., as follows: "Seems to be melancholy for long periods of time. Regrets deeply that he hurt another youngster rather badly in a gangfight before being sentenced. Has only one or two friends." These comments most nearly fit the description of Personality

   (A) W   (B) X   (C) Y   (D) Z

94. A counselor described a young offender, George H., as follows: "Didn't seem to care when I suggested that he didn't show enough interest in our activities. When in the shops he tends to stand off on one side, thinking instead of actively working. He's got a temper but doesn't start fights." These comments most nearly fit the description of Personality

   (A) W   (B) X   (C) Y   (D) Z

95. A counselor described a young offender, Charles D., as follows: "He is ready to argue at the slightest provocation. Once when he beat another youth he said he was not sorry for what he did, and he did exactly the same thing the next day, watching almost maliciously for my reaction. He seems to really want only his own way." These comments most nearly fit the description of Personality

   (A) W   (B) X   (C) Y   (D) Z

96. A counselor described a young offender, Larry M., as follows: "Admitted that he had been bullying some younger residents for 'kicks,' then told me to mind my own business. Kept interrupting me and continued to do so even when I asked him to stop." These comments most nearly fit the description of Personality

   (A) W   (B) X   (C) Y   (D) Z

Answer questions 97 to 100 on the basis of the following paragraph.

"A sheriff, or court officer or other person, who allows a prisoner, lawfully in his custody, in any action or proceedings, civil or criminal, or in any prison under his charge or control, to escape or go at large, except as permitted by law, or connives at or assists such escape, or omits an act or duty whereby such escape is occasioned, or contributed to, or assisted is: 1. If he corruptly and willfully allows, connives at, or assists the escape, guilty of a felony; 2. In any other case, is guilty of a misdemeanor. Any officer who is convicted of the offense specified, forfeits his office, and is forever disqualified to hold any office, or place of trust, honor, or profit, under the constitution or laws of this state."

97. Tom Rooks, a newly appointed court officer, is bringing Bob Thomas, under indictment for armed robbery, into court for the first day of trial. As they approach the rear courtroom door, they hear an exceptionally loud noise from the street below, and vibrations make the building shake and the windows rattle. Rooks runs to the window to see what has caused the impact. As Rooks releases his hold on Thomas, Thomas bolts down the stairs and into the milling crowd and disappears. Rooks faces an investigation and charges. On the basis of the facts above and the paragraph, Rooks

    (A) is innocent
    (B) is not guilty but should be reprimanded for carelessness
    (C) is guilty of a felony
    (D) is guilty of a misdemeanor

98. A counselor who has been working with an accused awaiting trial is very concerned for the accused's mental health. The defendant cannot raise bail and is very depressed about what he considers to be false charges that reflect on his morals and virtue. The counselor speaks with a correction officer suggesting that the defendant is a potential suicide if he must remain much longer awaiting trial. The correction officer, fearful lest a suicide occur during his tour, unlocks the gate and turns away. The accused leaves his cell but is apprehended in the prison yard.

    (A) Both the counselor and the correction officer are guilty of felony.
    (B) The counselor and the correction officer are both guilty of misdemeanor.
    (C) The counselor is not guilty; the correction officer is guilty of a felony.
    (D) The counselor is guilty of a misdemeanor; the correction officer is guilty of a felony.

99. A police officer walking his beat late at night comes upon a man who is beating a woman with the metal top of a garbage can. He tells the man to stop beating the woman, but the man continues. The police officer takes the man into custody and locks him into a jail cell for the night. The next morning, the woman who was being beaten arrives at the jail and demands the release of her husband. She loves her husband, accepts his manner of settling domestic disputes, and does not wish to press charges. The officer in charge releases the man.

    (A) Both the officer and the woman are guilty of felony.
    (B) Neither the officer nor the woman is guilty of anything.
    (C) Both the officer and the woman are guilty of misdemeanor.
    (D) The officer is guilty of felony; the woman is guilty of misdemeanor.

100. Bill Burns, a known underworld figure, regularly visits his friend, Fred Church, who is serving a long prison service for racketeering. Each time Burns comes to visit, he hands correction officer John Smith a small wad of $100 bills and asks him to treat his friend well. One week, Burns hands Smith a short hacksaw blade along with the $100 bills. The next week, along with the money Burns gives Smith a note warning that people who do not treat his friend well tend to suffer. During the next week, Church saws through the cell window bars and slips through. Officer Smith will

    (A) be executed by the mob
    (B) be suspended from his position
    (C) lose his job
    (D) be convicted for committing a misdemeanor

End of Exam

Correct Answers for Model Court Officer Exam II

1. B	21. A	41. C	61. C	81. D
2. D	22. C	42. C	62. A	82. B
3. D	23. D	43. B	63. D	83. D
4. B	24. A	44. B	64. A	84. C
5. B	25. A	45. C	65. A	85. A
6. C	26. C	46. C	66. C	86. D
7. B	27. B	47. A	67. D	87. C
8. D	28. D	48. D	68. C	88. D
9. A	29. D	49. B	69. C	89. B
10. D	30. A	50. C	70. C	90. D
11. B	31. A	51. C	71. A	91. B
12. C	32. D	52. B	72. C	92. D
13. A	33. B	53. D	73. D	93. B
14. B	34. B	54. D	74. C	94. A
15. D	35. C	55. A	75. D	95. C
16. D	36. C	56. C	76. A	96. C
17. A	37. D	57. B	77. B	97. D
18. B	38. C	58. D	78. D	98. B
19. A	39. D	59. D	79. D	99. B
20. D	40. A	60. A	80. B	100. C

Explanations of Correct Answers

If you made any errors in answering questions 1 to 15, look back at the pictures and find the relevant details.

16. **(D)** If the ideal of a correctional system is that different degrees of custody should be provided by different types of institutions, then clearly not all prisoners should be subjected to the same degree of custody. Choice (A) addresses only numbers of institutions; choice (B) reverses the statement; choice (C) does not make sense.

17. **(A)** Daily work reduces the amount of time devoted to enforced idleness, reducing the boredom and tensions that lead to riots and improving morale and discipline.

18. **(B)** The problems of neglect and delinquency are an established feature of everyday life everywhere, not only in the big cities. In other words, rural areas have their share of the same problems which plague the cities.

19. **(A)** Discouragement and hopelessness stemming from unemployment and actual economic need sometimes lead to criminal behavior as a means of supplying that need.

20. **(D)** Reform of neglectful parents, bad companions, unsatisfactory homes, selfishness, disregard for the rights of others, and bad social conditions constitutes general social reform.

21. **(A)** The statement suggests that comic books that glorify criminals and criminal acts may make an impression on their readers and help those readers on their way to

criminal careers. None of the other three answer choices is suggested by the paragraph.

22. **(C)** The paragraph states only that there is a correlation between delinquency and low scholastic achievement. The paragraph specifically states that delinquents are equal in intelligence to nondelinquents but lag in achievement.

23. **(D)** It is hoped that rehabilitation of prisoners will prevent further crime. Execution also prevents further crime, but its effects cannot be widespread because few criminals are candidates for execution.

24. **(A)** The first sentence states that the first report to the Safety Division, the one filed after every accident, is the Form S–23.

25. **(A)** The employee sends two copies of Form MV–104 to the Safety Division, which sends both copies on to the Corporation Counsel. The Corporation Counsel keeps one copy and sends the other to the State Bureau of Motor Vehicles. If you didn't pick up this sequence, look back at the paragraph now.

26. **(C)** If it appears that the employee was at fault, the dispatcher files a complaint on Form D–11 which is sent, along with other papers, to the Safety Division for investigation.

27. **(B)** The dispatcher prepares Form D–11, the complaint form.

28. **(D)** Doing a thing is gaining experience in doing it. The more often one performs a certain act, the more experience one gains and the better one becomes.

29. **(D)** This paragraph is saying that administrators or policymakers determine the purposes and the goals of an organization and should then pass these goals and purposes on to the supervisory personnel. Choice (A) contradicts the statement, in suggesting that supervisory personnel are party to the process of establishing purposes and goals. Choices (B) and (C) have nothing to do with the paragraph.

30. **(A)** Violations of traffic laws and illegal and dangerous driving behavior constitute bad driving.

31. **(A)** The subject of the paragraph is the best approach to take in correcting employee errors and improving work habits.

32. **(D)** See the last two sentences. The paragraph does suggest that the supervisor listen to the employee's story, but only for his own understanding, not to exonerate the employee. The supervisor makes the suggestions for improvement, not the employee. You may feel that asking the employee for suggestions about how he might improve would be a good supervisory policy, but you must answer questions on the basis of what is stated in the paragraph.

33. **(B)** Talking over a mistake quietly and privately is making the correction when other employees are not present. Public embarrassment is not a good supervisory technique.

34. **(B)** The sociological view, as represented in this paragraph, is that the facts are irrelevant in determining guilt and responsibility and that all weight should be given to the history and development of the individual.

35. **(C)** This is the "anti-gridlock" regulation. It has nothing to do with parking spaces. While the anti-gridlock rule requires that the driver not enter the intersection on a green light if he or she has no expectation of clearing the intersection during the duration of the green light, it does not give permission to ignore a red light just because the intersection is clear. A red light must always be obeyed unless a police officer gives contradictory instructions.

36. **(C)** See the first sentence.

37. **(D)** See the last sentence.

38. **(C)** Actually, a definition of *forfeit* follows the use of the word in the paragraph.

39. **(D)** This definition also follows use of the word. Always look for definitions of unfamiliar words within the context of reading paragraphs. You will usually find clues.

40. **(A)** While the writer of the paragraph does not state that he or she agrees with the experts cited, it is clear that the writer is in sympathy with the view that operation of the bail system is unfair because of its lack of relationship to guilt or innocence.

41. **(C)** The amount of increase was $360 - $320 = $40. To calculate the percentage of increase, divide the amount of increase by the original figure. $40 \div $320 = .125 = $12\frac{1}{2}$%.

42. **(C)** $1/3 \times 1/2 = 1/6$

43. **(B)** Convert to decimals to work out the math. Then return to %. $.10 \times .15 = .015 = 1.5$%.

44. **(B)** $1100 \times .15 = 165$ peace officers
    $165 \times .80 = 132$ attorneys
    $2/5 \times 132 = 52.8$ which is most nearly 53

45. **(C)** In the first half-hour, the employee who can pack 50 cartons per hour packed 25 cartons; 475 cartons remained to be packed. The two employees working together can pack 95 cartons per hour. 475 cartons $\div$ 95 per hour = 5 hours. Add to the 5 hours working together the half-hour the first employee worked alone, and the total time taken to pack the 500 cartons is $5\frac{1}{2}$ hours.

46. **(C)** Solve this problem by means of a proportion.
    $36:22 = x:12$ Multiply both sides:
    $12x = (36 \times 22) = 792$ Divide both sides by 12.
    $x = 66$ officers needed to complete assignment in 12 days.

47. **(A)** By subtracting the number of people within each category in the labor force in 1975 from the number in the labor force in 1980, we can determine the size of the increase for each group. The number of men in the 14 to 24 age group increased by 2,470 (10,900 − 8,430 = 2,470). The increases in the other groups suggested are smaller (men age 45 and over by 2,250, women between the ages of 14 and 24 by 2,465, and women age 45 and over by 2,145).

48. **(D)** First add the numbers of women in the three age groups in 1985 to learn that there were 32,410 women in the labor force in 1985. Then in the same way, find that the number of women in the labor force in 1980 was 26,395. To find the increase from 1980 to 1985 subtract 26,395 from 32,410. The result is 6,015. If the increase from 1985 to 1990 is to be the same, then add 6,015 to 32,410 to learn that in 1990 there will be 38,425 women of all ages in the labor force.

49. **(B)** The procedure for figuring the answer to this question is similar to that used in answering question 48. The number of women in the labor force increased from 20,855 in 1975 to 26,395 in 1980, a total increase of 5,540. The number of men increased from 48,180 in 1975 to 53,050 in 1980, a total increase of 4,870. The difference between the increases is 670, and the number of women increased more than the number of men.

50. **(C)**   1/5 (20%) of 4,450 =   890
                    1/4 (25%) of 9,080 = 2,270
            + 2/5 (40%) of 7,325 = <u>2,930</u>
                                        6,090 married women in 1975

If you made any errors in questions 51 to 60, look back at the questions and carefully compare middle initials, the spelling of both first and last names, and the orders of the numbers.

61. **(C)** (A) is wordy. In (B), the correct verb should be *have* in place of *leave*. In (D), the word *arose* should be *arisen*.

62. **(A)** In (B), *they* is incorrect. (C) contains an error of number; to be correct, the phrase must read either *this sort of worker* or *these sorts of workers*. In (D) the comparison is incomplete. It must read *than any other man*.

63. **(D)** In (A), the subject is *nobody,* which is singular and requires the singular verb *knows*. (B) and (C) are awkward and poorly written.

64. **(A)** In (B) the term *both alike* is a meaningless redundancy. In (C) the phrase *alike to him* is awkward. (C) might be correctly stated, "He is like him in this respect." In (D), *to this respect* is an incorrect idiom.

65. **(A)** The verb *is* is a linking verb which takes no object. The noun following a linking verb must be in the nominative case. Only choice (A) meets this requirement.

66. **(C)** Use the fewest possible words to make your message clear. "Where is he?" is perfectly adequate.

67. **(D)** All four sentences are somewhat awkward, but (D) is correct and does say what it means. Improvements might read: "I can believe only that he is guilty." "I cannot believe that he is not guilty." "I cannot believe anything, except that he is guilty."

68. **(C)** The word *data* is plural and must take a plural verb. The singular of *data* is *datum*.

69. **(C)** The proper idiom is *different from*.

70. **(C)** The past tense *hanged* is used only with reference to people. Things, including draperies, are *hung*. Choice (C) is correct because the adverb *well* is needed to describe how the draperies were hung. Choice (D) incorrectly uses the adjective *good*.

71. **(A)** dnb − 435 − tie

72. **(C)** nba − 359 − iel

73. **(D)** blz − 507 − eya

74. **(C)** lzdy − 0746 − yats

75. **(D)** ife − 218 − rwb

76. **(A)** fye − 168 − wsb

77. **(B)** alzd − 9074 − lyat

78. **(D)** nel − 380 − iby

79. **(D)** ilza − 2079 − ryal

80. **(B)** ndb − 345 − ite

81. **(D)** The juror is not allowed to read any matter that he or she may have or that may be given by any other person, including a court officer. That is an absolute rule. Furthermore, since the court is awaiting the prompt return of the juror, the distraction of the juror by reading material might constitute an extra, unnecessary delay.

82. **(B)** The alert court officer notices everything going on around the jurors and interprets it as well as he or she can. Unobtrusive intervention is the most diplomatic yet effective way to deal with an ambiguous situation. The person with the active hands may or may not be communicating by sign language, which the juror may or may not understand. If the juror cannot see the hands, no message can be transmitted. Questioning then can follow.

83. **(D)** If there is any possibility that a mistrial might result from communication from an outsider to a juror, the judge must know immediately. Since sign language communication is outside the usual communication against which a court officer must be on guard, the officer need not feel guilty. However, having noticed the event, even if it was of short duration, the court officer is bound to report it at once.

84. **(C)** The court officer must maintain silence in the courtroom, yet must keep all jurors in the jury box unless authorized to remove them. Perhaps a glass of water is all that is needed to calm the coughing. If not, the judge will most certainly take the initiative and suggest a respite.

85. **(A)** The court officer must confirm that every juror has his or her proper place in the box. The court officer does not have the authority to make or to permit changes.

86. **(D)** Richards was not an actual eyewitness to the shooting, so his testimony cannot be considered direct evidence, but what he did hear and see before and after the shooting constitutes circumstantial evidence.

87. **(C)** Smith's academic record has absolutely nothing to do with his guilt or innocence in this murder case.

88. **(D)** Smith's ownership of the murder weapon is very important evidence in this trial.

89. **(B)** The testimony of an eyewitness is direct evidence; if Rogers actually witnessed the murder, his testimony is certainly relevant.

90. **(D)** A correction officer is obliged to follow all rules exactly. A dental appointment is not a life or death matter, so there is no room for the officer to make his or her own judgment as to the inaccessibility of the key or the reliability of the prisoner.

91. **(B)** Jack K. is a typical "X," nervous and truly sorry for his shortcomings but unable to change his habits.

92. **(D)** Edward F. is a "Z." He gets along in prison and gets along with other inmates, but he keeps coming back.

93. **(B)** Arthur B., another "X," seems unhappy much of the time and, because he is selective, has few friends.

94. **(A)** George H. shows the lack of interest in activities or events that is typical of a "W."

95. **(C)** A "Y" is hostile and aggressive and gets pleasure from having others notice these aspects of his behavior. Charles D. fits this pattern.

96. **(C)** Larry M. is another hostile and aggressive "Y."

97. **(D)** You can chalk this up to inexperience and carelessness, but Rooks, through his own actions, permitted Bob Thomas to escape and is guilty of a misdemeanor.

98. **(B)** The matter of the correction officer's guilt is very clear. The correction officer's behavior in permitting the prisoner to escape was certainly willful, but it was in no way corrupt, so the crime must be classified as a misdemeanor rather than as a felony. The counselor contributed to the escape by raising fears in the correction officer's mind. As such, the counselor is also guilty of a misdemeanor.

99. **(B)** No charges were pressed, so the man is not in lawful custody under any action or proceedings. Since the man is not in lawful custody, his release is not a crime.

100. **(C)** Officer Smith has corruptly and willfully assisted the escape of the prisoner. If convicted, he will forfeit his position, be barred from future similar employment or office, and face other criminal penalties as well. Even if Smith's offense had been classified as a misdemeanor, he would have lost his job permanently.

Model Court Officer Exam III
Answer Sheet

1 Ⓐ Ⓑ Ⓒ Ⓓ	21 Ⓐ Ⓑ Ⓒ Ⓓ	41 Ⓐ Ⓑ Ⓒ Ⓓ	61 Ⓐ Ⓑ Ⓒ Ⓓ	81 Ⓐ Ⓑ Ⓒ Ⓓ
2 Ⓐ Ⓑ Ⓒ Ⓓ	22 Ⓐ Ⓑ Ⓒ Ⓓ	42 Ⓐ Ⓑ Ⓒ Ⓓ	62 Ⓐ Ⓑ Ⓒ Ⓓ	82 Ⓐ Ⓑ Ⓒ Ⓓ
3 Ⓐ Ⓑ Ⓒ Ⓓ	23 Ⓐ Ⓑ Ⓒ Ⓓ	43 Ⓐ Ⓑ Ⓒ Ⓓ	63 Ⓐ Ⓑ Ⓒ Ⓓ	83 Ⓐ Ⓑ Ⓒ Ⓓ
4 Ⓐ Ⓑ Ⓒ Ⓓ	24 Ⓐ Ⓑ Ⓒ Ⓓ	44 Ⓐ Ⓑ Ⓒ Ⓓ	64 Ⓐ Ⓑ Ⓒ Ⓓ	84 Ⓐ Ⓑ Ⓒ Ⓓ
5 Ⓐ Ⓑ Ⓒ Ⓓ	25 Ⓐ Ⓑ Ⓒ Ⓓ	45 Ⓐ Ⓑ Ⓒ Ⓓ	65 Ⓐ Ⓑ Ⓒ Ⓓ	85 Ⓐ Ⓑ Ⓒ Ⓓ
6 Ⓐ Ⓑ Ⓒ Ⓓ	26 Ⓐ Ⓑ Ⓒ Ⓓ	46 Ⓐ Ⓑ Ⓒ Ⓓ	66 Ⓐ Ⓑ Ⓒ Ⓓ	86 Ⓐ Ⓑ Ⓒ Ⓓ
7 Ⓐ Ⓑ Ⓒ Ⓓ	27 Ⓐ Ⓑ Ⓒ Ⓓ	47 Ⓐ Ⓑ Ⓒ Ⓓ	67 Ⓐ Ⓑ Ⓒ Ⓓ	87 Ⓐ Ⓑ Ⓒ Ⓓ
8 Ⓐ Ⓑ Ⓒ Ⓓ	28 Ⓐ Ⓑ Ⓒ Ⓓ	48 Ⓐ Ⓑ Ⓒ Ⓓ	68 Ⓐ Ⓑ Ⓒ Ⓓ	88 Ⓐ Ⓑ Ⓒ Ⓓ
9 Ⓐ Ⓑ Ⓒ Ⓓ	29 Ⓐ Ⓑ Ⓒ Ⓓ	49 Ⓐ Ⓑ Ⓒ Ⓓ	69 Ⓐ Ⓑ Ⓒ Ⓓ	89 Ⓐ Ⓑ Ⓒ Ⓓ
10 Ⓐ Ⓑ Ⓒ Ⓓ	30 Ⓐ Ⓑ Ⓒ Ⓓ	50 Ⓐ Ⓑ Ⓒ Ⓓ	70 Ⓐ Ⓑ Ⓒ Ⓓ	90 Ⓐ Ⓑ Ⓒ Ⓓ
11 Ⓐ Ⓑ Ⓒ Ⓓ	31 Ⓐ Ⓑ Ⓒ Ⓓ	51 Ⓐ Ⓑ Ⓒ Ⓓ	71 Ⓐ Ⓑ Ⓒ Ⓓ	91 Ⓐ Ⓑ Ⓒ Ⓓ
12 Ⓐ Ⓑ Ⓒ Ⓓ	32 Ⓐ Ⓑ Ⓒ Ⓓ	52 Ⓐ Ⓑ Ⓒ Ⓓ	72 Ⓐ Ⓑ Ⓒ Ⓓ	92 Ⓐ Ⓑ Ⓒ Ⓓ
13 Ⓐ Ⓑ Ⓒ Ⓓ	33 Ⓐ Ⓑ Ⓒ Ⓓ	53 Ⓐ Ⓑ Ⓒ Ⓓ	73 Ⓐ Ⓑ Ⓒ Ⓓ	93 Ⓐ Ⓑ Ⓒ Ⓓ
14 Ⓐ Ⓑ Ⓒ Ⓓ	34 Ⓐ Ⓑ Ⓒ Ⓓ	54 Ⓐ Ⓑ Ⓒ Ⓓ	74 Ⓐ Ⓑ Ⓒ Ⓓ	94 Ⓐ Ⓑ Ⓒ Ⓓ
15 Ⓐ Ⓑ Ⓒ Ⓓ	35 Ⓐ Ⓑ Ⓒ Ⓓ	55 Ⓐ Ⓑ Ⓒ Ⓓ	75 Ⓐ Ⓑ Ⓒ Ⓓ	95 Ⓐ Ⓑ Ⓒ Ⓓ
16 Ⓐ Ⓑ Ⓒ Ⓓ	36 Ⓐ Ⓑ Ⓒ Ⓓ	56 Ⓐ Ⓑ Ⓒ Ⓓ	76 Ⓐ Ⓑ Ⓒ Ⓓ	96 Ⓐ Ⓑ Ⓒ Ⓓ
17 Ⓐ Ⓑ Ⓒ Ⓓ	37 Ⓐ Ⓑ Ⓒ Ⓓ	57 Ⓐ Ⓑ Ⓒ Ⓓ	77 Ⓐ Ⓑ Ⓒ Ⓓ	97 Ⓐ Ⓑ Ⓒ Ⓓ
18 Ⓐ Ⓑ Ⓒ Ⓓ	38 Ⓐ Ⓑ Ⓒ Ⓓ	58 Ⓐ Ⓑ Ⓒ Ⓓ	78 Ⓐ Ⓑ Ⓒ Ⓓ	98 Ⓐ Ⓑ Ⓒ Ⓓ
19 Ⓐ Ⓑ Ⓒ Ⓓ	39 Ⓐ Ⓑ Ⓒ Ⓓ	59 Ⓐ Ⓑ Ⓒ Ⓓ	79 Ⓐ Ⓑ Ⓒ Ⓓ	99 Ⓐ Ⓑ Ⓒ Ⓓ
20 Ⓐ Ⓑ Ⓒ Ⓓ	40 Ⓐ Ⓑ Ⓒ Ⓓ	60 Ⓐ Ⓑ Ⓒ Ⓓ	80 Ⓐ Ⓑ Ⓒ Ⓓ	100 Ⓐ Ⓑ Ⓒ Ⓓ

MODEL COURT OFFICER EXAM III

TIME ALLOWED FOR ENTIRE EXAMINATION—3 HOURS.

DIRECTIONS: Each question has four suggested answers lettered A, B, C, and D. Decide which one is the best answer and, on your answer sheet, darken the space for that letter.

Memory Section

You will have 10 minutes to read, reread, and note the details of the following memorandum. Then you will have to answer fifteen questions about the memorandum without referring back to it.

M e m o r a n d u m

May 10

TO: All Court Officers
FROM: Clerk of the Court
SUBJECT: Assignment of Duties

Each of you will start a new assignment on May 13. You will be assigned to either Part 1, Part 2, or Part 4. Definite assignments will be made on Monday.

Those of you who are assigned to Part 4, at which the murder trial of George Jackson is now in progress, are cautioned to be especially alert. Information has been received from the office of the Police Commissioner that the accused may attempt to escape from the courtroom, aided by members of the "Blue Circle" gang with which the accused was connected prior to his arrest.

Known members of this gang include: Patsy "Boots" Brescia, a short, swarthy individual who invariably dresses conservatively. Although this member of the gang has no arrest record, he is known to carry firearms at all times and is now wanted by authorities in this State.

Fred Fick, alias Frederick Fidens: This individual is 6 feet 4 inches tall, weighs 230 pounds and may be identified by a knife scar on the right cheek. He has been convicted of felonious assault, manslaughter and burglary.

Patrick Ahern: This individual is 6 feet, 2 inches tall and weighs 145 pounds. He is known to be extremely dangerous when under the influence of drugs. Ahern's convictions include those for robbery, breaking and entering, and Sullivan Law violation. He is wanted for kidnapping by the California authorities.

All court officers, including those not assigned to the murder trial, are, of course, expected to be on the lookout for anyone acting peculiarly. If you observe anyone who answers any of the descriptions given above, or anyone else whose actions are such as to arouse your suspicion, send another officer to call the chief court officer. Avoid any indication that you are suspicious. Above all, avoid any action which may even remotely jeopardize the safety of spectators. While every precaution will be taken to prevent the admission to the courtroom of anyone carrying arms, do not gamble on the success of these precautions. These men are dangerous and, if convinced that their own safety is in peril, will have no hesitancy in using their weapons should they be able to smuggle them in.

DIRECTIONS: Below are 15 questions numbered 1 to 15, based on the memorandum you have just read. Each question is followed by several suggested answers. Blacken the space on your answer sheet with the same letter as the best ONE of the suggested answers.

1. The memorandum you have just read was issued by the

    (A) Clerk of the Court
    (B) Presiding Justice
    (C) Chief Court Attendant
    (D) Chief of Police

2. The number of members in the "Blue Circle" gang is

    (A) 1 or 2
    (B) 3 to 5
    (C) 6 to 9
    (D) not definitely stated in the memorandum

3. According to the memorandum, the man accused of murder is named

    (A) Johnson
    (B) Jamison
    (C) Jackson
    (D) Johnston

4. Information concerning the possibility of the attempted escape of the accused was received from

    (A) the office of the District Attorney
    (B) the office of the Police Commissioner
    (C) a member of the underworld
    (D) not stated in the memorandum

5. The memorandum indicates that, of the members of the "Blue Circle" gang mentioned,

    (A) all have been arrested at least once
    (B) only one has never been arrested
    (C) two have never been arrested
    (D) three have never been arrested

6. The murder trial mentioned in the memorandum

    (A) has already begun
    (B) will begin some time next week
    (C) will begin on Monday
    (D) will begin on May 13

7. According to the memorandum, all officers

    (A) are to be on the alert for escaped prisoners
    (B) assigned to the murder trial are to personally search all spectators for concealed weapons immediately upon entering the courtroom
    (C) will be assigned, at one time or another, to duty at the murder trial
    (D) will receive definite new assignments on Monday

8. Of the members of the gang mentioned in the memorandum

    (A) at least one, if apprehended, may be extradited (returned to another state).
    (B) at least two are said to be wanted by authorities in other states
    (C) at least three have been guilty of felonies
    (D) any one is likely to act peculiarly

9. The memorandum does not state that Fred Fick has ever been convicted of

    (A) burglary
    (B) manslaughter
    (C) robbery
    (D) felonious assault

10. From information given in the memorandum, Patrick Ahern may best be described as

    (A) short and stocky
    (B) tall and heavy
    (C) tall and thin
    (D) short and thin

11. According to the memorandum, the member of the "Blue Circle" gang who is known to use drugs is

    (A) "Boots" Brescia
    (B) Patrick Ahern
    (C) Fred Fick
    (D) George Jackson

12. "Boots" Brescia may most readily be identified by

    (A) his swarthy complexion
    (B) the scar on his right cheek
    (C) his flashy clothes
    (D) his footwear

13. According to instructions contained in the memorandum, if a court officer observes anyone acting suspiciously he or she should

    (A) sound an alarm
    (B) report the situation in person to the chief court officer
    (C) keep the suspect under surveillance until he or she can turn the job over to another court officer
    (D) send another court officer to summon the Chief Court Officer

14. On the basis of the information contained in the memorandum, it may be positively stated that

    (A) most members of the "Blue Circle" gang habitually carry firearms
    (B) two or more members of the gang are armed at all times
    (C) at least one member of the gang is always armed
    (D) the murder was committed with a hand gun

15. In dealing with any suspicious characters seen in the courtroom, a court officer's first concern should be with

    (A) maintenance of order
    (B) protection of spectators
    (C) detention of the suspect
    (D) confiscation of arms

16. "Referees of the Civil Court are former judges of this court who have served at least ten years and whose term of office terminated at the age of 55 or over, or any judge who has served in a court of record and has retired." According to this statement, a person can be a referee of the Civil Court only if he or she

    (A) has been a judge
    (B) has retired
    (C) has served at least 10 years in the court
    (D) meets certain age requirements

17. "One theory states that all criminal behavior is taught by a process of communication within small intimate groups. An individual engages in criminal behavior if the number of criminal patterns which he or she has acquired exceeds the number of non-criminal patterns." This statement indicates that criminal behavior is

    (A) learned
    (B) instinctive
    (C) hereditary
    (D) reprehensible

18. "The law enforcement staff of today requires training and mental qualities of a high order. The poorly or partially prepared staff member lowers the standard of work, retards personal earning power, and fails in a career meant to provide a livelihood and social improvement." According to this statement,

    (A) an inefficient member of a law enforcement staff will still earn a good livelihood
    (B) law enforcement officers move in good social circles
    (C) many people fail in law enforcement careers
    (D) persons of training and ability are essential to a law enforcement staff

19. "In New York State, no crime can occur unless there is a written law forbidding the act or omission in question, and even though an act may not be exactly in harmony with public policy, such act is not a crime unless it is expressly forbidden by legislative enactment." According to the above statement

    (A) a crime is committed with reference to a particular law
    (B) acts not in harmony with public policy should be forbidden by law
    (C) noncriminal activity will promote public welfare
    (D) legislative enactments frequently forbid actions in harmony with public policy

20. "The unrestricted sale of firearms is one of the main causes of our shameful crime record." According to this statement, one of the causes of our crime record is the

    (A) development of firepower
    (B) ease of securing weapons
    (C) increased skill in using guns
    (D) scientific perfection of firearms

21. "Every person must be informed of the reason for arrest unless arrested in the actual commission of a crime. Sufficient force to effect the arrest may be used, but the courts frown on brutal methods." According to this statement, a person does not have to be informed of the reason for arrest if

    (A) brutal force was not used in effecting it
    (B) the courts will later turn the defendant loose
    (C) the person arrested knows force will be used if necessary
    (D) the reason for it is clearly evident from the circumstances

22. "An important duty of a court officer is to keep order in the court." On the basis of this statement it is probably true that

    (A) it is more important for a court officer to be strong than to be smart
    (B) people involved in court trials are noisy if not kept in check
    (C) not every duty of a court officer is important
    (D) the maintenance of order is important for the proper conduct of court business

23. "The criminal is rarely or never reformed." Acceptance of this statement as true would mean that greatest emphasis should be placed on

    (A) imprisonment
    (B) parole
    (C) probation
    (D) malingering

Answer questions 24 to 26 on the basis of the following paragraph.

Undoubtedly, the ultimate solution to the housing problem of the hard-core slum does not lie in code enforcement, however defined. The only solution to that problem is demolition, clearance, and new construction. However, it is also clear that, even with government assistance, new construction is not keeping pace with the obsolescence and deterioration of the existing housing inventory of our cities. Add to this the facts of an increasing population and the continuing migration into metropolitan areas, as well as the demands for more and better housing that grow out of continuing economic prosperity and high employment, and some intimation may be gained of the dimensions of the problem of maintaining our housing supply so that it may begin to meet the need.

24. The one of the following that would be the most appropriate title for the preceding passage is

    (A) Problems Associated with Maintaining an Adequate Housing Supply
    (B) Demolition as a Remedy for Housing Problems
    (C) Government's Essential Role in Code Enforcement
    (D) The Ultimate Solution to the Hard-Core Slum Problem

25. According to the passage, housing code enforcement is

    (A) a way to encourage local initiative in urban renewal
    (B) a valuable tool that has fallen into disuse
    (C) inadequate as a solution to slum housing problems
    (D) responsible for some of the housing problems, since the code has not been adequately defined

26. The passage makes it clear that the basic solution to the housing problem is to

    (A) erect new buildings after demolition and site clearance
    (B) discourage migration into the metropolitan area
    (C) increase rents paid to landlords
    (D) enforce the housing code strictly

Answer questions 27 and 28 on the basis of the following paragraph.

The employees in a unit or division of a government agency may be referred to as a work group. Within a government agency that has existed for some time, the work groups will have evolved traditions of their own. The persons in these work groups acquire these traditions as part of the process of work adjustment within their groups. Usually a work group in a large organization will contain "old-timers," "newcomers," and "in-betweeners." Like the supervisor of a group, who is not necessarily an old-timer or the oldest member, old-timers usually have great influence. They can recall events unknown to others and are a storehouse of information and advice about current problems in the light of past experience. They pass along the traditions of the group to the others who in turn become old-timers themselves. Thus the traditions of the group that have been honored and revered by long acceptance are continued.

27. According to the preceding paragraph, the traditions of a work group within a government agency are developed

    (A) at the time the group is established
    (B) over a considerable period of time
    (C) in order to give recognition to old-timers
    (D) for the group before it is established

28. According to the preceding paragraph, the old-timers within a work group

    (A) are the means by which long accepted practices and customs are perpetuated
    (B) would best be able to settle current problems that arise
    (C) are honored because of the changes they have made in the traditions
    (D) have demonstrated that they have learned to do their work well

29. "There are many theories of the causes of delinquent behavior. One approach sees delinquent behavior as the normal response of many adolescents to conditions of social and economic deprivation characteristic of the lower class." This statement implies that

    (A) delinquent behavior is a neurotic response to repeated personal failure
    (B) the root of the delinquency problem is to be found in destructive family relationships
    (C) delinquency is more related to a particular kind of social environment than it is to individual character
    (D) delinquent behavior can be treated by modifying individual patterns of personal feeling, behavior, and relationships

30. "When an employee is encouraged by his or her supervisor to think of new ideas in connection with work, the habit of improving work methods is fostered." The one of the following that is the most valid implication of this statement is that

  (A) the improvement of work methods should be the concern not only of the supervisor but of the employee as well
  (B) an employee without initiative cannot perform the job well
  (C) an employee may waste too much time in experimenting with new work methods
  (D) an improved method for performing a task should not be used without the approval of the supervisor

Answer questions 31 to 34 on the basis of the following paragraph.

A summons is an official statement ordering a person to appear in court. In traffic violation situations, summonses are used when arrests need not be made. The main reason for traffic summonses is to deter motorists from repeating the same traffic violation. Occasionally motorists may make unintentional driving errors, and sometimes they are unaware of correct driving regulations. In cases such as these, the policy is to have the officer verbally inform the motorist of the violation and warn him or her against repeating it. The purpose of this practice is not to limit the number of summonses, but rather to prevent the issuing of summonses when the violation is not due to deliberate intent or to inexcusable negligence.

31. According to the preceding passage, the principal reason for issuing traffic summonses is to

  (A) discourage motorists from violating these laws again
  (B) increase the money collected by the city
  (C) put traffic violators in prison
  (D) have them serve as substitutes for police officers

32. The reason a verbal warning may sometimes be substituted for a summons is to

  (A) limit the number of summonses
  (B) distinguish between excusable and inexcusable violations
  (C) provide harsher penalties for deliberate intent than for inexcusable negligence
  (D) decrease the caseload in the courts

33. The author of the preceding passage feels that someone who violated a traffic regulation because he or she did *not* know about the regulation should be

  (A) put under arrest
  (B) fined less money
  (C) given a summons
  (D) told not to do it again

34. Using the distinctions made by the author of the preceding passage, the one of the following motorists to whom it would be most desirable to issue a summons is the one who exceeded the speed limit because he or she

  (A) did not know the speed limit
  (B) was late for an important business appointment
  (C) speeded to avoid being hit by another car
  (D) had a speedometer which was not working properly

35. "Even minor cuts should be properly cared for so that there will be no chance for infection to set in. Amputations and even death have resulted from small neglected wounds." According to this statement,

   (A) a small wound is more likely to become infected than a large one
   (B) minor cuts should not be neglected
   (C) more people die from small wounds than from large ones
   (D) small wounds are always worse then they look

36. "It shall be unlawful for any person to manufacture, pack, possess, sell, offer for sale and/or expose for sale any compound or blended oil of any kind that purports to be an olive oil mixture unless the container be permanently and conspicuously labeled "compound oil" or "blended oil" with a statement of the different ingredients thereof and the specific percentage of olive oil, the total percentage of other vegetable oils and the specific percentage of each other ingredient comprising more than one-half of one percent of the mixture." According to this paragraph, a mixture consisting of olive oil and other oils that is offered for sale

   (A) may be labeled as "olive oil" if it contains at least $98\frac{1}{2}\%$ olive oil
   (B) may not contain more than $\frac{1}{2}$ of 1% of other oils
   (C) must be labeled "compound oil" or "blended oil"
   (D) must contain only olive oil and other vegetable oils

Answer questions 37 to 40 on the basis of the following paragraph.

"Because of the importance of preserving physical evidence, the officer should not enter a scene of a crime if it can be examined visually from one position and if no other pressing duty requires his presence there. There are some responsibilities, however, that take precedence over preservation of evidence. Some examples are as follows: rescue work, disarming dangerous persons, and quelling a disturbance. The officer should learn how to accomplish these more vital tasks while at the same time preserving as much evidence as possible. If he finds it necessary to enter upon the scene, he should quickly study the place of entry to learn if any evidence will suffer by his contact; then he should determine the routes to use in walking to the spot where his presence is required. Every place where a foot will fall or where a hand or other part of his body will touch should be examined with the eye. Objects should not be touched or moved unless there is a definite and compelling reason. For identification of most items of physical evidence at the initial investigation, it is seldom necessary to touch or move them.

37. The one of the following titles that is the most appropriate for the above paragraph is

   (A) Determining the Order of Tasks at the Scene of a Crime
   (B) The Principal Reasons for Preserving Evidence at The Scene of a Crime
   (C) Precautions to Take at the Scene of a Crime
   (D) Evidence to be Examined at the Scene of a Crime

38. When an officer feels that it is essential for him to enter the immediate area where a crime has been committed, he should

   (A) quickly but carefully glance around to determine whether his entering the area will damage any evidence present
   (B) remove all objects of evidence from his predetermined route in order to avoid stepping on them
   (C) carefully replace any object immediately if it is moved or touched by his hands or any other part of his body.
   (D) use only the usual place of entry to the scene in order to avoid disturbing any possible clues left on rear doors and windows

39. The one of the following which is the *least* urgent duty of an officer who has just reported to the scene of a crime is to

(A) disarm the hysterical victim who is wildly waving a loaded gun in all directions
(B) give first-aid to a possible suspect who has been injured while attempting to leave the scene of the crime
(C) prevent observers from attacking and injuring the persons suspected of having committed the crime
(D) preserve from damage or destruction any evidence necessary for the proper prosecution of the case against the criminals

40. An officer has just reported to the scene of a crime in response to a phone call. The best of the following actions for him to take with respect to objects of physical evidence present at the scene is to

(A) make no attempt to enter the crime scene if his entry will disturb any vital physical evidence
(B) map out the shortest straight path to follow in walking to the spot where the most physical evidence may be found
(C) move such objects of physical evidence as are necessary to enable him to assist the wounded victim of the crime
(D) quickly examine all objects of physical evidence in order to determine which objects may be touched and which may not

Answer questions 41 to 49 based only on the information given in the table below:

Court	Arraignments	Fines	Summonses	Warrants
Lower Manhattan	48,175	$74,386	6,388	6,926
Upper Manhattan	20,953	45,183	10,745	5,721
Bay Ridge	6,943	14,238	2,674	1,457
Coney Island	8,481	16,805	2,076	1,476
Flatbush	8,935	15,354	3,301	1,090
Williamsburg	8,017	13,170	4,454	1,412
Flushing	3,527	8,297	1,971	708
Long Island City	2,261	4,855	1,719	552
Criminal Court, Manhattan	10,521	200,617	2,312	1,324
Criminal Court, Bronx	4,450	78,625	273	683
Criminal Court, Brooklyn	11,242	164,482	1,782	1,342
Criminal Court, Queens	2,680	31,658	576	365
Total		$667,670	38,271	23,056

41. The total of the arraignments for all the courts listed in the table is most nearly

(A) 138,000
(B) 137,000
(C) 136,000
(D) 135,000

42. The difference between the total collected in fines in Criminal Court, Brooklyn, and the total collected in fines in Criminal Court, Bronx, is most nearly

   (A) $85,860
   (B) $85,855
   (C) $85,850
   (D) $85,845

43. The number of summonses for Criminal Court, Bronx, when multiplied by 36, is most nearly equal to the number of arraignments for

   (A) Lower Manhattan
   (B) Flatbush
   (C) Criminal Court, Brooklyn
   (D) Criminal Court, Manhattan

44. The average collected in fines per court for the 12 courts listed is most nearly

   (A) $55,640
   (B) $55,635
   (C) $55,630
   (D) $55,625

45. Of the following, the court with the greatest amount in fines in proportion to the number of arraignments is

   (A) Lower Manhattan
   (B) Upper Manhattan
   (C) Criminal Court, Queens
   (D) Coney Island

46. Of the following, the court which has most nearly a 4:1 ratio of arraignments to summonses is

   (A) Flatbush
   (B) Criminal Court, Brooklyn
   (C) Criminal Court, Manhattan
   (D) Flushing

47. Of the courts with more than 8,000 arraignments, the one which had more than three times as many summonses as warrants is

   (A) Williamsburg
   (B) Coney Island
   (C) Upper Manhattan
   (D) Lower Manhattan

48. Of the criminal courts,

   (A) Manhattan had fewer arraignments but more summonses than Brooklyn
   (B) Bronx had more summonses but fewer arraignments than Queens
   (C) Queens had fewer arraignments, fewer summonses, and fewer warrants than any other court
   (D) Brooklyn had more arraignments, more summonses, and more warrants than any other court

49. The court, with fewer than 3,000 summonses and more than 5,000 arraignments, which had the smallest number of warrants is

    (A) Flatbush
    (B) Criminal Court, Queens
    (C) Criminal Court, Manhattan
    (D) Criminal Court, Brooklyn

50. At a forced sale, a bankrupt farmer sold his farm for $7,500. If this amount was $33\frac{1}{3}\%$ less than its real value, the value of the farm would be

    (A) $11,250
    (B) $5,000
    (C) $7,500
    (D) $10,000

DIRECTIONS for questions 51 to 60: Each question consists of letters or numbers in Columns I and II. For each question, compare each line of Column I with its corresponding line in Column II and decide how many lines in Column II are exactly the same as their counterparts in Column I. Mark your answers as follows:

Mark (A) if only *ONE* line in Column II is exactly the same as its corresponding line in Column I

Mark (B) if *TWO* lines in Column II are exactly the same as their corresponding lines in Column I

Mark (C) if *THREE* lines in Column II are exactly the same as their corresponding lines in Column I

Mark (D) if all *FOUR* lines in Column II are exactly the same as their corresponding lines in Column I

	Column I	Column II			Column I	Column II
51.	3816	3816		55.	lbct	lbct
	5283	5832			18o3	1803
	4686	4868			Xtux	Xtux
	1252	1252			45NM	45NM
52.	acdt	acdt		56.	AbuR	AbuR
	xuer	xuer			52VC	52VC
	ltbf	lbtf			rehg	rehg
	oypn	oypn			3416	3416
53.	9063	9063		57.	awg3	awg3
	itop	itop			tyE3	ty3E
	nzne	nzne			abhn	abhn
	7549	7549			24po	24op
54.	TYBF	TYIF		58.	6tru	6tru
	5631	5361			sw4k	sw4K
	BcOp	BcOP			lgh8	lgh8
	ag7B	ag7B			u2up	u2up

	Column I	Column II		Column I	Column II
59.	agxp	agXp	60.	agbt	agbt
	ruy5	ruy5		1LiI	lliI
	aglb	agLb		ty4f	ty4f
	8a9c	8z9c		arwd	erwd

DIRECTIONS for questions 61 to 70: Each of the following questions contains several sentences. You are to select the sentence in each question that is *best* with respect to grammar and good usage. On your answer sheet, mark the letter preceding the sentence you choose.

61. (A) The receptionist must answer courteously the questions of all them callers.
    (B) The receptionist must answer courteously the questions what are asked by the callers.
    (C) There would have been no trouble if the receptionist had have always answered courteously.
    (D) The receptionist should answer courteously the questions of all callers.

62. (A) This letter, together with the reports, are to be sent to the principal.
    (B) The reports, together with this letter, is to be sent to the principal.
    (C) The reports and this letter is to be sent to the principal.
    (D) This letter, together with the reports, is to be sent to the principal.

63. (A) One of us have to make the reply before tomorrow.
    (B) Making the reply before tomorrow will have to be done by one of us.
    (C) One of us has to reply before tomorrow.
    (D) Anyone has to reply before tomorrow.

64. (A) According to the preceding paragraph, the laws have no affect on practice.
    (B) The laws have no effect on practice, according to the preceding paragraph.
    (C) The laws have, according to the preceding paragraph, no effect on practice.
    (D) The preceding paragraph states no effect is made by law on practice.

65. (A) Brown's & Company employees have recently received increases in salary.
    (B) Brown & Company recently increased the salaries of all its employees.
    (C) Recently Brown & Company has increased their employees' salaries.
    (D) Brown & Company have recently increased the salaries of all its employees.

66. (A) Since the report lacked the needed information, it was of no use to him.
    (B) This report was useless to him because there were no needed information in it.
    (C) Since the report did not contain the needed information, it was not real useful to him.
    (D) Being that the report lacked the needed information, he could not use it.

67. (A) If properly addressed, the letter will reach my mother and I.
    (B) The letter had been addressed to myself and my mother.
    (C) I believe the letter was addressed to either my mother or I.
    (D) My mother's name, as well as mine, was on the letter.

68. (A) The supervisor reprimanded the typist, whom she believed had made careless errors.
    (B) The typist would have corrected the errors had she of known that the supervisor would see the report.
    (C) The errors in the typed report were so numerous that they could hardly be overlooked.
    (D) Many errors were found in the report which she typed and could not disregard them.

69. (A) It is quite possible that we shall reemploy anyone whose training fits them to do the work.
    (B) It is probable that we shall reemploy those who have been trained to do the work.
    (C) Such of our personnel that have been trained to do the work will be again employed.
    (D) We expect to reemploy the ones who have training enough that they can do the work.

70. (A) The paper we use for this purpose must be light, glossy, and stand hard usage as well.
    (B) Only a light and a glossy, but durable, paper must be used for this purpose.
    (C) For this purpose, we want a paper that is light, glossy, but that will stand hard wear.
    (D) For this purpose, paper that is light, glossy, and durable is essential.

DIRECTIONS For questions 71 to 80: Each letter should be matched with its number in accordance with the following table:

Letter	Y	J	X	C	M	B	V	W	U	L
Number	0	1	2	3	4	5	6	7	8	9

For each question, compare each line of letters and numbers carefully to see if each letter has the correct matching number. Mark your answer based on how many lines in each question are correctly matched.

Mark (A) if *NONE* of the lines matches
Mark (B) if only *ONE* of the lines matches
Mark (C) if *TWO* of the lines match
Mark (D) if all *THREE* lines match

71. BXUC   5283
    JLMB   1945
    CYWM   3074

72. MXWB   4285
    CUJL   3819
    MYVX   4073

73. XWLB   2695
    MUBY   5860
    LXJB   9215

74. CWLY   3790
    MXJV   4216
    YWMC   0473

75. LMXB   9452
    BCWY   5370
    JBWU   1587

76. MWCJ   4731
    VYBU   6085
    LXMB   9254

77. UCJL   8419
    WXYB   7206
    CWMX   3842

78. LMWX   9472
    BYCU   5038
    XULJ   2891

79. JBVW   1576
    YXLM   0295
    WXCJ   7213

80. JUWL   1897
    CBXW   3527
    JVYB   1065

Base your answers to questions 81 to 85 on the following enumeration of some of the duties of a court officer.

The jury room must be properly ventilated, heated, and lighted, and the jurors must have an ample supply of paper, pens, and any other needed stationery items. The court officer immediately locks the door when leaving the jury room and remains at calling or hearing distance. If any jury member requires services, the officer must respond at a moment's notice. In all cases, two officers are assigned to guard a jury. This ensures constant guard over the jury. Should one court officer be dispatched with a message or sent to the courtroom for an exhibit, the other would remain on guard. If only one guard were assigned, the chances of wrongdoing would be heightened.

There arises, at times, a situation in which a jury member desires to communicate with some family member while the jury is behind closed doors. The court officer cannot allow this except with the permission of the judge or the clerk. If the jury member requires the sending of a message to the judge or court, it must be put in writing with the request that it be delivered by the court officer.

81. In a civil case, the jurors are sometimes instructed to deliver a sealed verdict. In such case, the jurors deliberate until they reach a verdict, put it in writing, and seal it in an envelope. The envelope may be delivered to the court the next morning. After a sealed verdict has been ordered and the judge has gone home for the day, a juror asks permission to telephone his wife to tell her that he will be late. The court officer should

   (A) not permit the juror to use the phone
   (B) permit the juror to use the phone
   (C) call the juror's wife and let the juror talk to her
   (D) call the juror's wife and ask her to come to the courthouse to talk to her husband

82. While one court officer assigned to guard a deliberating jury is on her way to the judge's chambers with a request from the jurors for clarification of a point of law, the foreman of the jury knocks on the door and asks the court officer to procure for the jury Exhibits E and G. The court officer should

   (A) shout loudly after the first officer to ask her to return and pick up the additional requests
   (B) complain to the foreman that the jury makes too many requests
   (C) run after the first officer and hand her notes making requests for the Exhibits
   (D) wait for the first officer to return and then go for the Exhibits

83. A court officer has conscientiously supplied the jury room with paper, pencils, pens, and a generous assortment of office supplies. After several days of deliberation, a member of the jury tells the officer that the jury needs more rubber bands and paper clips. The officer should

   (A) ask the jury what has happened to all the supplies
   (B) tell the judge that this jury is costing the taxpayers too much money
   (C) get more rubber bands and paper clips for the jury
   (D) tell the jury that it must get along with what it has

84. A juror tells a court officer that he is claustrophobic and is afraid to remain in a closed and locked jury room. Under these circumstances, the court officer should

   (A) leave the door partly open
   (B) close the door but not lock it
   (C) close and lock the door
   (D) have the juror sit outside the locked door with the court officers

85. A court officer with a 5:30 p.m. appointment has been assigned to a jury room to guard the jury until 4 p.m., at which time she is to be relieved if the jury has not yet come to an agreement. At 4 p.m. the jury is still deliberating, and the relief has not appeared. The court officer should

   (A) ask the foreman of the jury to assume responsibility until the relief arrives
   (B) find out what the jurors may need, get it, and then lock the jurors in for the night
   (C) inform her supervisor but remain on duty until she is relieved
   (D) wait until 5 p.m. and then leave the jury in the care of the of the second court officer, even if the relieving officer has not arrived

Answer questions 86 to 95 on the basis of the following legal definitions.

Larceny is committed when a person wrongfully takes, obtains, or withholds the property of another.

Grand larceny is committed when a person wrongfully takes, obtains, or withholds the property of another and the value of the property is over $250 or the property taken is a credit card.

Theft of services is committed when a person uses a stolen credit card to purchase goods or services or when a person avoids payment for restaurant, hotel, motel, transportation, gas, electric, or telecommunications (telephone) services.

Menacing is committed when a person, by physical menace, places another person in fear of immediate serious injury. "Physical menace" means that a person must have the means available to carry out the threat, i.e., if the person threatens to shoot someone, he must have a gun present; if he threatens to beat someone with a bat, he must have the bat present, etc.

Arson is committed when a person *intentionally* causes damage to a building or motor vehicle by either setting fire to said building or motor vehicle or by causing an explosion that damages said building or motor vehicle.

86. Thomas Evans, while riding on a subway train, reaches into the pocketbook of Janet Brown and removes two credit cards. Evans could be charged with

    (A) larceny
    (B) grand larceny
    (C) theft of services
    (D) no crime, as he did not use the cards

87. John Murphy overslept and because of this he may be late reporting to his job. He has been tardy for work several times in the recent past and has been warned that future lateness may result in his being fired from his job. As John enters the subway station, he hears his train approaching. He does not have a token for the turnstile, and the line to purchase tokens is very long. He knows that if he waits in line he will definitely miss the train and thereby be late for work and perhaps lose his job. John jumps over the turnstile without paying and enters the train. John could be charged with

    (A) larceny and theft of services
    (B) grand larceny and theft of services
    (C) theft of services
    (D) no crime because waiting in the token line could have caused him to lose his job

88. Mary Simmons was doing some shopping in a department store. She observed another customer place a credit card on the counter as she examined some merchandise. Mary took the credit card off the counter and put it in her pocketbook. She then proceeded to another section of the store where she purchased some articles with the credit card she had just taken. Mary could be charged with

    (A) larceny only
    (B) grand larceny only
    (C) larceny and theft of services
    (D) grand larceny and theft of services

89. John Smith enters an appliance store and takes a portable stereo-cassette player valued at $100 without paying for it. As he starts to exit the store, the manager of the store yells to Smith to stop. Smith turns and puts his hand in his pocket and states "I'll shoot you if you come near me." Smith does not actually have a gun in his possession. He flees with the cassette player. Smith could be charged with

    (A) menacing only
    (B) larceny only
    (C) grand larceny only
    (D) menacing and larceny

90. Mary Johnson enters a jewelry store and takes a watch worth $250 without paying for it. As she is leaving the store, the manager approaches her and Mary starts to run for the front door. While trying to make her escape, Mary accidentally knocks over a portable electric heater, which starts a fire. Mary escapes with the watch and the store suffers minor damage from the fire. Mary could be charged with

    (A) grand larceny only
    (B) larceny only
    (C) larceny and arson
    (D) arson only

91. Bill Walsh was assaulted by the owner of an apartment building. He wants revenge for the injuries he suffered and has decided to burn the apartment house down. Bill does not want to hurt any innocent people, so he calls the superintendent of the building to warn him to get the tenants out. Walsh had to use a slug to make the phone call, as he had no change, only paper money, in his possession. He enters the building and starts a fire which damages the building extensively before it is extinguished. Walsh could be charged with

    (A) arson only
    (B) larceny and theft of services
    (C) arson and larceny
    (D) arson and theft of services

92. Bill enters the basement of John's house and takes a saw worth $250. As he is about to escape, John attempts to stop him. Bill then picks up a baseball bat and says, "If you come one step closer, I'll break your head." John retreats. Just before he flees, Bill tosses a lighted match into a group of paint cans that are stacked in a corner of the basement. A fire starts and causes minor damage to the basement before it is extinguished. Bill could be charged with

    (A) grand larceny and arson
    (B) larceny and arson
    (C) larceny, menacing, and arson
    (D) grand larceny, menacing, and arson

93. While visiting Lisa at her apartment, Frank takes a credit card from her pocketbook without Lisa's knowledge. Frank then goes to a restaurant and charges his meal with the credit card he had just taken. He takes a cab to his home and, when he realizes that he does not have enough money to pay the cab fare, he opens the door and flees without paying. Frank could be charged with

    (A) larceny and theft of services
    (B) grand larceny and theft of services
    (C) larceny only
    (D) grand larceny only

94. Bill Martin is a passenger in a taxi cab. He lights a cigarette and then proceeds to fall asleep. The lighted cigarette drops between the seat cushions. When Bill awakens, he does not realize that the cigarette has fallen from his mouth. He pays his fare and leaves the cab, taking with him a woman's pocketbook that he found on the seat. A fire starts in the back of the cab and causes minor damage to the rear of the taxi before it is extinguished. Bill could be charged with

   (A) larceny
   (B) grand larceny
   (C) larceny and arson
   (D) grand larceny and arson

95. Mike steals a telephone credit card from Joe. He then makes a long distance phone call to his girlfriend and charges it to the credit card he has just taken. Mike could be charged with

   (A) larceny
   (B) grand larceny
   (C) theft of services
   (D) grand larceny and theft of services

Answer questions 96 to 98 on the basis of the information in the following paragraph.

"A person who gives or offers a bribe to any executive officer, or to a person elected or appointed to become an executive officer, of this state with intent to influence him in respect to any act, decision, vote, opinion, or other proceedings as such officer, is punishable by imprisonment in a state prison not exceeding 10 years or by a fine not exceeding $5,000 or by both."

96. George Sloan has just been elected to his first term as the county executive. Among the issues facing the county is disposal of solid waste. Phil Crane is a private contractor involved in collection and transportation of garbage from restaurants and businesses. Crane has definite ideas as to methods of solving the solid waste question. Crane offers Sloan a bribe and attempts to convince Sloan of the value of his opinion. Sloan listens politely but refuses to accept the bribe. Crane's attempt comes to the attention of the county prosecutor.

   (A) Sloan and Crane could both be subject to fines.
   (B) Crane faces imprisonment in the county jail.
   (C) Crane could spend 5 years in a state prison.
   (D) Crane could be imprisoned for 10 years or be fined $5,000 but not both.

97. Don Williams is an Assistant Attorney General. The Attorney General's office has been investigating an alleged civil rights violation. Joe Marshall, a friend of the suspect, approaches Williams and asks him to use his influence to curtail the investigation and to overlook certain evidence against the accused violator. He backs his request with a cash offer which Williams accepts. The investigation is later dropped for lack of evidence.

   (A) Williams is subject to imprisonment or fine.
   (B) Marshall is subject to imprisonment or fine.
   (C) Williams is subject to imprisonment; Marshall to fine.
   (D) Williams is subject to fine; Marshall to imprisonment.

98. Joe White is very eager for the planning commission to give him permission to build a twelve-unit subdivision in an area tentatively designated open space. White speaks at every public meeting, takes out ads in local newspapers and generally makes himself heard. He also writes and calls the chief of the commission, Jack Fisk, threatening, cajoling, and promising a generous donation to Fisk's favorite charity if Fisk will expedite his application.

    (A) White could be fined and/or imprisoned.
    (B) White could be fined but not imprisoned.
    (C) White could be imprisoned but not fined.
    (D) White cannot be imprisoned or fined.

Use the information in the paragraph below to answer questions 99 and 100.

"A person concerned in the commission of a crime, whether he directly commits the act constituting the offense or aids and abets in its commission, and whether present or absent, and a person who directly or indirectly counsels, commands, induces or procures another to commit a crime is a 'principal.' A person who, after the commission of a felony, harbors, conceals, or aids the offender, with intent that he may avoid or escape from arrest, trial, conviction, or punishment, having knowledge or reasonable ground to believe that such offender is liable to arrest, has been arrested, is indicted or convicted, or had comitted a felony, is an 'accessory' to the felony."

99. Glen Wilson, Tim Tripp, Bob Burns, and Don Ford made elaborate plans to rob the Buy-Rite Liquor Store on Saturday night just before closing. On the designated night, Bob Burns had a bad case of flu and stayed home in bed. Glen Wilson drove Tripp and Ford in his car, then waited with the engine running while Tripp and Ford went in with guns drawn, emptied the cash register, and emerged with the money and two bottles of vodka. Tripp and Ford jumped into Wilson's car. Wilson drove them to the Holiday Inn where they registered and spent the night.

    (A) Tripp and Ford are principals; Wilson is an accessory.
    (B) Tripp, Ford, and Wilson are principals; Burns is an accessory.
    (C) Tripp, Ford, Wilson, and Burns are principals.
    (D) Tripp, Ford, Wilson, and Burns are principals; the night clerk at the Holiday Inn is an accessory.

100. Ron Johnson is a crack dealer. He has been a regular supplier to Harry Walker, a user introduced to crack by Johnson some months ago. Walker finds his habit increasingly expensive, so Johnson suggests that Walker begin dealing himself in order to make money. Walker takes the suggestion and begins by selling small vials in a corner of the schoolyard at PS 380. One day, a child accuses Walker of delivering short measure and threatens to tell the principal of Walker's activity. Walker becomes frightened and drives out of the city to the farm of his friend Molly Miller. He tells Molly Miller that he may be in trouble and asks to stay at her home for awhile. Molly refuses to let Harry into her house but tells him he may stay in the barn for as long as he likes.

    (A) Harry Walker is a principal; Ron Johnson and Molly Miller are accessories.
    (B) Harry Walker and Ron Johnson are principals; Molly Miller is an accessory.
    (C) Harry Walker, Ron Johnson, and Molly Miller are all principals.
    (D) Harry Walker and Ron Johnson are principals; Molly Miller and the child are accessories.

End of Exam

Correct Answers for Model Court Officer Exam III

1. A	21. D	41. C	61. D	81. A
2. D	22. D	42. B	62. D	82. D
3. C	23. A	43. D	63. C	83. C
4. B	24. A	44. A	64. A	84. C
5. B	25. C	45. C	65. B	85. C
6. A	26. A	46. C	66. A	86. B
7. D	27. B	47. A	67. D	87. C
8. A	28. A	48. A	68. C	88. D
9. C	29. C	49. C	69. B	89. B
10. C	30. A	50. A	70. D	90. B
11. B	31. A	51. B	71. D	91. D
12. A	32. B	52. C	72. B	92. C
13. D	33. D	53. D	73. B	93. B
14. C	34. B	54. A	74. C	94. A
15. B	35. B	55. C	75. B	95. D
16. A	36. C	56. D	76. B	96. C
17. A	37. C	57. A	77. A	97. B
18. D	38. A	58. C	78. D	98. D
19. A	39. D	59. A	79. A	99. C
20. B	40. C	60. B	80. B	100. B

Explanations of Correct Answers

1. **(A)** The memorandum was issued by the clerk of the court.

2. **(D)** Four members of the gang are named, but the total number of members of the gang is not stated.

3. **(C)** The accused on trial for murder is George Jackson.

4. **(B)** Information concerning the possible escape came from the office of the Police Commissioner (second paragraph).

5. **(B)** Patsy "Boots" Brescia has no arrest record. Fick and Ahearn have previous convictions, so they obviously have been previously arrested. Jackson is under arrest right now.

6. **(A)** A murder trial now in progress has already begun.

7. **(D)** The first paragraph states that all officers will begin new assignments on May 13 and that all will receive definite assignments on Monday.

8. **(A)** Patrick Ahern is wanted for kidnapping in California and, if apprehended, may be extradited to California. No mention is made of any other gang member's being wanted by another state.

9. **(C)** Fred Fick's list of convictions does not include robbery.

10. **(C)** A person who stands 6 feet, 2 inches yet weighs only 145 pounds is tall and thin.

11. **(B)** If Patrick Ahern is extremely dangerous when under the influence of drugs, he must be a user.

12. **(A)** Brescia is a conservative dresser with a swarthy complexion. Fick is the one with a knife scar. We were not told how Brescia got his nickname.

13. **(D)** So stated in the last paragraph.

14. **(C)** Brescia is known to carry firearms at all times. Chances are pretty good that others of the gang carry arms as well, but the memorandum does not say so.

15. **(B)** The court officers must avoid any action which may jeopardize the safety of spectators.

16. **(A)** Referees of the civil court are drawn from the ranks of former judges of this court or from the ranks of judges who have retired from any court of record.

17. **(A)** If criminal behavior is taught, then it is learned.

18. **(D)** The law enforcement staff of today requires training and mental qualities of a high order.

19. **(A)** Regardless of how antisocial an act may be, it is not a crime unless it is a violation of a written law.

20. **(B)** Our crime rate is so high because it is so easy for criminals to obtain guns.

21. **(D)** A person who is arrested while in the process of committing a crime knows full well why he or she is being arrested and need not be told.

22. **(D)** If it is important that the court officer keep order in the court, obviously order is important to the functioning of the court.

23. **(A)** If one's attitude is "once a criminal always a criminal," then probation and parole should not be options and imprisonment must be emphasized. *Malingering* is pretending to be sick to avoid work.

24. **(A)** The subject of the paragraph is precisely the various problems that arise in maintaining an adequate housing supply.

25. **(C)** The passage states that code enforcement alone will not alleviate the problem of slums and inadequate housing supply.

26. **(A)** The only solution is demolition, clearance, and new construction.

27. **(B)** Evolved traditions are traditions that have developed over a period of time.

28. **(A)** Chances are that the old-timers are old-timers because they have learned to do their work well, but the paragraph discusses the old-timers as the source of long accepted practices and customs and as the means by which these practices and customs are handed on to newer workers.

29. **(C)** This paragraph links delinquent behavior to social and economic deprivation, in other words, to the social environment.

30. **(A)** The supervisor should encourage employees to devise new work methods.

31. **(A)** See the third sentence.

32. **(B)** Your answer must be based upon the paragraph, whether or not you believe the content to be true. The last two sentences state that summonses are not issued in cases of ignorance of the law or simple error.

33. **(D)** The author appears to approve of the policy.

34. **(B)** The person who speeds because he or she is late is speeding intentionally.

35. **(B)** The paragraph does not state that small wounds are more dangerous than large ones—only that they must not be neglected.

36. **(C)** As long as the oil is properly labeled, any blend may be packed and sold.

37. **(C)** The paragraph discusses the precautions which must be taken at the scene of the crime so as to disturb as little evidence as possible.

38. **(A)** Danger to persons is more compelling than preservation of evidence, but the officer should size up the situation so as to do as little damage as possible.

39. **(D)** Preservation of evidence is important, but it pales in the face of danger to any person, victim or perpetrator.

40. **(C)** The same point is repeated. Save lives.

41. **(C)** Add up arraignments in all twelve courts. The total is 136,185, which is closest to 136,000.

42. **(B)** $164,482 − $78,625 = $85,857, which is most nearly $85,855.

43. **(D)** 273 × 36 = 9,828, which is closest to the 10,521 arraignments in Manhattan.

44. **(A)** $667,670 ÷ 12 = $55,639.17, which is most nearly $55,640.

45. **(C)** In Criminal Court, Queens the amount of fines is nearly 12 times the number of arraignments. In the other three courts, fines outpace arraignments by only about 2 to 1.

46. **(C)** By inspection, it is clear that the 10,521 to 2,312 in Criminal Court, Manhattan, is much closer to 4 to 1 than is the 8,935 to 3,301 of Flatbush, the 11,242 to 1,782 of Criminal Court, Brooklyn, or the 3,527 to 1,971 of Flushing.

47. **(A)** 1412 × 3 = 4236, which is very close to 4454.

48. **(A)** Manhattan had 10,521 arraignments, while Brooklyn had 11,242; on the other hand, Manhattan had 2,312 summonses, while Brooklyn had only 1,782.

49. **(C)** Study the table. The court that meets the criteria of the question is Criminal Court, Manhattan.

50. **(A)** $7,500 is $33\frac{1}{3}$% less than its real value so it is $66\frac{2}{3}$% or $\frac{2}{3}$ of its real value. If $\frac{2}{3}$ = $7500, then $\frac{1}{3}$ = $3750, and $\frac{3}{3}$ or the full value is $3,750 × 3 = $11,250.

51. **(B)** Lines 1 and 4 are exactly the same.

52. **(C)** Lines 1, 2, and 4 are exactly the same.

53. **(D)** All four lines are exactly the same.

54. **(A)** Only the fourth line is exactly the same.

55. **(C)** Lines 1, 3, and 4 are exactly the same.

56. **(D)** All four lines are exactly the same.

57. **(A)** Only the first line is exactly the same.

58. **(C)** Lines 1, 3, and 4 are exactly the same.

59. **(A)** Only the second line is exactly the same.

60. **(B)** Lines 1 and 3 are exactly the same.

61. **(D)** (A), (B), and (C) are all badly written sentences with extraneous and incorrect words.

62. **(D)** The first three choices all present errors of agreement between subject and verb.

63. **(C)** (B) and (D) are awkward and poorly written. (A) contains an agreement error that is corrected in (C).

64. **(A)** *Effect* means *cause; affect* means *influence.*

65. **(B)** In referring to the employees of a company in this manner, you need not use a possessive. (A) is incorrect. *Brown & Company* is the singular subject of (C) and (D).

66. **(A)** In (B), the subject of the second clause is *information*, which is singular. In (C), the adverb should be *really. Being that,* in (D), is not an acceptable form.

67. **(D)** In (A), *my mother and me* are the objects of the verb *reach*, while in (C), *my mother or me* are the objects of the preposition *to.* In (B), the object of the preposition *to* should be *me* not the reflexive *myself,* since I did not address the letter.

68. **(C)** In (A), *who* is the subject of *had made.* In (B), the word *of* before *known* should be omitted. In (D), the second clause is missing a subject.

69. **(B)** In (A), *them* should be *him* because it refers to *anyone*, which is singular. (C) and (D) are very awkward.

70. **(D)** The first three sentences lack parallel construction. All the words that modify *paper* must appear in the same form.

71. **(D)** All three lines are correctly coded.

72. **(B)** In the first line, W is miscoded; in the third line, V and X are both miscoded.

73. **(B)** In the first line, W is miscoded; in the second line, M and B are miscoded.

74. **(C)** In the third line, the code numbers for W and M are reversed.

75. **(B)** In the first line, the code numbers for X and B are reversed; in the third line, the code numbers for W and U are reversed.

76. **(B)** In the second line, the code numbers for B and U are reversed; in the third line, the code numbers for M and B are reversed.

77. **(A)** In the first line, C is miscoded; in the second line, B is miscoded; in the third line, W is miscoded.

78. **(D)** All three lines are correctly coded.

79. **(A)** In the first line, the code numbers for V and W are reversed; in the second line, M is miscoded; in the third line, the code numbers for V and Y are reversed.

80. **(B)** In the first line, the code numbers for W and L are reversed; in the third line, the code numbers for V and Y are reversed.

81. **(A)** The sealed verdict has been ordered, and the jury is now deliberating. This is a period of time during which no juror may communicate with anyone outside, unless with the permission of the judge. Since the judge has left the courthouse, permission cannot be requested nor granted, so the juror cannot use the telephone. (Since the message is a simple "I'll be home late," a court officer might make the call and give this information to the wife. Court officers, who are not privy to deliberations, are not under the same tight restrictions concerning communication.)

82. **(D)** The jury must never be left unguarded, so both court officers must not run errands at the same time. Courthouse decorum suggests that shouting down the corridor is not appropriate. The jury must wait until one request is filled before a court officer can leave to fill the next one.

83. **(C)** The court officer must supply the jury with whatever supplies its members feel that they need.

84. **(C)** Rules demand that the court officer close and lock the door of the jury room and remain outside the door within easy calling distance of the jurors.

85. **(C)** Two officers are assigned to guard the jury at all times. This job cannot be delegated to any other person. If, for some reason, a relieving officer does not arrive on time, both officers must remain with the jury, even if doing so interferes with personal responsibility.

86. **(B)** Evans took two credit cards, thereby committing grand larceny.

87. **(C)** John Murphy avoided payment for transportation. He thus committed theft of services.

88. **(D)** By taking the credit card, Mary committed grand larcency. In using the credit card, Mary committed theft of services as well.

89. **(B)** Refer to the definition of larceny. There is no charge of menacing because Smith did not have the means to carry out the threat.

90. **(B)** Larceny is the only charge that could be brought against Mary. Grand larceny and arson are discounted as possible answers because the former involves values *over* $250 and the latter requires the fire to be set intentionally.

91. **(D)** Bill could be charged with arson and theft of services because the fire was started intentionally and because he used a slug to make a phone call.

92. **(C)** The charges that could be brought against Bill are larceny, because the saw was not worth more than $250; arson, because the fire was started intentionally; and menacing, because he had the means available to carry out his threat.

93. **(B)** In taking Lisa's credit card, Frank committed grand larceny. Frank committed theft of services two times, once when he used the credit card to pay for his dinner and again when he did not pay for the cab ride.

94. **(A)** Bill Martin's taking the pocketbook constituted larceny. He cannot be charged with arson because the fire was not started intentionally.

95. **(D)** Mike's stealing the credit card constitutes grand larceny; his using it is theft of services.

96. **(C)** Sloan has been elected to become an executive officer of the county. Bribing or attempting to bribe him is a crime. Crane has attempted to bribe this elected officer. If convicted, Crane could serve 5 years in a state prison—he could even serve up to 10 years and be fined as well. Sloan, in refusing the bribe, has done no wrong.

97. **(B)** Joe Marshall has bribed a public officer. He is subject to imprisonment and/or fine. Don Williams is clearly guilty of accepting a bribe and probably of delivering the action for which the bribe was made. The paragraph, however, deals only with penalties for the person who offers the bribe. Williams's punishment cannot enter into the answer.

98. **(D)** White is trying very hard and may be making himself obnoxious, but he really is not offering a bribe to a public official. There is no basis for punishment in the context of the quoted paragraph.

99. **(C)** All four men conspired to commit an armed robbery and, as such, contributed to its success. The fact that Bob Burns was unable to physically participate does not make him any less party to the crime. Likewise, Wilson, who did not actually enter the liquor store, was a participant and principal in the action. The night clerk at the Holiday Inn had no reason to suspect that two men seeking accommodations for the night were fugitives from justice. He is not an accessory.

100. **(B)** Ron Johnson is a crack dealer. Selling crack is a crime. Further, Johnson has counseled and induced Walker to commit the same crime. Both are principals. Hiding Harry in the barn is aiding him to avoid detection, even though he is not in her house. Molly is an accessory.

Model Court Officer Exam IV
Answer Sheet

PART ONE

1 Ⓐ Ⓑ Ⓒ Ⓓ	7 Ⓐ Ⓑ Ⓒ Ⓓ	13 Ⓐ Ⓑ Ⓒ Ⓓ	19 Ⓐ Ⓑ Ⓒ Ⓓ	25 Ⓐ Ⓑ Ⓒ Ⓓ
2 Ⓐ Ⓑ Ⓒ Ⓓ	8 Ⓐ Ⓑ Ⓒ Ⓓ	14 Ⓐ Ⓑ Ⓒ Ⓓ	20 Ⓐ Ⓑ Ⓒ Ⓓ	26 Ⓐ Ⓑ Ⓒ Ⓓ
3 Ⓐ Ⓑ Ⓒ Ⓓ	9 Ⓐ Ⓑ Ⓒ Ⓓ	15 Ⓐ Ⓑ Ⓒ Ⓓ	21 Ⓐ Ⓑ Ⓒ Ⓓ	27 Ⓐ Ⓑ Ⓒ Ⓓ
4 Ⓐ Ⓑ Ⓒ Ⓓ	10 Ⓐ Ⓑ Ⓒ Ⓓ	16 Ⓐ Ⓑ Ⓒ Ⓓ	22 Ⓐ Ⓑ Ⓒ Ⓓ	28 Ⓐ Ⓑ Ⓒ Ⓓ
5 Ⓐ Ⓑ Ⓒ Ⓓ	11 Ⓐ Ⓑ Ⓒ Ⓓ	17 Ⓐ Ⓑ Ⓒ Ⓓ	23 Ⓐ Ⓑ Ⓒ Ⓓ	29 Ⓐ Ⓑ Ⓒ Ⓓ
6 Ⓐ Ⓑ Ⓒ Ⓓ	12 Ⓐ Ⓑ Ⓒ Ⓓ	18 Ⓐ Ⓑ Ⓒ Ⓓ	24 Ⓐ Ⓑ Ⓒ Ⓓ	30 Ⓐ Ⓑ Ⓒ Ⓓ

PART TWO

1 Ⓐ Ⓑ Ⓒ Ⓓ	15 Ⓐ Ⓑ Ⓒ Ⓓ	29 Ⓐ Ⓑ Ⓒ Ⓓ	43 Ⓐ Ⓑ Ⓒ Ⓓ	57 Ⓐ Ⓑ Ⓒ Ⓓ
2 Ⓐ Ⓑ Ⓒ Ⓓ	16 Ⓐ Ⓑ Ⓒ Ⓓ	30 Ⓐ Ⓑ Ⓒ Ⓓ	44 Ⓐ Ⓑ Ⓒ Ⓓ	58 Ⓐ Ⓑ Ⓒ Ⓓ
3 Ⓐ Ⓑ Ⓒ Ⓓ	17 Ⓐ Ⓑ Ⓒ Ⓓ	31 Ⓐ Ⓑ Ⓒ Ⓓ	45 Ⓐ Ⓑ Ⓒ Ⓓ	59 Ⓐ Ⓑ Ⓒ Ⓓ
4 Ⓐ Ⓑ Ⓒ Ⓓ	18 Ⓐ Ⓑ Ⓒ Ⓓ	32 Ⓐ Ⓑ Ⓒ Ⓓ	46 Ⓐ Ⓑ Ⓒ Ⓓ	60 Ⓐ Ⓑ Ⓒ Ⓓ
5 Ⓐ Ⓑ Ⓒ Ⓓ	19 Ⓐ Ⓑ Ⓒ Ⓓ	33 Ⓐ Ⓑ Ⓒ Ⓓ	47 Ⓐ Ⓑ Ⓒ Ⓓ	61 Ⓐ Ⓑ Ⓒ Ⓓ
6 Ⓐ Ⓑ Ⓒ Ⓓ	20 Ⓐ Ⓑ Ⓒ Ⓓ	34 Ⓐ Ⓑ Ⓒ Ⓓ	48 Ⓐ Ⓑ Ⓒ Ⓓ	62 Ⓐ Ⓑ Ⓒ Ⓓ
7 Ⓐ Ⓑ Ⓒ Ⓓ	21 Ⓐ Ⓑ Ⓒ Ⓓ	35 Ⓐ Ⓑ Ⓒ Ⓓ	49 Ⓐ Ⓑ Ⓒ Ⓓ	63 Ⓐ Ⓑ Ⓒ Ⓓ
8 Ⓐ Ⓑ Ⓒ Ⓓ	22 Ⓐ Ⓑ Ⓒ Ⓓ	36 Ⓐ Ⓑ Ⓒ Ⓓ	50 Ⓐ Ⓑ Ⓒ Ⓓ	64 Ⓐ Ⓑ Ⓒ Ⓓ
9 Ⓐ Ⓑ Ⓒ Ⓓ	23 Ⓐ Ⓑ Ⓒ Ⓓ	37 Ⓐ Ⓑ Ⓒ Ⓓ	51 Ⓐ Ⓑ Ⓒ Ⓓ	65 Ⓐ Ⓑ Ⓒ Ⓓ
10 Ⓐ Ⓑ Ⓒ Ⓓ	24 Ⓐ Ⓑ Ⓒ Ⓓ	38 Ⓐ Ⓑ Ⓒ Ⓓ	52 Ⓐ Ⓑ Ⓒ Ⓓ	66 Ⓐ Ⓑ Ⓒ Ⓓ
11 Ⓐ Ⓑ Ⓒ Ⓓ	25 Ⓐ Ⓑ Ⓒ Ⓓ	39 Ⓐ Ⓑ Ⓒ Ⓓ	53 Ⓐ Ⓑ Ⓒ Ⓓ	67 Ⓐ Ⓑ Ⓒ Ⓓ
12 Ⓐ Ⓑ Ⓒ Ⓓ	26 Ⓐ Ⓑ Ⓒ Ⓓ	40 Ⓐ Ⓑ Ⓒ Ⓓ	54 Ⓐ Ⓑ Ⓒ Ⓓ	68 Ⓐ Ⓑ Ⓒ Ⓓ
13 Ⓐ Ⓑ Ⓒ Ⓓ	27 Ⓐ Ⓑ Ⓒ Ⓓ	41 Ⓐ Ⓑ Ⓒ Ⓓ	55 Ⓐ Ⓑ Ⓒ Ⓓ	69 Ⓐ Ⓑ Ⓒ Ⓓ
14 Ⓐ Ⓑ Ⓒ Ⓓ	28 Ⓐ Ⓑ Ⓒ Ⓓ	42 Ⓐ Ⓑ Ⓒ Ⓓ	56 Ⓐ Ⓑ Ⓒ Ⓓ	

TEAR HERE

MODEL COURT OFFICER EXAM IV

Part One

45 MINUTES, 30 QUESTIONS, 25% OF TOTAL SCORE.
ALL QUESTIONS ARE EQUALLY WEIGHTED.

DIRECTIONS for questions 1 through 20: Each question consists of three sets of information appearing in three columns. In some of the questions, the same information appears on the same line in all three sets. In other questions, the information appears on a different line in each set. The position of the information is irrelevant. You are to compare the information in the three sets, searching for any differences in the information presented. Keep in mind that *any* difference at all makes the sets different. Mark your answer sheet as follows:

Mark (A) if *ALL THREE* sets are exactly alike
Mark (B) if only the *FIRST* and *THIRD* sets are exactly alike
Mark (C) if only the *FIRST* and *SECOND* sets are exactly alike
Mark (D) if *NONE* of the sets are exactly alike

1. Petrillo, A T Co Inc.   Petrillo, A T Co Inc.   Petrillo, A T Co Inc.
   1-201-748-4999   1-201-748-4999   1-201-748-4999
   Troy: Red and Tan   Troy:Red and Tan   Troy: Red and Tan
   PG683.D781045   PG683.D781045   PG683.D781045
   Peiser, Isadore   Peiser, Isadore   Peiser, Isadore

2. Uniform Commercial Code   Uniform Commercial Code   Uniform Commercial Code
   ISBN 0-13-18476-2-8   ISBN 0-13-18476-2-8   ISBN 0-13-184762-8
   Moscovitz, Simeon   Moscowitz, Simeon   Moscovitz, Simeon
   Guaranty Title Co.   Guaranty Title Co.   Guaranty Title Co.
   155 East 3300 South   155 East 3300 South   155 East 3300 South

3. Manhattan Referral Svce   Manhattan Referral Svce   Manhattan Referral Svce
   XT9846.L4010   XT9846.L4010   XT9846.L4010
   H. Kauffman & Sons   H. Kauffman & Sons   H. Kauffman & Sons
   011-34-52-882291   011-34-52-882291   011-34-882291
   Maison Sapho School   Maison Sapho School   Maison Sapho School

4. Harvey Geary Assocs Inc   Harvey Geary Assocs Inc   Harvey Geary Assocs Inc
   9-1-817-625-3394   9-1-817-625-3394   9-1-817-625-3394
   Deluxe Courier & Air   Deluxe Courier & Air   Deluxe Courier & Air
   BX44182.J908764   BX44182.J908764   BX44182.J908764
   McGregor, Angus W.   McGregor, Angus W.   MacGregor, Angus W.

5. Spadaro and Heller, PC
Rent-A-Mailbox Inc.
ISBN 0-668-05604-5
NY Civil Practice Law
33164,8972.7

Spadaro and Heller, PC
Rent-A-Mailbox Inc.
ISBN 668-05604-5
NY Civil Practice Law
33164,8972.7

Spadaro and Heller, PC
Rent-a-Mailbox Inc.
ISBN 0-668-05604-5
NY Civil Practice Law
33164,8972.7

6. Misericordia Hospital
619-60-4683
PTB3.9760.G109
Schildwachter Fuel Oil
Summer-Wiggins, Ltd.

Misericordia Hospital
619-60-4683
PT83.9760.G109
Schildwachter Fuel Oil
Summer-Wiggins, Ltd.

Misericordia Hospital
619-60-4683
PTB3.9760.G109
Schildwachter Fuel Oil
Sumner-Wiggins, Ltd.

7. Montessori-Piaget
ISBN 0-8120-3886-X
Bouregy, Thomas PC
TT980.765,412
Ohaus Itin Scales

Bouregy, Thomas PC
ISBN 0-8120-3886-X
Ohaus Itin Scales
TT980.765,412
Montessori-Piaget

TT980.765,412
Ohaus Itin Scales
Bouregy, Thomas PC
Montessori-Piaget
ISBN 0-8120-3886-x

8. First Megasafe Indus.
D703Y380-SAI-413
Black's Law Dictionary
22 Street Electronics
708.732DWI/4168

22 Street Electronics
708.732DWI/4168
D703Y380-SAI-413
First Megasafe Indus.
Black's Law Dictionary

708.732DWI/4168
Black's Law Dictionary
22 Street Electronics
D703Y380-SAI-413
First Megasafe Indus.

9. Title L 205.00-205.65
Cirabella, Carmen Mi
Alco Grauvre Inc.
Miller & Dollard
ISBN 0-931794-14-5

Miller & Dollard
ISBN 0-931794-14-5
Cirabella, Carmen Mi
Alco Grauvre Inc.
Title L 205.00-205.56

Cirabella, Carmen Mi
Title L 205.00-205.65
ISBN 0-931794-14-5
Miller & Dollard
Alco Grauvre Inc.

10. Corbin on Contracts
9-011-021-28-17-33
ISBN 0-913094-37-4
Scheichet and Elger
Bunting and Lyon, Inc.

Bunting and Lyon, Inc.
Scheichet and Elgar
Corbin on Contracts
ISBN 0-913094-37-4
9-011-021-28-17-33

ISBN 0-913094-37-4
Bunting and Lyon, Inc.
9-011-021-28-17-33
Corbin on Contracts
Scheichet and Elger

11. Immigration Law & Proc.
Jofram Ambulette Serv.
Biegeleisen, J. Co.
11th '89 $17.95
FH3281.K27919

11th '89 $19.95
Immigration Law & Proc.
FH3281.K27919
Biegeleisen, J. Co.
Jofram Ambulette Serv.

FH3281.K27919
Jofran Ambulette Serv.
Immigration Law & Proc.
11th '89 $17.95
Biegeleisen, J. Co.

12. Spink & Gaborc Inc.
Leavenworth Prison
PE1628.W5633
McKinney's Consol. Laws
2550-923-258-7530

2550-923-258-7530
McKinney's Consol. Laws
Leavenworth Prison
PE1628.W5633
Spink & Gaborc Inc.

Leavenworth Prison
Spink & Gaborc Inc.
McKinney's Consol. Laws
2550-923-258-7530
PE1628.W5633

13. Forzano and Sons, Ltd.   FAX # 302-741-0809   Constitutional Issues
    Constitutional Issues   ISBN 0-525-03543-1   Forzano and Sons, Ltd.
    FAX # 302-741-0809   Constitutional Issues   ISBN 0-03643-1
    Hwang v. Mathews   Forzano and Sons, Ltd.   Hwang v. Mathews
    ISBN 0-525-03643-1   Hwang v. Mathews   FAX # 302-741-0809

14. Hohenfels Abstract Svce   9-1-723-282-4451x67   Angelika Film Corp.
    Angelika Film Corp.   Francais, Jacques   Hohenfels Abstract Svce
    1487-3.09/865   Hohenfels Abstract Svce   Francais, Jacques
    9-1-723-282-4551x67   Angelika Film Corp.   9-1-723-282-4551x67
    Francais, Jacques   1487-3.09/865   1487-3.09/865

15. Siegel Chalif & Winn   Siegel Chalif & Winn   Siegel Chalif & Winn
    PC1.582-68314EX77531   PC1.582-63814EX77531   PC1.582-68314EX77531
    Hahnemann, Jos. & Bro.   Hahnemann, Jos. & Bro.   Hahnemann, Jos. & Bro.
    TT46814.3209/5911-7   TT46814.3209/5911-7   TT46814.3209/5911-7

16. Criminal Justice Admin.   Criminal Justice Admin.   Criminal Justice Admin.
    Amitai, Jonah ben   Amitai, Jonah Ben   Amitai, Johan ben
    TZ-39184-672/091.4   TZ-39184-672/091.4   TZ-39184-672/091.4
    Sills Beck Cummins Radin   Sills Beck Cummins Radin   Sills Beck Cummins Radin

17. Espejo, Manning & Esposito PC   RD45Y,90UPN-0056.2   Kurumazushi Sushi Shoppe
    Geoghan Tutrone & Grossman   Kurumazushi Sushi Shoppe   RD45Y,90UPN-0056.2
    RD45Y,90UPN-0056.2   Geoghan Tutrone & Grossman Espejo, Manning & Esposito PC
    Kurumazushi Sushi Shoppe   Espejo, Manning & Esposito PC   Geoghan Tutrone & Grossman

18. White & Snow Beck & Koss   Song Yook Hong Law Offices   118.9FR-9230/10585.6
    Song Yook Hong Law Offices 118.9FR-9230/10585.6   Lorson Electrical Contractors
    118.9FR-9230/10585.6   White & Snow Beck & Koss   Song Yook Hong Law Offices
    Lorson Electrical Contractors Lorson Electrical Contractors White Snow Beck & Koss

19. Feet First Reflexology Center   FTD475-3412.FBP838/2684   Feet First Reflexology Center
    Spagna, Saul & Rose, Rene PC   8976JV765.33/3975WE.644   FTD475-3412.FPB838/2684
    8976JV765.33/3975WE.644   Feet First Reflexology Center Spagna, Saul & Rose, Rene PC
    FTD475-3412.FPB838/2684   Spagna, Saul & Rose, Rene PC   8976JV765.33/3975WE.644

20. Gouverneur Hospital Facility   PT68432.UZ83921-91   TSS-ONY Production Centre
    PT68432.UZ83921-91   Tsigonia Industries Corp.   Gouverneur Hospital Facility
    TSS-ONY Production Centre   Gouverneur Hospital Facility PT68432.UZ83921-91
    Tsigonia Industries Corp.   TSS-ONY Production Center   Tsigonia Industrial Corp.

DIRECTIONS: Answer questions 21 through 30 on the basis of the information contained in the following tables and their accompanying code keys. You may find it helpful to complete Tables 4 and 5, the summary tables, before you attempt to answer the questions. Use of a calculator is permitted.

Table 1
Sentences—Wessex County—May 11–15

Offense	Age and Sex of Offender									
	under 15		15–17		18–21		22–30		over 30	
	M	F	M	F	M	F	M	F	M	F
vandalism	c;d;d	c	a;d	c;j	a;e	d	b&e			
burglary			a&c		b;e&f	b&e	g;h;j	e;f	h;h;j	b&e;f
larceny	c	c;j	d;d	b&c	b;f;j	a&d	d&f	e&g	b&d;c	e&f;j
assault	a;b		j;j	a	b;f	a;j	b;e	d;f	g;j	f;h
robbery			a;b		b;g	b;e	e&f	h;j	g;g;g	d&f;j
drunk driving			e;j	d;d	b&e	e;j;j	e;f	e&f	b;d;j	e;e
prostitution		a;j	b	b;d		b;f	e	g;j	d;e	e;g
manslaughter			j	j	b	a;j	d&f	f	b;g	e;j
narcotics (sale)	a;a;b		b;e	c;d	e&g;g	e&f	e&h;g	h;j	g;h;j	e;j
narcotics (possession)	c;c	c	a&c	a;c	b;b;b	b;c	b;j	d;j	b;f;j	b&d;f

Table 2
Sentences—Essex County—May 11–15

Offense	Age and Sex of Offender									
	under 15		15–17		18–21		22–30		over 30	
	M	F	M	F	M	F	M	F	M	F
vandalism	d;j	c	a;e	c	e;e;e	b&d	b;e	d		
burglary	j		b		b;e;j	d;j	e&g;f	d&f	e&g;h	b&e;d
larceny	d;c	c	a;c	d;j	a;j	a;b;e	d;g	d&g	e;f;j	a
assault	b;j	a	b;e;j	b	b&d	a	d&g;f	b	b;e;f	b;j
robbery	b&e		b;d	a	b;e;j	d&f	e;f;g	e&g	e;h;h	b;f;h
drunk driving	b		e	j	b;e	a;j	e;f;j	e&f;j	e;e;f	d;g
prostitution		b;d	a	b&c;j	b;d	a;c;c		d;e	e	b;e;j
manslaughter			e		b;b;e	b;j	a&e;j	a	b;d	e;j;j
narcotics (sale)	b;a&d		b;b	e	e;g;h	e&h	h;j	h;h;j	e&h;j	e&h;j
narcotics (possession)	j	c;j	a;a&d	c;d	b&d	d;d	d;f	e&f	b;j	b&e;j

Code key:

a = probation 1 to 2 yrs.
b = probation more than 2 yrs.
c = fine under $100
d = fine $100-$350
e = fine over $350

f = imprisonment 1–6 months
g = imprisonment 6 mos. to 1 yr.
h = imprisonment over 1 yr.
j = acquitted

Table 3
Sentences—Sussex County—May 11–15

Offense	under 15 M	under 15 F	15–17 M	15–17 F	18–21 M	18–21 F	22–30 M	22–30 F	over 30 M	over 30 F
vandalism	d;e;e	d	b&e	c;d	a;b;e	b;d	b;e	j		
burglary	a		b;j		b;f	e&f	e&g	g;j	e&h;h	f
larceny	a	a&c	d;e	a;c	b;d	c;d	f;f	j;j	e&f;j	e&g;h
assault	b	a	b;d	d;j	e&f	b;b	b;d;j	d;j	f;f	d;f
robbery	b		b;e;j	a	e&f	b&d	a;e;h	h;j	e;e&g	e;f;g
drunk driving		b	b&e	a&c	e;j	d;j	e;e	b;e	f;j	e&f
prostitution	j	a;b		b;b;j	a	d;e	d	f;j		e&f;j
manslaughter			a;a		b;e	b;j	e;j	j	e;e;e	e;j
narcotics (sale)	b	b	b;e	e;j	d&f	f	g;j	e&g	e&h;j	g;h;j
narcotics (possession)	a&c	a	a&d	a;j	e	d	a&d	b&d	e;e	e;j;j

Code key:

a = probation 1 to 2 yrs.
b = probation more than 2 yrs.
c = fine under $100
d = fine $100–$350
e = fine over $350

f = imprisonment 1–6 months
g = imprisonment 6 mos. to 1 yr.
h = imprisonment over 1 yr.
j = acquitted

Table 4
Summary of Disposition of Cases—Three Counties

Disposition	under 15 M	under 15 F	under 15 T	15–17 M	15–17 F	15–17 T	18–21 M	18–21 F	18–21 T	22–30 M	22–30 F	22–30 T	over 30 M	over 30 F	over 30 T	Total M	Total F	Total T
acquitted	卌			卌 卌 (9)							卌III 卌卌								
probation only							卌 卌卌							67					
fine only		卌卌 卌卌								卌 卌卌								138
prison only				0	卌 II									卌卌卌 卌卌卌卌				
probation & fine				卌 I							IIII							29
prison & fine																		
Total			21						108									

Table 5
Summary of Dispositions By Offense—Three Counties

Offense	Sentence						
	acquitted	probation only	fine only	prison only	probation & fine	prison & fine	Total
vandalism			‖‖ ‖‖ ‖‖ ‖‖ ‖‖ ‖				
burglary							
larceny		‖‖ ‖‖		‖‖ ‖	‖‖		53
assault						1	
robbery			‖‖ ‖‖			‖‖ ‖	
drunk driving	‖‖ ‖‖ ‖						
prostitution							
manslaughter		‖‖ ‖‖ ‖‖					39
narcotics (sale)				‖‖ ‖‖ ‖‖			
narcotics (possession)					‖‖ ‖‖		
Total			138	29			

21. The total number of women age 21 and younger who were acquitted is

(A) 21
(B) 22
(C) 23
(D) 24

22. The total number of people between the ages of 18 and 21 who will spend more than one year in prison is

(A) 0
(B) 1
(C) 2
(D) 3

23. The number of people sentenced to probation only upon conviction for prostitution is

(A) 13
(B) 14
(C) 15
(D) 16

24. How many more people were convicted and sentenced for assault than were acquitted?

    (A) 10
    (B) 32
    (C) 42
    (D) 52

25. The number of men tried for manslaughter is

    (A) 19
    (B) 22
    (C) 24
    (D) 27

26. How many more women than men in the 18–21 age group were sentenced to pay fines only?

    (A) 2
    (B) 3
    (C) 15
    (D) 17

27. The number of women over age 30 who will spend any time in prison is

    (A) 15
    (B) 16
    (C) 20
    (D) 21

28. How many men between the ages of 15 and 30 were convicted of drunk driving?

    (A) 13
    (B) 14
    (C) 16
    (D) 20

29. The total number of people who paid fines under $100 for narcotics convictions is

    (A) 8
    (B) 9
    (C) 10
    (D) 11

30. How many more people will serve prison time for burglary than will spend time on probation?

    (A) 7
    (B) 9
    (C) 12
    (D) 18

END OF PART ONE

Memory Story

DIRECTIONS: Read and study the story below for five minutes. Concentrate on the details and try to remember as many as possible. You will later be asked questions about this story.

On Tuesday, March 13, Supreme Court of Princess County was gearing up for trial in the latest of a series of bias-related crimes. Two Korean merchants, UnJin Ehee and Ed Paik, had been badly beaten in their store on the evening of July 12, and Ehee remained in a coma eight months after the attack.

Three black teenagers, Harry Wilson, George Jones, and Glenda Pratt, had been indicted, and jury selection for their trial was scheduled to begin at 10 A.M. All court personnel were alert to the possibility of demonstrations, disruptions, and even violence.

Court Officers Maria Martinez, Monty Pipko, and Ben Bradson stood just inside the door of the courthouse, manning the front desk and the metal detector. Senior Court Officer Warren Chen stood on the front steps of the courthouse with Officers Pat Kelly, John Pinero, Kuniko Parker, and Fred White.

At 9:20 A.M., a large, noisy group, led by Hal Sharkey, rounded the corner and began to converge on the courthouse. Members of the group carried signs demanding justice for all blacks. They shouted that blacks are always singled out, picked on, and accused.

As the group attempted to mount the courthouse steps, Senior Court Officer Chen barred their way and asked them to please congregate in the grassy area directly across the street from the courthouse. Hal Sharkey complained that blacks were never even permitted to express their opinions, but a cordon of court officers and city police slowly moved the group back to the designated area. In the course of this action, one protester hit Court Officer Parker over the head with a sign, opening a nasty gash on Parker's scalp. Officer Parker was assisted by paramedics who were called to the scene by Officer Pinero.

Part Two

2 Hours, 69 questions, 75% of total score.
Questions 1 through 55 count 1 point each.
Questions 56 through 69 count ½ point each.

DIRECTIONS for questions 1 through 10: These questions are based on the Memory Story which you have just read and studied. Answer each question on the basis of the story as you remember it. After answering the memory questions, proceed directly to question 11 without waiting for another signal.

1. The trial about to take place concerns an incident that occurred on

    (A) July 10
    (B) March 13
    (C) August 8
    (D) July 12

2. The victim who remains in a coma is

    (A) Warren Chen
    (B) UnJin Ehee
    (C) Ed Paik
    (D) Kuniko Parker

3. The trial is being held in

    (A) Criminal Court, Princess County
    (B) Supreme Court, Kent County
    (C) Supreme Court, Princess County
    (D) Superior Court, Prince County

4. The name of one accused teenager is

    (A) Harry Wilson
    (B) Ben Bradson
    (C) Hal Sharkey
    (D) Fred White

5. The location of the metal detector is

    (A) at the top of the courthouse steps
    (B) inside the front door of the courthouse
    (C) outside the door of the courtroom
    (D) in the grassy area across the street from the courthouse

6. The demonstrators approached the courthouse from

    (A) across the street
    (B) around the corner
    (C) the park
    (D) down the block

7. The protest by the demonstrators concerned

   (A) police brutality
   (B) equal justice
   (C) poor medical services
   (D) the right to protest

8. The demonstrators were controlled by

   (A) court officers
   (B) court officers and paramedics
   (C) court officers and city police
   (D) court officers, city police, and paramedics

9. The injury to the officer occurred

   (A) before 9:20 A.M.
   (B) around 9:30 A.M.
   (C) after 10:30 A.M.
   (D) in the evening

10. The paramedics who assisted the injured officer were summoned by

    (A) Officer Pinero
    (B) Officer Parker
    (C) Officer Pipko
    (D) Officer Pratt

DIRECTIONS: Answer each question on the basis of your reading, understanding, and interpretation of the material provided. Use only the information
given and your own common sense. Do not allow any additional or contrary
knowledge you may have to influence your answer choice.

11. "Many children who are exposed to contacts and experiences of a delinquent nature
    become educated and trained in crime in the course of participating in the daily life of
    the neighborhood." From this statement, we may reasonably conclude that

    (A) delinquency passes from parent to child
    (B) neighborhood influences are usually bad
    (C) schools are training grounds for delinquents
    (D) none of the above conclusions is reasonable

12. "Old age insurance, a benefit for which city employees are eligible, is one feature of
    the Social Security Act that is wholly administered by the federal government." On the
    basis of this statement, it may most reasonably be inferred that

    (A) all city employees are now drawing old age insurance
    (B) no city employees have elected to become eligible for old age insurance
    (C) the city has no part in administering Social Security old age insurance
    (D) only the federal government administers the Social Security Act

13. A court officer is a peace officer. A peace officer's revolver is a defensive, not an
    offensive, weapon. From this statement, you know that a court officer should draw a
    revolver

    (A) to fire at an unarmed burglar
    (B) to force a suspect to confess
    (C) to frighten a juvenile delinquent
    (D) in self-defense

14. "The depositions must set forth the facts tending to establish that an illegal act was committed and that the defendant is guilty." According to this statement, the one of the following which need *not* be included in a deposition is evidence that establishes the .

    (A) fact that an illegal act was committed
    (B) fact that the defendant committed the illegal act
    (C) guilt of the defendant
    (D) method of commission of the illegal act

15. "Each court officer should understand how his or her own work helps to accomplish the purpose of the entire agency." This statement means most nearly that the court officer should understand the

    (A) efficiency of a small agency
    (B) importance of his or her own job
    (C) necessity of initiative
    (D) value of a large organization

16. "All concerned are most likely to recognize the court officer's authority and cooperate if the officer conveys in his or her manner a complete confidence that they will do so." According to this statement, an effective court officer should display

    (A) arrogance
    (B) agitation
    (C) assurance
    (D) excitement

17. "It is a frequent misconception that court officers can be recruited from those registers established for the recruitment of city police or firefighters. While it is true that many common qualifications are found in all of these, specific standards for court officer work are indicated, varying with the size, geographical location, and policies of the office." According to this statement, it may be inferred that

    (A) a successful court officer must have some qualifications not required of a police officer or a firefighter
    (B) qualifications that make a successful police officer will also make a successful firefighter
    (C) the same qualifications are required of a court officer, regardless of the office to which he or she is assigned
    (D) the successful court officer is required to be both more intelligent and stronger than a firefighter

Answer questions 18 and 19 on the basis of the following paragraph.

Proper firearms training is one phase of law enforcement that cannot be ignored. No part of the training of a police officer is more important or more valuable. The officer's life and often the lives of his fellow officers depend directly upon his skill with the weapon he is carrying. Proficiency with the revolver is not attained exclusively by the volume of ammunition used and the number of hours spent on the firing line. Supervised practice and the use of training aids and techniques help make the shooter. It is essential to have a good firing range where new officers are trained and older personnel practice in scheduled firearms sessions. The fundamental points to be stressed are grip, stance, breathing, sight alignment, and trigger squeeze. Coordination of thought, vision, and motion must be achieved before the officer gains confidence in his shooting ability. Attaining this ability will make the student a better officer and enhance his value to the force.

18. A police officer will gain confidence in his shooting ability only after he has

    (A) spent the required number of hours on the firing line
    (B) been given sufficient supervised practice
    (C) learned the five fundamental points
    (D) learned to coordinate revolver movement with his sight and thought

19. Proper training in the use of firearms is one aspect of law enforcement which must be given serious consideration chiefly because it is the

    (A) most useful and essential single factor in the training of a police officer
    (B) one phase of police officer training that stresses mental and physical coordination
    (C) costliest aspect of police officer training, involving considerable expense for the ammunition used in target practice
    (D) most difficult part of police officer training, involving the expenditure of many hours on the firing line

20. "Complaints from the public are no longer regarded by government officials as mere nuisances. Instead, complaints are often welcomed because they frequently bring into the open conditions and faults in operation and service that should be corrected." This selection means most nearly that

    (A) government officials now realize that complaints from the public are necessary
    (B) faulty operations and services are not brought into the open except by complaints from the public
    (C) government officials now realize that complaints from the public are in reality a sign of a well-run organization
    (D) complaints from the public can be useful in indicating need for improvement in operation and service

Base your answers to questions 21 to 25 on the following enumeration of some of the duties of a court officer.

Another important duty of the court officers is to see that no witnesses are left standing while others who have no business in the courtroom have seats. They must also direct witnesses to seats when they present themselves in court to testify. If the case being tried is a criminal case, the court officers must collect all the subpoenas from those who have been summoned and turn them over to the District Attorney.

In order to bring about a smoother conduct of the day's business, it is best that the court officers reserve a portion of the courtroom for the witnesses, thus making it easier to call them to the witness stand. This eliminates much confusion and saves the court much time. When a witness is called to testify, the court officers must direct him or her to the witness stand. The officer at the witness stand should direct the witness to face the court while being sworn. The officer should remain close by to render further assistance.

21. A witness takes his seat in the courtroom and hands his subpoena to the court officer who has shown him to his seat. The court officer should

    (A) tell the witness to hold onto the subpoena until he is called to the stand
    (B) accept the subpoena and give it to the attorney for the defense
    (C) accept the subpoena and give it to the District Attorney
    (D) accept the subpoena and put it into his pocket

22. A witness has been called, and the court officer has directed the witness to the stand for swearing in. The court officer should now

    (A) administer the oath to the witness
    (B) leave the courtroom and stand guard outside the jury room
    (C) remain in the courtroom in sight of the judge
    (D) stand guard outside the courtroom door to keep people from entering and thereby disrupting the proceedings

23. With no clear knowledge of how many witnesses are scheduled to testify, a court officer has reserved three rows for witnesses in a sensational trial. Spectators have arrived early, and the courtroom is nearly full when a delegation from the defendant's church, led by their pastor, arrives. The court officer tells the group that there are not enough remaining seats for all their members. The pastor asks that they be seated in the vacant three rows. The court officer should

    (A) refuse, explaining that those seats are reserved for witnesses
    (B) seat the church delegation in the three rows but not seat any further spectators so as to have seats in the courtroom for witnesses
    (C) seat the church group telling them that they may be asked to leave as witnesses arrive
    (D) seat part of the delegation and hold one row for witnesses

24. As people enter the courtroom before the hour of trial, the court officer should

    (A) ask them to remain standing until all witnesses are seated
    (B) ask them why they are in the courtroom and seat them according to their business
    (C) ask them how long they plan to stay and seat those who will leave early near the back of the courtroom
    (D) direct them to seats near the front of the courtroom, reserving the back for latecomers

25. During the course of testimony by a witness, an attorney raises a point of information. The judge requests that the court officer who has been stationed near the witness go to her chambers and bring a specific book that might clarify the point. The court officer should

    (A) refuse because his duty is to remain near the witness
    (B) go for the book
    (C) send a messenger for the book
    (D) ask the judge for a clarification of the duties of a court officer

Use the information in the paragraph below to answer questions 26 and 27.

Criminal acts are classified according to several standards. One is whether the crime is major or minor. A major offense, such as murder, would be labeled a felony, whereas a minor offense, such as reckless driving, would be considered a misdemeanor. Another standard of classification is the specific kind of crime committed. Examples are burglary and robbery which are terms often used incorrectly by individuals who are not aware of the actual difference as defined by law. A person who breaks into a building to commit a theft or other major crime is guilty of burglary, while robbery is the felonious taking of an individual's property from his person or in his immediate presence by the use of violence or threat. Other common criminal acts with distinct legal definitions are those of larceny and assault. The unlawful taking away of another's property without his consent and with the intent of depriving him belongs to the first classification, while a violent attack on someone or an unlawful threat or attempt to do physical harm belongs to the second category.

26. A young woman was threatened at knife point by a criminal who demanded that she give him her pocketbook and gold watch. The woman screamed and the criminal, frightened, ran off without taking anything. According to the information in the above paragraph, the crime committed was

    (A) assault
    (B) robbery
    (C) larceny
    (D) burglary

27. A man who has been asleep on a bus awakes to find that $350 in cash has been taken from him. According to the above passage, he was subjected to

    (A) robbery
    (B) burglary
    (C) larceny
    (D) assault

Use the information in the paragraph below to answer questions 28 to 30.

"A person, who, with intent to effect or facilitate the escape of a prisoner, whether the escape is effected or attempted or not, enters a prison, or conveys to a prisoner any information, or sends into a prison any disguise, instrument, weapon, or other thing, is guilty of felony, if the prisoner is held upon a charge, arrest, commitment, or conviction for a felony; and of a misdemeanor, if the prisoner is held upon a charge, arrest, commitment, or conviction of a misdemeanor."

28. Johnny O. is serving time after conviction for the felony crime of armed robbery. Johnny's friend Frank devises an escape scheme and writes a letter to Johnny detailing the plans. Frank, without telling of the contents of the letter, asks Mary P. to deliver the letter for Johnny when she visits her husband, Bob, in on a misdemeanor conviction. The letter is intercepted by a correction officer.

    (A) Frank and Mary are both guilty of felonies.
    (B) Frank is guilty of a felony; Mary is guilty of misdemeanor.
    (C) Frank is guilty of a felony; Mary is not guilty.
    (D) Frank is guilty of a misdemeanor; Mary is not guilty.

29. On a visit to her boyfriend, Bill, who is awaiting trial in the county jail on a felony charge of grand larceny, Joan orally transmits to Bill instructions for fashioning a cutting tool from objects available to him in the jail. This tool had been an invention of Joan's brother, Tom. Bill follows these instructions, creates the tool, and escapes.

    (A) Joan and Tom are both guilty of felonies.
    (B) Joan is guilty of a felony; Tom is guilty of misdemeanor.
    (C) Joan is guilty of felony; Tom is not guilty.
    (D) Neither Joan nor Tom is guilty.

30. While charming little Debbie, age 4, distracts a guard, Barbara manages to smuggle a gun to Jim, who is completing a sentence on a misdemeanor conviction. In the course of his escape, Jim shoots and severely injures a correction officer.

    (A) Barbara is guilty of a felony; Debbie is guilty of misdemeanor.
    (B) Barbara is guilty of a felony; Debbie is not guilty.
    (C) Barbara and Debbie are both guilty of misdemeanors.
    (D) Barbara is guilty of misdemeanor; Debbie is not guilty.

31. When a person is frustrated in his desires, whether those desires are for economic advancement, for power, influence, love, or simply for getting his work done, one of the most common reactions is to become aggressive. His aggressive thoughts or actions may be directed at the thing or person that frustrated him or at some imagined source of his frustration; or his aggression may be released indiscriminately against some minority group he feels to be different from himself. The frustrated individual seeks a scapegoat as a target for the hostility he cannot safely express toward the real source of his frustration. A group whose members have troubles due to their own shortcomings will not quarrel among themselves; hence the external enemy becomes the target for this hostility. Any visible minority can be made a scapegoat. The chief function of a scapegoat is to

    (A) solve the problems of minorities
    (B) serve as an object of frustration
    (C) counter hostility
    (D) remedy inequalities of economic opportunity

Answer questions 32 and 33 on the basis of the following paragraph.

"An assumption commonly made in regard to the reliability of testimony is that when a number of persons report upon the same matter, those details upon which there is an agreement may, in general, be considered to be substantiated. Experiments have shown, however, that there is a tendency for the same errors to appear in the testimony of different individuals, and that, quite apart from any collusion, agreement of testimony is no proof of dependability."

32. According to the above statement, it is commonly assumed that details of an event are substantiated when

    (A) a reliable person testifies to them
    (B) several witnesses are in agreement about them
    (C) a number of persons report upon them
    (D) no errors are apparent in the testimony of different individuals

33. According to the above statement, agreement in the testimony of different witnesses to the same event is

    (A) not a guarantee of the accuracy of the facts
    (B) evaluated more reliably when considered apart from collusion
    (C) not the result of chance
    (D) the result of a mass reaction of the witnesses

Answer questions 34 and 35 on the basis of the following paragraph.

A steadfast concert for peace cannot be maintained except by a partnership of democratic nations. No autocratic government could be trusted to keep faith within it or observe its covenants. It must be a league of honor, a partnership of opinion. Intrigue would eat its vitals away; the plottings of inner circles who could plan what they would and render account to no one would be a corruption seated at its very heart. Only free people can hold their purpose and their honor steady to a common end, and prefer the interests of mankind to any narrow interest of their own.

34. According to the selection quoted, only democratic nations can

    (A) be free of plotting, intrigue, and corruption
    (B) be trusted to do what is right and honorable
    (C) plan programs that promote the interests of their country
    (D) subordinate their own interests to those that benefit the entire world

35. It may be implied from this passage that an autocratic government could not be trusted to respect its international agreements because it

    (A) exemplifies the proverb that there is no honor among thieves
    (B) is full of corruption, plots, and intrigue
    (C) is principally concerned with the welfare of its own people
    (D) would plot with other governments to advance their own mutual interests

36. "Security of tenure in the public service must be viewed in the context of the universal quest for security. If we narrow our application of the term to employment, the problem of security in the public service is seen to differ from that in private industry only in the need to meet the peculiar threats to security in governmental organizations—principally the danger of making employment contingent on factors other than the performance of the worker." According to this passage, the employment status of the public servant

    (A) as well as that of the private employee is affected only by performance
    (B) may be endangered by factors other than poor performance
    (C) depends to a great extent on election returns
    (D) changes less rapidly than that of the private employee

Answer questions 37 to 40 on the basis of the following paragraph.

The authority to examine records conferred by the Internal Revenue Code can be exercised only with the consent of the taxpayer, freely and voluntarily given, or by means of appropriate process. Any taxpayer may refuse an informal request to produce records. The individual, as distinguished from the corporate taxpayer, may even refuse to comply with the legal process by relying on his constitutional privilege against self-incrimination. Corporate records will be subpoenaed if an informal request is declined, but the Revenue Service will not issue a subpoena for records belonging to an individual when criminal prosecution is under consideration. It should be noted that the language of the Internal Revenue Code authorizing the compulsory production of records is directed solely to the determination and collection of the civil tax liability.

37. According to this paragraph, the authority to examine records informally under the Internal Revenue Code

    (A) is unlimited
    (B) can be exercised without the consent of the taxpayer
    (C) can be exercised only by means of appropriate process
    (D) can be exercised with the consent of the taxpayer

38. According to this paragraph, an informal request to produce records may be refused

    (A) only by an individual taxpayer
    (B) by any taxpayer, individual or corporate
    (C) only by a corporate taxpayer
    (D) by neither a corporate nor an individual taxpayer

39. According to this paragraph, the constitutional privilege against self-incrimination as justification for refusal to comply with legal process may be invoked by

    (A) any taxpayer
    (B) an individual taxpayer but not a corporate taxpayer
    (C) a corporate taxpayer but not an individual taxpayer
    (D) neither an individual nor a corporate taxpayer

40. According to this paragraph, the Internal Revenue Code authorizes compulsory production of records

    (A) in aid of criminal investigation
    (B) for any investigatory purpose
    (C) to determine civil liability
    (D) for submission to the grand jury

Use the information in the paragraph below to answer questions 41 to 43.

"A male between the ages of sixteen and thirty, convicted of a felony, who has not theretofore been convicted of a crime punishable by imprisonment in a state prison, may, in the discretion of the trial court be sentenced to imprisonment in the state reformatory. Where a male person between the ages of 16 and 21 is convicted of a felony, or where the term of imprisonment of a male convict for a felony is fixed by the trial court at one year or less, the court may direct the convict to be imprisoned in a county penitentiary, instead of a state prison, or in the county jail located in the county where sentence is imposed."

41. Harry, age 32, has been convicted of a felony and has been sentenced to a term of eleven months.

    (A) Harry must serve his term in a state prison.
    (B) The court may sentence Harry to the state reformatory.
    (C) Harry must serve his term in either the county penitentiary or the county jail.
    (D) The court may direct that Harry serve at a state prison, the county penitentiary or the county jail.

42. Mark, age 20, recently released from state prison after serving time for a felony committed when he was 16, has just been convicted of another felony.

    (A) Mark must serve his new term in a state prison.
    (B) Mark may not serve his term at the state reformatory.
    (C) Mark must serve his term at the county penitentiary.
    (D) Mark may serve his term in any one of the following: state penitentiary, county penitentiary, state reformatory, or county jail.

43. George, age 21, has just been convicted for his first crime ever and has been sentenced to a term of 4 to 7 years.

    (A) George must serve his term in a state prison.
    (B) George may be sentenced to either state prison or the state reformatory.
    (C) George may serve his time in a state prison or in the county penitentiary but not in the state reformatory.
    (D) George may serve his sentence at a state prison or at the county jail of the county in which he is sentenced.

44. A fracture is a broken bone. In a simple fracture, the skin is not broken. In a compound fracture, a broken end of the bone pierces the skin. Whenever a fracture is feared, the first thing to do is to prevent motion of the broken part. A defendant awaiting trial has just tripped on a stairway and twisted her ankle. She says it hurts badly, but the court officer cannot tell what is wrong merely by looking at it. The court officer should

    (A) tell the defendant to stand up and see whether she can walk
    (B) move the ankle gently to feel for any broken ends of bones
    (C) tell the defendant to rest a few minutes and promise to return later to see whether her condition has improved
    (D) tell the defendant not to move her foot and put in a call for medical assistance.

Base your answers to questions 45 to 49 on the following description of some court procedures.

When the jurors agree upon a verdict, one of the court officers should make it known to the courtroom and then proceed to announce the court's command, "Return the jury to the courtroom." After delivery of this command, the officers should conduct the jurors back to the jury box and remain near them. The clerk then receives and records the verdict.

A slightly different procedure is followed if the jurors are deliberating on a civil case and are instructed to deliver a sealed verdict. It then becomes necessary for the court officers to procure an envelope and blank form from the clerk. The jurors are instructed to sign the form when they have reached a decision, and the foreman is instructed to seal the envelope and keep it until the following morning or until the opening of the court at the next session. No one is to read the contents of the envelope, not even the court officers.

45. The jury has been deliberating for a number of hours and has finally agreed upon a verdict. The court officer should

    (A) lead the jury back into the courtroom
    (B) ask the jury to put their decision in writing
    (C) go to the courtroom and announce to the judge that the jury has reached a decision
    (D) tell the verdict to the court clerk

46. The jurors deliberating on a civil case have been instructed to deliver a sealed verdict. The jurors have reached their decision. The court officer should

    (A) read the decision, then seal the envelope
    (B) read the decision, then ask the foreman to seal the envelope
    (C) tell the foreman to seal and keep the envelope
    (D) tell the foreman to seal the envelope and mail it to the court clerk

47. The jury that has been deliberating a criminal case has reached its decision and has returned to the jury box. The court officer who has accompanied the jury should now

    (A) stay in the courtroom with the jury
    (B) guard the door to the courtroom so that no one else may enter
    (C) tell the defendant about the verdict
    (D) go home

48. The jury, having reached its conclusion, has returned to the courtroom and announced its verdict. The clerk of the court must now

    (A) hand an envelope and blank form to the court officer for the use of the jury
    (B) receive the envelope from the foreman of the jury
    (C) poll the jury
    (D) record the verdict

49. It is very late at night, and the jurors in a criminal case have finally agreed upon a verdict. The court officer should

    (A) tell the jurors to put the verdict in writing and go home
    (B) inform the court that the jurors have reached a verdict
    (C) tell the jurors to go home to sleep and to return first thing in the morning without telling anyone of their decision
    (D) send the jurors home and tell the judge what their verdict is

50. Most employees of foreign governments serving in Embassies, Consulates, or United Nations delegations, above the clerical level, have the privilege of "diplomatic immunity." In dealing with persons with diplomatic immunity, court officers face the same restrictions as do police officers. Persons with diplomatic immunity may not be issued summonses and may not be arrested or otherwise detained.

Court Officer Collins is on duty in the courtroom during the trial of a legally resident national of a foreign country. The defendant has been accused of armed robbery. As a witness is being questioned, a well-dressed gentleman seated in the spectators' section jumps up on his chair and begins shouting obscenities and threats concerning the United States, its people, its government, and this court. His final threat concerns the safety of the prosecuting attorney. As he finishes his diatribe, the man runs from the courtroom. Court Officer Collins follows the man and stops him in the corridor. Collins asks for identification, and the man produces a State Department Diplomat's Identity Card. Satisfied with the card's authenticity, Collins watches the man exit the courthouse. This action by Collins is

(A) proper; the man did nothing wrong
(B) improper; Collins should have made the man wait until his consulate was summoned
(C) proper; there was nothing more Collins could do
(D) improper; Collins should have turned the man over to a police officer

51. A court officer being called to a disciplinary hearing on any charges is entitled to request that the personnel office produce all documents that the court officer feels could bolster his or her defense.

Court Officer Blakelee's new supervisor has placed charges that Blakelee has reported late on two occasions within the supervisor's three-week tenure. Blakelee's attorney requests Blakelee's attendance records for all seven years of her employment in the court system and copies of all performance reviews. Court Officer Arthur of the court personnel office readily produces the attendance records for all seven years but releases only two years' performance reviews. This action by Officer Arthur is

(A) appropriate; performance reviews are irrelevant to a charge of lateness
(B) inappropriate; Blakelee is entitled to any documents that she feels will be helpful
(C) appropriate; if Blakelee persists in being late, she should be disciplined
(D) inappropriate; two years' worth of attendance records would be adequate

52. The rules governing a court officer's mandate are very clear: maintain order through the use of minimum necessary force.

Court Officer Janssen has been assigned to a jury room during the jury's deliberations in a felony trial. The jury has been sequestered for three days and seems nowhere near reaching a verdict. Tempers are heating up. As he stands outside the jury room, Janssen hears furniture crashing, shouts, and a scuffle. He enters the jury room and finds two jurors involved in a violent struggle on the floor. Other jurors are watching and cheering, and one or two look ready to join the fray. Officer Janssen calls loudly for assistance. The next thing he should do is

(A) shoot into the air
(B) tell the jurors to stop fighting
(C) hit the fighting jurors with his billy club
(D) clear the other jurors to the other side of the room

Use the information in the paragraph below to answer questions 53 and 54.

"It is not always understood that the term 'physical evidence' embraces any and all objects, living or inanimate. A knife, gun, signature, or burglar tool is immediately recognized as physical evidence. Less often is it considered that dust, microscopic fragments of all types, even an odor, may equally be physical evidence and often the most important of all. It is well established that the most useful types of physical evidence are generally microscopic in dimensions, that is, not noticeable by the eye and therefore most likely to be overlooked by the criminal and by the investigator. For this reason microscopic evidence persists for months or years after all other evidence has been removed and found inconclusive. Naturally, there are limitations to the time of collecting microscopic evidence as it may be lost or decayed. The exercises of judgment as to the possibility or profit of delayed action in collecting the evidence is a field in which the expert investigator should judge."

53. The one of the following which would not be considered to be physical evidence is

(A) a typewritten note
(B) an odor of raw onions
(C) criminal intent
(D) a minute speck of dust

54. The most accurate of the following statements, according to the above paragraph, is that

(A) a delay in collecting evidence must definitely diminish its value to the investigator
(B) microscopic evidence is generally the most useful type of physical evidence
(C) microscopic evidence exists for longer periods of time than other physical evidence
(D) physical evidence is likely to be overlooked by the criminal and by the investigator.

55. "Credibility of a witness is usually governed by his character and is evidenced by his reputation for truthfulness. Personal or financial reasons or a criminal record may cause a witness to give false information to avoid being implicated. Age, sex, physical and mental abnormalities, loyalty, revenge, social and economic status, indulgence in alcohol, and the influence of other persons are some of the many factors which may affect the accuracy, willingness, or ability with which witnesses observe, interpret, and describe occurrences."

According to the above paragraph, factors which influence the witness of an occurrence may affect

(A) what he sees but not what he describes
(B) what he is willing to see but not what he is able to see
(C) only what he describes and interprets later but not what he actually sees at the time of the event
(D) not only what he says about it but what he was able and wanted to see of it.

DIRECTIONS: Each of the two passages below contains seven numbered blanks. Read each passage through quickly to get the overall sense of the passage. Following each passage are sets of words numbered to match the blanks. Read the passage a second time and choose the word from each set that best fits into the blank. Consider the meaning of the sentence and of the total passage.

The criminal __56__ system is generally regarded as having the __57__ objective of reducing crime. However, one must __58__ consider its larger objective of minimizing the total social costs associated with crime and crime control. Both of these components are complex and difficult to measure completely. The social __59__ associated with crime come from the long and short-term physical damage, psychological harm, and property losses to __60__ as a result of crimes committed. __61__ also creates serious indirect effects. It can induce a feeling of insecurity that is only partially reflected in business losses and economic disruption due to anxiety __62__ venturing into high crime-rate areas.

56. (A) behavior
    (B) justice
    (C) action
    (D) patrol

57. (A) sole
    (B) occasional
    (C) basic
    (D) peripheral

58. (A) never
    (B) consequently
    (C) also
    (D) fortunately

59. (A) security
    (B) activities

    (C) resources
    (D) costs

60. (A) criminals
    (B) victims
    (C) justice
    (D) prisoners

61. (A) Security
    (B) Justice
    (C) Control
    (D) Crime

62. (A) about
    (B) into
    (C) for
    (D) and

If the interviewer does not __63__ the witness, it is better to proceed __64__ permitting the witness to know that __65__ statements are being __66__. A __67__ who believes that his deception is successful is encouraged to complete his prepared story by supplementing it with other false details. Only __68__ a witness has completed his story should the interviewer, if the occasion arises, tell him that his story is __69__.

63. (A) understand
    (B) like
    (C) know
    (D) believe

64. (A) unless
    (B) cautiously
    (C) without
    (D) quickly

65. (A) your
    (B) one's
    (C) his
    (D) their

66. (A) recorded
    (B) doubted

    (C) changed
    (D) dramatic

67. (A) victim
    (B) lawyer
    (C) witness
    (D) liar

68. (A) after
    (B) if
    (C) while
    (D) before

69. (A) funny
    (B) untrue
    (C) interesting
    (D) well-written

END OF EXAM

Correct Answers for Model Court Officer
Exam IV

PART ONE

1. B	7. C	13. D	19. B	25. B
2. D	8. A	14. B	20. D	26. A
3. C	9. B	15. B	21. A	27. D
4. C	10. B	16. D	22. C	28. A
5. D	11. D	17. A	23. B	29. C
6. D	12. A	18. C	24. B	30. B

PART TWO

1. D	15. B	29. A	43. B	57. C
2. B	16. C	30. D	44. D	58. C
3. C	17. A	31. B	45. C	59. D
4. A	18. B	32. B	46. C	60. B
5. B	19. A	33. A	47. A	61. D
6. B	20. D	34. D	48. D	62. A
7. B	21. C	35. B	49. B	63. D
8. C	22. C	36. B	50. C	64. C
9. B	23. A	37. D	51. B	65. C
10. A	24. B	38. B	52. D	66. B
11. D	25. B	39. B	53. C	67. C
12. C	26. A	40. C	54. B	68. A
13. D	27. C	41. D	55. D	69. B
14. D	28. C	42. B	56. B	

Explanations of Correct Answers

PART ONE

1. **(B)** In the second set, the spacing of *Troy:Red and Tan* differs from the spacing in the first and third sets.

2. **(D)** The first and third sets differ in the placement of dashes in the ISBN number. The first and second sets differ in the spelling of the person's last name.

3. **(C)** In the third set, fourth line, the digits "52" are omitted.

4. **(C)** In the third set, *MacGregor* differs from the *McGregor* of the first and second sets.

5. **(D)** In the second set, the ISBN number is missing a zero. In the third set, the letter "a" is lowercase.

6. **(D)** The first and third sets differ in the spelling of the last company's name. The first and second sets differ in that PTB3 is not the same as PT83.

7. **(C)** In the third set, the ISBN number ends with a lowercase "x."

8. **(A)** All three sets are exactly alike.

9. **(B)** In the second set, the final two digits of the Title number are reversed.

10. **(B)** In the second set, the spelling of the name *Elgar* differs from the *Elger* of the first set.

11. **(D)** In the third set, the name of the ambulette service differs from that in the first. In the second set, the book price exceeds that in the first set by $2.00.

12. **(A)** All three sets are exactly alike.

13. **(D)** All three ISBN numbers are different.

14. **(B)** In the second set, the digits "4451" differ from the "4551" of the first set.

15. **(B)** The second set contains a digit reversal—638 in place of 683.

16. **(D)** In the second set, *Ben* begins with an initial capital letter. In the third set, *Johan* is substituted for *Jonah.*

17. **(A)** All three sets are exactly alike.

18. **(C)** In the third set, an ampersand has been omitted.

19. **(B)** In the second set, we find the letters "FBP" instead of "FPB" as in the first and third sets.

20. **(D)** In the second set, *Center* differs from *Centre* of the first set. In the third set, *Industrial* differs from *Industries* of the first set.

21. **(A)** If you filled in Table 4, just add together $3 + 9 + 9$ from the three columns, "under 15," "15–17," and "18–21." If you chose not to spend time filling in tables 4 and 5, quickly run down the "F" column in the three age categories on Tables 1, 2, and 3, and keep a tally of all the *j*'s.

22. **(C)** The summary tables will not help you here, but the task is not difficult. The code letter *h* refers to imprisonment of more than one year, and the question does not specify whether or not a fine is to be paid in addition. Look straight down both the "M" and "F" columns in the 18–21 range on all three county tables and count the *h*'s.

23. **(B)** If you filled in Table 5, just convert your tally lines to a number. If you skipped over Table 5, remember that both *a* and *b* refer to probation sentences and that the question specifies "probation *only*." Then look across the "probation" line on all three county charts and tally up all appearances of *a* or *b* not in combination with another letter.

24. **(B)** Table 5 is very helpful here. All alleged offenders who were not acquitted were convicted. Ten people were acquitted. The total number of assault cases is 52. $52 - 10 = 42$, so 42 were convicted. $42 - 10 = 32$, so 32 more were convicted than were acquitted. If you did not fill in Table 5, your best bet is to fill in the "assault" category in conjunction with answering this question.

25. **(B)** You must turn to the three county charts and count. As you count, remember that the question specifies *men*, that the code *j* does not refer to conviction, and that a dual sentence (probation plus fine or prison plus fine) is meted out to one person.

26. **(A)** If you filled in Table 4, follow the "fine only" line across to the 18–21 "M" and "F" columns. Turn your tallies into numbers. $17F - 15M =$ a difference of 2. Again, if you did not fill out Table 4 in advance, you might deal with just this category now. Remember to count only the single letters *c, d,* and *e.*

27. **(D)** Table 4 gives you a quick answer. Fifteen women over 30 are sentenced to prison only and six to prison and fine. 15 + 6 = 21. You will get the same answer, of course, by doing the counting when you get to the question.

28. **(A)** You have to use the county tables to answer this question. Limit your counting to the three central age categories and to the M columns only. Then, remember that *j* is not a conviction and that a sentence with & is given to one person.

COMPLETED TABLES

Table 4
Summary of Disposition of Cases—Three Counties

| Disposition | Age and Sex of Offender | | | | | | | | | | | | | | | | | |
| | under 15 | | | 15–17 | | | 18–21 | | | 22–30 | | | over 30 | | | Totals | | |
	M	F	T	M	F	T	M	F	T	M	F	T	M	F	T	M	F	T
acquitted	5	3	8	7	9	16	5	9	14	8	14	22	11	15	26	36	50	86
probation only	13	9	22	20	10	30	22	15	37	6	3	9	6	4	10	67	41	108
fine only	12	8	20	16	17	33	15	17	32	15	8	23	17	13	30	75	63	138
prison only	0	0	0	0	0	0	7	2	9	16	11	27	20	15	35	43	28	71
probation & fine	3	1	4	6	3	9	3	4	7	3	1	4	1	4	5	16	13	29
prison & fine	0	0	0	0	0	0	5	4	9	7	8	15	6	6	12	18	18	36
Totals	33	21	54	49	39	88	57	51	108	55	45	100	61	57	118	255	213	468

Table 5
Summary of Dispositions By Offense—Three Counties

| Offense | Sentence | | | | | | |
	acquitted	probation only	fine only	prison only	probation & fine	prison & fine	Total
vandalism	3	8	27	0	3	0	41
burglary	7	6	4	12	4	7	40
larceny	9	9	19	6	4	6	53
assault	10	20	9	10	1	2	52
robbery	5	12	9	15	2	6	49
drunk driving	11	6	19	5	3	3	47
prostitution	8	14	16	4	1	1	44
manslaughter	12	12	11	2	1	1	39
narcotics (sale)	11	10	8	14	1	9	53
narcotics (possession)	10	11	16	3	9	1	50
Totals	86	108	138	71	29	36	468

29. **(C)** This is an easy count. Just remember that both categories *narcotics (sale)* and *narcotics (possession)* must be included and that a fine is a fine even when paid in conjunction with a prison or probationary sentence.

30. **(B)** Table 5 is helpful here. Add together the 6 burglars who will serve only probation and the 4 burglars who will pay fines with their probation and subtract those 10 from the 19 burglars who will serve time in prison (12 in prison only + 7 paying fines and serving time as well).

An ARCO suggestion: Tables 4 and 5 here, and their counterparts on an actual exam, include a great many categories which are totally irrelevant to answering test questions. However, filling out these tables in their entirety is very time-consuming. Some questions must be answered without the summary tables; others can easily be answered bypassing the summaries. Where a summary table might prove useful, as where categories must be combined or comparisons made, use the summary tables as work sheets, tallying as you count along, and fill out only those segments that you need. Remember, only the answer sheet is scored; the summary tables are for your own use even though they will be collected along with the question booklets.

PART TWO

Questions 1 through 10: If you made any errors, reread the Memory Passage to confirm the correct answer.

11. **(D)** The paragraph states that *if* the neighborhood is composed of people and circumstances that might serve as a breeding ground for crime, *then* children might gain a criminal education in that neighborhood. Neither (A) nor (B) nor (C) may reasonably be concluded from the paragraph.

12. **(C)** Since old age insurance is *wholly* administered by the federal government, the city has no part in it. However, old age insurance is *one feature* of the Social Security Act that is wholly administered by the federal government, so presumably other governments administer other features. In light of this information, choice (D) cannot be correct.

13. **(D)** A defensive weapon is used in self-defense.

14. **(D)** Method of commission of the illegal act is not included among the requirements for the depositions.

15. **(B)** Understanding how one's own work contributes to the effort of the entire agency is appreciating the importance of that job.

16. **(C)** Conveying self-confidence is displaying assurance.

17. **(A)** The paragraph says that a court officer needs specific qualifications that are different from those required of police officers or of firemen and which may differ from court to court. The paragraph does not spell out the nature of these qualifications. It further does not equate the qualifications of policemen with those of firemen, saying only that they have many qualifications in common.

18. **(B)** "Supervised practice and the use of training aids and techniques help make the shooter."

19. **(A)** See the second sentence.

20. **(D)** Complaints from the public may be helpful in pointing out areas for improvement, but they are not required.

21. **(C)** One of the duties of court officers is to collect subpoenas and turn them over to the District Attorney.

22. **(C)** While a witness is being sworn in and while that witness is testifying, a court officer should remain close by the witness and in easy distance of the judge so as to render any assistance requested.

23. **(A)** Especially in a crowded courtroom, it is important that the witnesses be seated in one area for easy access. Attending a trial as a spectator is a privilege based on available space; it is not a right, even for a religious delegation.

24. **(B)** Witnesses in a civil case and witnesses for the defense do not come with subpoenas in hand. In order to seat witnesses in the area reserved for them, the court officer must know which people they are.

25. **(B)** Going for a book requested by the judge is precisely the type of assistance for which the court officer is standing nearby.

26. **(A)** An unlawful threat or attempt to do physical harm, even if unsuccessful, constitutes assault.

27. **(C)** Larceny is the taking away of another's property. It differs from robbery because violence is not involved.

28. **(C)** Frank was attempting to help a convicted felon to escape, so Frank is guilty of a felony. Mary was an innocent courier; she did not intend to help Johnny to escape, so, within the scope of the quoted paragraph, she is not guilty.

29. **(A)** The prisoner being assisted to escape is being held on a felony charge, therefore those who assist in his escape are guilty of felonies. While all the assistance is given orally, it is obviously useful. Both Joan and Tom are parties to Bill's escape.

30. **(D)** Debbie is a very young child, far too young to be charged with criminal intent; she is innocent. Since Jim was serving a sentence on a misdemeanor conviction, Barbara is guilty only of a misdemeanor. Jim, on the other hand, is now in serious trouble. The next person who tries to help Jim escape will be guilty of a felony.

31. **(B)** The unsolicited function of a scapegoat is to serve as the object of the frustrations of an impotent person or group. The true value of a scapegoat is, of course, nil. While the scapegoat suffers, the problems of the scapegoaters remain unsolved.

32. **(B)** This is a restatement of the first sentence. Note that (C) is not the best answer because it omits the important requirement of agreement on the details, not merely reporting.

33. **(A)** The paragraph refers to experimental evidence that a number of witnesses' "seeing" the same thing may be a matter of chance.

34. **(D)** See the last sentence.

35. **(B)** The paragraph attributes to autocratic nations intrigue, plotting, and corruption, which would render them unable to respect international agreements.

36. **(B)** If employment is contingent on factors other than performance, then employment security may be endangered by factors other than poor performance.

37. **(D)** If the taxpayer gives consent, appropriate process is unnecessary.

38. **(B)** See the second sentence.

39. **(B)** The constitutional privilege against self-incrimination is a right guaranteed only to individuals, not to corporations.

40. **(C)** See the last sentence.

41. **(D)** Harry is too old to be sent to the state reformatory, but since his term is only for 11 months, he may be sent to county penitentiary, county jail, or state prison.

42. **(B)** Mark, as a second offender, cannot serve his term in the state reformatory. Even though Mark's sentence is for a term well in excess of 1 year, he may serve his time at the county penitentiary or at the county jail because he is between the ages of 16 and 21. Mark may, of course, be sent to a state prison.

43. **(B)** As a first offender between the ages of 16 and 30, George may be sent to the state reformatory. State prison is also an option. George's term is too long for a man his age to serve at the county penitentiary or the county jail.

44. **(D)** If there is any possibility of a fracture, the injured part should not be moved.

45. **(C)** The correct procedure: the jurors tell a court officer that they have reached a decision; the court officer reports to the court that the jury has reached a decision; the judge orders the court officer to return the jury to the courtroom; the court officer leads the jury back.

46. **(C)** The foreman of the jury seals the envelope containing the verdict signed by the jurors. The foreman then personally keeps custody of the envelope until turning it in to the court at the next session. The court officer may know that a verdict has been reached, but not what that verdict is.

47. **(A)** The court officer who accompanies the jury from the jury room back to the courtroom to deliver its verdict remains with that jury in the courtroom.

48. **(D)** If the verdict is announced in open court, it is not a sealed verdict. No forms or envelopes are involved. The clerk receives and records the verdict as announced. The jury is not routinely polled but only upon request of the judge.

49. **(B)** Only the judge has the authority to send the jurors home. Once the jurors have reached their verdict, the court officer must go to the court and announce that the verdict has been reached.

50. **(C)** The law with respect to diplomatic immunity is clear. The court officer had no choice. The man could not be detained, but follow-up contact with his consulate would not be out of order.

51. **(B)** If the officer or the officer's attorney feels that the documents would be helpful to the defense, the documents should be provided.

52. **(D)** The jurors are unarmed, and assistance has been summoned. Preventing the fight from spreading to other jurors seems adequate for the immediate moment. Shooting always presents a danger and adding to the violence seems unnecessary. However, just asking them to stop fighting is unlikely to be an effective way to restore order. When reinforcements arrive, the fighters can easily be separated.

53. **(C)** Criminal intent is purely mental.

54. **(B)** Microscopic evidence is likely to be the most useful not because of its size per se but because it is likely to have been overlooked and so not to have been disturbed. (C) is not necessarily true. Some microscopic evidence readily dissipates or degenerates; however, that which remains intact and undisturbed may be very useful.

55. **(D)** The answer is in the last line. The factors which influence the witness affect what he observes (what he is able to see), how he interprets (what he wants to see), and how he describes (what he says about it).

56. **(B)** Reducing crime is an objective of the criminal *justice* system.

57. **(C)** Obviously, crime reduction must occur more than occasionally or peripherally. Your choice that reducing crime is its *basic* objective is based on reading ahead to the next sentence. The word "however" indicates that this is not the sole objective.

58. **(C)** *Also* is the only sensible completion here.

59. **(D)** The losses described are social *costs*.

60. **(B)** Obviously, the people who suffer the losses are the *victims*.

61. **(D)** Read on to the next sentence. *Crime* induces a feeling of insecurity.

62. **(A)** This is an idiomatic phrase, "anxiety *about*."

63. **(D)** You may have to read well into the paragraph to learn that the paragraph is about deception and false details. Then, you will know that the paragraph deals with the interviewer who does not *believe* the witness.

64. **(C)** The case is better if filled out with false details; therefore it is better to proceed *without* letting on that the interviewer is suspicious.

65. **(C)** We are speaking of a single witness. *His* is the only possible word for this blank.

66. **(B)** We don't want him to know that he is being *doubted*.

67. **(C)** The *witness* is telling the story.

68. **(A)** The whole point of the paragraph is to let the witness complete the story and only *after* the testimony to express doubt.

69. **(B)** Deception and false details describe a story that is *untrue*.

Part Two

Promotion to Senior Court Officer or Court Clerk

THE PROMOTIONAL EXAMS

Examinations for the promotional positions of senior court officer and court clerk are very different from the open competitive examination for the entry position of court officer. While the entry examination is geared to measure the applicant's ability to learn the duties of the job quickly and thoroughly and to perform effectively on the job, the promotional exam asks, "What do you know? What have you learned?" Aside from a reading comprehension section on the court clerk exam, all the questions on the promotional exams are based on knowledge of the functioning of the courts, of the law itself, and about the actual duties of court officers.

Applicants for the position of senior court officer must have served for at least 1 year in the position of court officer. Those who seek to become court clerks must have served for at least 2 years as court officers or in similar responsible positions within the court system. These years of exposure should have led to familiarity with the vocabulary of the court system, to an understanding of the responsibilities of and limitations on, the court officer, and to an appreciation of emergencies that may arise and how to handle them.

The knowledge for answering questions on the promotional exams comes from three sources: experience; the training, instruction, and handouts given to court officers and responsible employees of the court; and study of the laws themselves. Part of your preparation for the exam must involve going back to training materials and handouts and rereading the contents in light of your own experiences. Part of your preparation should consist of going into the law library and browsing through articles and sections that seem applicable to the exam as enumerated on the announcement. The rest of your preparation is right here in this book.

On the next few pages, you will find a glossary of legal terms. This is by no means a comprehensive list, as there are, of course, many more legal terms. The glossary will, however, give you a good start in pinning down a legal vocabulary. Following the glossary are four chapters: Civil Practice Law and Rules, Criminal Procedure Law, Family Court Act, and Penal Law. Each of these chapters begins with a full listing of all topics covered by that law. Look over each list of articles. Tick those articles that you consider relevant. Think about what you already know in each of these areas. Then go into each chapter and study the portions that have been selected. Since the examination is heavily weighted toward understanding terminology and how it applies within the scope of each law, this part of the book is devoted to definition-type articles and sections. Again, it is impossible to include all necessary information in one book. You will find much that is very useful, but the complete laws are not included here. You will have to refer to some law books yourself. The listing of topics for each law that we have provided should help you plan your time in the library, so that you know what to look for and where to find it.

The remainder of this part of the book consists of questions that have appeared on previous examinations. You can answer many, but not all, of these questions on the basis of the glossary and the sections of the laws included in this book. To answer other questions, you may have to draw on your own knowledge and the various reference materials. The explanations that follow the answers at the end of the chapter give information beyond simply explaining what makes a particular answer correct. You can learn additional facts from the explanations.

GLOSSARY OF LEGAL TERMS

This is some of the language you are likely to see on your examination. You may not need to know all the words in this carefully prepared glossary, but if even a few appear, you'll be that much ahead of your competitors. Perhaps the greater benefit from this list is the frame of mind it can create for you. Without reading a lot of technical text you'll steep youself in just the right atmosphere for high test marks.

A

a posteriori—from effect to cause.

a priori—from cause to effect.

abate—destroy; remove.

abet—encourage; aid.

ab initio—from the beginning.

abjure—renounce.

abridge—reduce; contract.

abrogate—repeal; annul.

abscond—hide; absent oneself.

accident—unforeseen event.

accomplice—associate in crime.

acknowledgment—act of going before an authorized official to declare an act as one's own, thus giving it legal validity.

acquit—release; absolve.

act—something done voluntarily.

ad litem—for the suit.

adduce—offer; present.

adjacent—near to; close.

adjective law—rules of procedure.

adjudicate—to determine judicially.

admiralty—court having jurisdiction over maritime cases.

adult—one who has attained the age of majority or legal maturity.

affiant—one who makes an affidavit.

affidavit—a sworn, written statement.

affiliation—order stating one to be the father of a child.

affinity—relationship between persons through marriage with the kindred of each other; distinguished from consanguinity, which is relationship by blood.

affirm—ratify.

affirmation—a solemn declaration made under penalty of perjury by a person who conscientiously declines taking an oath.

agent—one who represents and acts for another.

aggressor—one who begins a quarrel.

aid and comfort—help; encourage.

alias—a name that is not one's true name.

alibi—a claim of not being present at a certain place at a certain time.

alienist—a doctor specializing in legal aspects of psychiatry.

allegation—the assertion, declaration, or statement of a party to an action, made in a pleading, setting out what he expects to prove.

158

ambiguous—not clear, having two meanings; equivocal.

amentia—mental deficiency.

amercement—a pecuniary penalty or a fine imposed as punishment on conviction; same as *mulct*.

amicus curiae—a friend of the court who advises on some legal matter.

animus—mind; intent.

animus furandi—intent to steal.

annul—cancel; void.

annus—a year.

ante—before.

ante mortem—before death.

aphasia—inability to speak, although vocal cords are normal.

appeal—to request a higher court to review a decision of a lower court.

appearance—the coming into court as defendant, attorney, etc.

appellant—one who appeals.

appellee—one who opposes an appellant; a respondent.

apprehend—arrest.

appurtenant—belonging to.

arbiter—one who decides a dispute; a referee.

arbitrary—an act having no cause or reason; absolute; despotic; peremptory.

arraign—to call a prisoner before the court to answer to a charge.

artifice—trickery; deception.

asportation—moving a thing from one place to another, as in larceny.

assert—to state as true.

asseveration—an affirmation; a solemn declaration.

asylum—a place of refuge.

at bar—before the court.

at issue—the point of contention between parties in a legal action.

attach—seize property by court order and sometimes arrest a person.

attainder—forfeiture of property and corruption of honor of one sentenced to death. (Compare with *bill of attainder* below.)

attempt—an act done with intent to commit a crime but falling short of consummating it.

attest—to witness a will, etc.

authentic—genuine; true.

authenticate—to give authority to a law, writing, or record.

axio—a self-evident truth.

B

bail—the security given to obtain the temporary release of a prisoner.

bailee—one of whom goods are bailed.

bailment—the giving of property to a bailee.

bailor—the one who gives his property to a bailee.

barratry—the persistent incitement of groundless judicial proceedings.

bill of attainder—a law pronouncing a person guilty without trial. It is illegal.

bludgeon—a club heavier at one end than at the other.

blue laws—rigid Sunday laws.

blue-sky laws—laws regulating investment companies to protect investors from frauds.

bona fide—in good faith.

bondsman—one who bails another by putting up a bond.

boycott—a joining together in refusal to deal with, so as to punish or to coerce a desired result without force.

breach of the peace—disturbing the public peace by disorder, violence, force, noise, etc.

bucket shop—a place where people bet on the stock market under pretense of buying and selling stocks.

bunco game—any trick or cunning calculated to win confidence and to deceive whether by conversation, conduct, or suggestion.

C

cadaver—a dead human body.

camera—a judge's chamber.

canon—a law; rule.

capias—an order to arrest.

carnal—relating to the body.

carnal abuse—a sex act not amounting to penetration.

carnal knowledge—sexual intercourse.

cause of action—matter for which an action may be brought.

caveat—a warning.

caveat emptor—let the buyer beware.

certiorari—an order from a high court to a lower court calling up for review the minutes of a trial.

challenge—an exception taken to a juror.

change of venue—the removal of the place of trial from one county to another.

character—the qualities or traits that make up or distinguish an individual.

charge—a complaint, information, or indictment.

chastity—abstention from unlawful sexual intercourse.

chattel—personal property.

chattel mortgage—a mortgage on personal property.

child—one under 16 years in criminal law.

cite—to summon; command one's presence.

civil rights—rights granted to citizens by the Constitution or by statute.

codicil—an addition to a will.

coercion—compulsion, duress.

cognomen—a family name.

cohabit—to live together as husband and wife.

comity—courtesy, respect; agreement between states to recognize each other's laws.

commitment—an order to take one to prison.

common law—law as it developed in England based on customs, usage, decisions, etc.

commute—change punishment to one less severe.

complainant—one who seeks legal redress.

complaint—a sworn allegation to a magistrate charging one with crime. Also called information.

compos mentis—sound of mind.

compromise—an agreement between one charged with certain crimes and the complainant to withdraw charges on payment of money, with court's consent.

concubinage—habitual cohabitation of persons not legally married.

concurrent—occurring at the same time.

condemnation—taking private property for public use on payment thereof.

confess—to admit the truth of a charge.

confession—voluntary statement of guilt of a crime.

confidence game—a swindle.

confrontation—the right of the defendant to have the witness stand face-to-face with the defendant when the accusation is made.

connivance—secret or indirect consent by one to a criminal act by another.

consanguinity—blood relationship.

consecutive—successive.

conspiracy—a plan by two or more to commit a crime.

constitution—the fundamental law of a state or nation.

constructive intent—if one intends one act and in carrying it out does another, the intent to do the first is construed to apply to the second.

contiguous—adjacent.

contingency—an event that may or may not happen.

contra—against.

contraband—illegal or prohibited trade.

controvert—to dispute or oppose by reasoning.

conviction—judgment that one is guilty as charged.

corporal—bodily.

corpus deliciti—the substantial and fundamental fact necessary to prove a crime.

corroborate—to strengthen.

corrupt—spoiled, tainted, debased.

counselor—a lawyer.

counterfeit—to forge, copy, imitate.

credible—worthy of belief.

crimen falsi—crimes involving deceit or falsification.

criminal action—the process by which one is accused of a crime and brought to trial and punishment.

criminal information—same as complaint.

criminal intent—intent to commit crime.

criminology—the scientific study of crime, criminals, and penal treatment.

culpable—blamable.

cumulative—tending to prove the same point in evidence; increasing severity with repetition of the offense.

curtilage—ground adjacent to a dwelling and used in connection with it. Usually this space is fenced off.

custody—control exercised by legal authority over a ward or suspect.

D

deadly weapon—an instrument likely to produce death or serious bodily injury.

debauch—to corrupt by intemperance or sensuality.

decision—a judgment rendered by a propert court.

deed—a signed instrument containing a legal transfer, bargain, or contract.

defalcation—the act or instance of embezzling.

de facto—actually or really existing.

defamation—injuring a reputation by false statements.

defendant—one who defends or denies a charge.

defraud—to deprive of property by fraud or deceit.

de jure—by right of law.

deliberate—to weigh or ponder before forming a decision.

delict—an offense against the law.

demented—mad or insane.

deponent—one who gives written testimony under oath.

deposition—sworn written testimony.

design—plan, scheme, intent.

dictum—an opinion on a point in a case expressed by a judge.

dipsomaniac—one who has an irresistible desire for alcohol.

disfranchise—to deprive of a legal right.

dismiss—to discharge a court action.

disorderly house—a place where people behave so badly as to become a nuisance to the neighborhood.

document—a written instrument.

domicile—one's permanent home.

duress—forcible restraint.

E

ego—the self.

eleemosynary—related to or supported by charity.

embezzlement—appropriation of entrusted property fraudulently for one's own use.

embracery—an attempt to influence a juror improperly.

eminent domain—the right of a government to take private property for public use.

empirical—based on experience.

entice—to solicit, persuade, allure by flattery, coaxing, etc.

entrapment—the act of luring one into a compromising statement or act.

essence—the ultimate nature of a thing.

evidence—all means used to prove or disprove a fact in issue.

ex officio—by virtue of office.

ex parte—on one side only.

ex post facto law—a law passed after an act was done which retroactively makes such an act a crime.

examined copy—one compared with the original and sworn to as a correct copy.

exception—a formal objection to the action of the court in denying a request or overruling an objection.

executed—completed.

extradition—surrender of a fugitive from one geographic jurisdiction to another.

extrajudicial—outside judicial proceeding.

extremis—near death, beyond hope of recovery.

F

facsimile—an exact or accurate copy of an original instrument.

false pretenses—intentionally untrue representations.

felo de se—one who kills himself; suicide.

felonious—criminal, malicious.

fence—one who buys stolen property.

fiduciary—holding in trust.

filiation, order of—a court order declaring one to be the father of an illegitimate child.

finding—the result of the deliberation of a court or jury.

firearm—a weapon that propels bullets by explosion of gunpowder.

forge—to counterfeit or make falsely.

fornication—sexual intercourse between persons not married to each other.

foundling—a deserted child.

franchise—a special privilege granted to an individual or group; elective franchise refers to the voting privilege.

fratricide—killing of one's brother or sister.

freeholder—one who owns real property.

fugitive from justice—one who commits a crime in one state and goes to another.

G

gamble—to bet on an event of which the outcome is uncertain.

general verdict—a verdict in which a jury finds a defendant guilty or not guilty.

genocide—the deliberate systematic destruction of certain races, nationalities or religious groups.

gift enterprise—a scheme for distribution of property by chance among persons who have paid or agreed to pay a consideration; the common term is lottery.

grand jury—not fewer than 16 but no more than 23 citizens of a county sworn to inquire into crimes committed or triable in that county.

grantee—one to whom a grant is made.

grantor—the one who makes the grant.

gravamen—the substantial part of a complaint.

guardian ad litem—a person designated by a court to represent a child bringing or defending a civil action.

H

habeas corpus—an order to produce a person before a court to determine the legality of detention.

hearsay—evidence based on repeating the words told by another and not based on the witness's own personal observation or knowledge of that to which he testifies.

hung jury—one so divided they can't agree on a verdict.

hypothecate—to pledge without delivery of title or possession.

hypothetical question—a question asked of an expert witness based on supposition from which the witness is asked to state his opinion.

I

illicit—unlawful.

impeach—to accuse, charge.

inalienable—those rights that cannot be lawfully transferred or surrendered.

in loco parentis—in place of a parent.

incommunicado—denial of the right of a prisoner to communicate with friends or relatives.

indictment—a written accusation of a crime presented by a grand jury.

inducement—cause or reason why a thing is done or that which incites the person to do the act or commit a crime; the motive for the criminal act.

infamous crime—a felony.

infant—in civil cases, one under 21 years of age.

information—a formal accusation of a crime.

injunction—legal process requiring a person to do or refrain from doing a certain action.

intent—state of mind to do or omit an act.

ipso facto—by the fact itself.

issue—what is affirmed by one and denied by another in an action.

J

jeopardy—danger, peril.

judicial notice—acceptance by a court or judge of some fact of common knowledge thereby dispensing with the need of offering evidence to prove it, i.e., 24 hours equal one day.

judiciary—relating to a court of justice.

jurat—the part of an affidavit stating where, when, and before whom it was signed and sworn.

jurisdiction—power or authority to apply or interpret the law.

jury—a group of citizens sworn to inquire into facts and deliver a verdict. A trial jury tries cases; a grand jury indicts.

K

kleptomaniac—one who has an irresistible propensity to steal.

L

laches—unreasonable delay in asserting a legal right or privilege.

latent—hidden, concealed.

leading question—one so put as to suggest the answer.

lien—a claim a creditor has on property until a debt is paid.

lis pendens—a pending civil or criminal action.

litigant—a party to a lawsuit.

locus delicti—place of the crime (See *situs delicti.*)

lucri causa—for sake of gain.

M

mala in se—bad in themselves; such crimes usually require a specific criminal intent.

mala prohibita—bad because it is prohibited by legislation, not because it is evil in its nature.

malfeasance—wrongdoing or misconduct, especially by a public official.

malice, intentional—wrongdoing to injure, vex or annoy.

malo animo—evil mind.

mandamus—a court order to a public official to perform a specified act.

maritime—pertaining to the sea or to commerce thereon.

masochism—sexual pleasure in being abused or dominated.

mens rea—criminal intent.

meretricious—relating to a prostitute; flashy

minor—one who has not attained majority.

miscegenation—marriage or sexual intercourse between persons of different races.

misfeasance—improper performance of a lawful act.

mittimus—a warrant of commitment to prison.

moral certainty—evidence that convinces the mind beyond a reasonable doubt, hence the degree of proof required to prove defendant's guilt in a criminal action.

moral turpitude—base or vile behavior.

motive—reason for doing an act.

mulct—a pecuniary fine imposed as punishment upon conviction of a crime; same as amercement.

N

natural child—a child born out of wedlock.

nolle prosequi—an entry of record signifying that the plaintiff or prosecutor will not press the complaint.

nolo contendere—equal to a plea of guilty.

nominal damages—award of a trifling sum where no substantial injury is proved to have been sustained.

nonfeasance—neglect of duty.

noscitur a sociis—meaning of doubtful words in a statute may be ascertained by referring to the meaning of other words associated with it in the definition; also called *ejusdem generis*. (See *sui generis*.)

novation—substitution of a new obligation for an old one.

nunc pro tunc—now for then; dated as if occurring on an earlier date.

O

oath—an attestation of the truth.

obiter dictum—opinion expressed by a court on a matter not essentially involved in a case and hence not a decision; also called *dicta* if plural.

onus probandi—burden of proof.

opinion evidence—inferences or conclusions stated by a witness in testimony as distinguished from facts known to him; generally inadmissible.

overt—open, manifest.

P

panel—a group of jurors selected to serve during a term of the court.

pardon—to release an offender from punishment for his crime.

parens patriae—sovereign power of a state to protect or be a guardian over children and incompetents.

parol—oral, verbal.

parole—to release one from prison conditionally before the expiration of his sentence.

peculation—embezzlement.

petit treason—common law crime in which a wife kills her husband, or a servant kills his master, or a subordinate kills his superior. Abolished as such under N.Y. Statute law when all such killings were classified as criminal homicides.

police power—inherent power of the state or its political subdivisions to enact laws within constitutional limits to promote the general welfare of society or the community.

polling the jury—calling the names of persons on a jury and requiring each juror to declare what his verdict is before it is legally recorded.

post mortem—after death.

power of attorney—an instrument authorizing one to act for another.

premeditate—to think or consider beforehand.

presentment—a report by a grand jury of an offense from their own knowledge, without any bill of indictment.

presumption—an inference as to the existence of some fact not known arising from its connection with facts that exist or are known to exist.

prima facie—at first sight.

prima facie case—a case in which the evidence is very strong against the defendant.

primary evidence—term applied to originals of written documents when placed in evidence.

pro and con—for and against.

probation—release of one after conviction, conditionally, without confining him in prison.

probative—tending to prove.

Q

quasi crime—violations of law not constituting crimes but punishable as wrongs against the local or general public welfare; thus, minor offenses.

quo warranto—a legal procedure to test an official's right to a public office or the right to hold a franchise, or to hold an office in a domestic corporation.

R

reasonable—fit and appropriate.

reasonable doubt—a doubt regarding the guilt of the accused person, which entitles him to an acquittal.

rebuttal—evidence to the contrary.

recidivist—habitual criminal.

recognizance—a written statement before a court to do an act specified or to suffer a penalty.

recrimination—accusation made by an accused person against his accuser.

rehabilitate—to reform.

remand—to send a prisoner back to jail after a hearing.

removal—a federal procedure by which a fugitive from justice under U.S. laws is returned for trial to the federal district wherein he committed his crime. May also refer to removing the trial for a criminal action from one county to another county or to another court.

replevin—an action to recover goods unlawfully taken or withheld.

res adjudicata—doctrine that an issue or dispute litigated and determined in a case between opposing parties is deemed permanently decided between these parties.

rescission—annulment of a contract.

respondeat superior—general rule charging the master or employer with liability for his servant's or employee's negligence in an act causing injury to third persons.

S

scienter—allegation that the defendant had knowledge or willfully committed the crime with which he is charged.

situs delicti—the place where a crime originates. (See *locus delicti*.)

special verdict—a verdict written by the jury that finds the facts only, leaving the legal judgment to the judge.

stare decisis—general rule that when an issue has been settled by a court decision, it forms a precedent which is not to be departed from in deciding similar future issues.

struck jury—a special jury or a blue ribbon jury.

suborn—to induce to commit perjury.

subpoena—a court process requiring one to appear as a witness.

subpoena duces tecum—a subpoena to produce records, books, and documents.

subrogation—substitution of one person for another in respect to rights and claims, debts, etc.

sui generis—of the same kind. (See *noscitur a sociis*.)

summons—a court order requesting one to appear to answer a charge.

surety—a bondsman.

surname—a family name.

suspend sentence—hold back a sentence pending a prisoner's good behavior.

T

talesman—person summoned to fill a panel of jurors when the regular panel is exhausted.

testimony—spoken or written evidence.

tolling the statute—facts that remove the statute of limitations as a bar to a criminal prosecution.

tort—a breach of legal duty caused by a wrongful act or neglect resulting in injury or loss for which the injured party may sue for damages.

trespass—illegal entry into another's property.

true bill—indictment.

trustee—one who lawfully holds property in custody for the benefit of another.

turpitude—anything done contrary to justice, honesty, morals; same as moral turpitude.

U

undertaking—a written agreement to appear in court when released on bail.

usury—unlawful interest on a loan.

V

veniremen—persons ordered to appear to serve on a jury or composing a panel of jurors.

venue—the place or location where the cause of legal action arises.

verdict—the findings of jury or judge in a criminal proceeding.

vi et armis—phrase used in indictments and information indicating the crime was committed with force, by violence, weapons, etc.

voir dire—preliminary examination of a witness or a juror to test competency, etc.

W

waive—to give up a right.

warrant—a written court order given to a peace officer to arrest the one named in it.

Z

zoning laws—laws specifying the use to which land in a city may be put; for example, residential, commercial, industrial, etc. May regulate height, width, and size of structures in a certain district. It is justified as a form of police power by the city or state.

Civil Practice Law and Rules

Selected Articles and Sections of the Civil Practice Law and Rules

(Full text of the CPLR, along with notes, commentaries, and amendments may be found in Volume 7B of McKinney's *Consolidated Laws of New York State*)

105. Definitions

(a) Applicability. Unless the context requires otherwise, the definitions in this section apply to the civil practice law and rules.

(b) Action and special proceeding. The word "action" includes a special proceeding; the words "plaintiff" and "defendant" include the petitioner and the respondent, respectively, in a special proceeding; and the words "summons" and "complaint" include the notice of petition and the petition, respectively, in a special proceeding.

(c) Attorney. The word "attorney" includes a party prosecuting or defending an action in person.

(d) Civil judicial proceeding. A "civil judicial proceeding" is a prosecution, other than a criminal action, of an independent application to a court for relief.

(e) Clerk. The word "clerk," as used in any provision respecting an action or any proceedings therein, means the clerk of the court in which the action is triable.

(f) Court and judge. The word "court," as used in any provision concerning a motion, order or special proceeding, includes a judge thereof authorized to act out of court with respect to such motion, order, or special proceeding.

(g) Domestic and foreign corporation. A "domestic corporation" is a corporation created by or under the laws of the state, or a corporation located in the state and created by or under the laws of the United States, or a corporation created by or pursuant to the laws in force in the colony of New York before April nineteenth, seventeen hundred seventy-five. Every other corporation is a "foreign corporation."

(h) Garnishee. A "garnishee" is a person who owes a debt to a judgment debtor, or a person other than the judgment debtor who has property in his possession or custody in which a judgment debtor has an interest.

(i) Judgment. The word "judgment" means a final or interlocutory judgment.

(j) Judgment creditor. A "judgment creditor" is a person in whose favor a money judgment is entered or a person who becomes entitled to enforce it.

(k) Judgment debtor. A "judgment debtor" is a person, other than a defendant not summoned in the action, against whom a money judgment is entered.

(l) Law. The word "law" means any statute or any civil practice rule.

(m) Matrimonial action. The term "matrimonial action" includes actions for a separation, for an annulment or dissolution of a marriage, for a divorce, for a declaration of the nullity of a void marriage, for a declaration of the validity or nullity of a foreign judgment of divorce and for a declaration of the validity or nullity of a marriage.

(n) Money judgment. A "money judgment" is a judgment, or any part thereof, for a sum of money or directing the payment of a sum of money.

(o) Place where action triable. The place where an action is "triable" means the place where the action is pending; or, if no action has been commenced, any proper place of trial or any proper place to commence the action; or, after entry of judgment, the place where the judgment was entered.

(p) Real property. "Real property" includes chattels real.

(q) Verified pleading. A "verified pleading" may be utilized as an affidavit whenever the latter is required.

106. Civil and criminal prosecutions not merged

Where the violation of a right admits of both a civil and criminal prosecution, the one is not merged in the other.

308. Personal service upon a natural person

Personal service upon a natural person shall be made by any of the following methods:

1. by delivering the summons within the state to the person to be served; or

2. except in matrimonial actions, by delivering the summons within the state to a person of suitable age and discretion at the actual place of business, dwelling place or usual place of abode of the person to be served and by mailing the summons to the person to be served at his last known residence; proof of such service shall be filed within twenty days thereafter with the clerk of the court designated in the summons; service shall be complete ten days after such filing; proof of service shall identify such person of suitable age and discretion and state the date, time and place of service; or

3. except in matrimonial actions, by delivering the summons within the state to the agent for service of the person to be served as designated under rule 318;

4. except in matrimonial actions, where service under paragraphs one and two cannot be made with due diligence, by affixing the summons to the door of either the actual place of business, dwelling place or usual place of abode within the state of the person to be served and by mailing the summons to such person at his last known residence; proof of such service shall be filed within twenty days thereafter with the clerk of the court designated in the summons; service shall be complete ten days after such filing;

5. in such manner as the court, upon motion without notice, directs, if service is impracticable under paragraphs one, two, and four of this section.

321. Attorneys

(a) **Appearance in person or by attorney.** A party, other than one specified in section 1201, may prosecute or defend a civil action in person or by attorney, except that a corporation or voluntary association shall appear by attorney. If a party appears by attorney he may not act in person in the action except by consent of the court.

(b) **Change of attorney.** An attorney of record may be changed by court order or, unless the party is a person specified in section 1201, by filing with the clerk a consent to the change signed by the retiring attorney and signed and acknowledged by the party. Notice of such change of attorney shall be given to the attorneys, for all parties in the action or, if a party appears without an attorney, to the party.

(c) **Death, removal or disability of attorney.** If an attorney dies, becomes physically or mentally incapacitated, or is removed, suspended or otherwise becomes disabled at any time before judgment, no further proceeding shall be taken in the action against the party for whom he appeared, without leave of the court, until thirty days after notice to appoint another attorney has been served upon that party either personally or in such manner as the court directs.

Rule 3402. Note of issue.

(a) **Placing case on calendar.** At any time after issue is first joined, or at least forty days after service of a summons has been completed irrespective of joinder of issue, any party may place a case upon the calendar by filing, within five days after service, with proof of such service two copies of a note of issue with the clerk and such other data as may be required by the applicable rules of the court in which the note is filed. The clerk shall enter the case on the calendar as of the date of the filing of the note of issue.

(b) New parties. A party who brings in a new party shall within five days thereafter serve him with the note of issue and file a statement with the clerk advising him of the bringing in of such new party and of any change in the title of the action, with proof of service of the note of issue upon the new party, and of such statement upon all parties who have appeared in the action. The case shall retain its place upon the calendar unless the court otherwise directs.

Rule 3403. Trial preferences

(a) Preferred cases. Civil cases shall be tried in the order in which notes of issue have been filed, but the following shall be entitled to a preference:

1. an action brought by or against the state, or a political subdivision of the state, or an officer or board of officers of the state or a political subdivision of the state, in his or its official capacity, on the application of the state, the political subdivision, or the officer or board of officers;

2. an action where a preference is provided for by statute; and

3. an action in which the interests of justice will be served by an early trial.

(b) Obtaining preference. Unless the court otherwise orders, notice of a motion for preference shall be served with the note of issue by the party serving the note of issue, or ten days after such service by any other party.

Rule 4011. Sequence of trial

The court may determine the sequence in which the issues shall be tried and otherwise regulate the conduct of the trial in order to achieve a speedy and unprejudiced disposition of the matters at issue in a setting of proper decorum.

Rule 4016. Opening and closing statements

Before any evidence is offered, an attorney for each plaintiff having a separate right, and an attorney for each defendant having a separate right, may make an opening statement. At the close of all the evidence on the issues tried, an attorney for each such party may make a closing statement in inverse order to opening statements.

4103. Issues triable by a jury revealed at trial; demand and waiver of trial by jury

When it appears in the course of a trial by the court that the relief required, although not originally demanded by a party, entitles the adverse party to a trial by jury of certain issues of fact, the court shall give the adverse party an opportunity to demand a jury trial of such issues. Failure to make such demand within the time limited by the court shall be deemed a waiver of the right to trial by jury. Upon such demand, the court shall order a jury trial of any issues of fact which are required to be tried by jury.

4104. Number of jurors

(a) Specification of number of jurors. A party demanding jury trial under sections 2218, 4102 or 4103 shall specify in demand whether he demands trial by a jury composed of twelve persons or six persons. Where a party has not specified the number of jurors, he shall be deemed to have demanded a trial by a jury composed of twelve persons.

(b) Increased number of jurors. If, under this section, a party demands a jury of six, any other party may, within ten days after service of the demand, serve upon all other parties and file a demand for a jury of twelve. If, under sections 2218 or 4103, a party demands a jury of six, the court shall give the other parties an opportunity to demand a jury of twelve.

4105. Persons who constitute the jury

The first twelve, or, if a jury of six is demanded, the first six, persons who appear as their names are drawn and called, and are approved as indifferent between the parties, and not discharged or excused, must be sworn and constitute the jury to try the issue.

4106. Alternate jurors

The court, in its discretion, may direct the calling of one or two additional jurors, to be known as "alternate jurors." Such jurors shall be drawn at the same time, from the same source, in the same manner, and have the same qualifications as the regular jurors, and be subject to the same examinations and challenges. They shall be seated with, take the oath with, and be treated in the same manner as the regular jurors, except that after final submission of the case, the court shall discharge the alternate jurors. If, before the final submission of the case, a regular juror dies, or becomes ill, or for any other reason is unable to perform his duty, the court may order him to be discharged and draw the name of an alternate, who shall replace the discharged juror in the jury box, and be treated as if he had been selected as one of the regular jurors.

Rule 4111. General and special verdicts and written interrogatories

(a) **General and special verdict defined.** The court may direct the jury to find either a general verdict or a special verdict. A general verdict is one in which the jury finds in favor of one or more parties. A special verdict is one in which the jury finds the facts only, leaving the court to determine which party is entitled to judgment thereon.

(b) **Special verdict.** When the court requires a jury to return a special verdict, the court shall submit to the jury written questions susceptible of brief answer or written forms of the several findings which might properly be made or it shall use any other appropriate method of submitting the issues and requiring written findings thereon. The court shall give sufficient instruction to enable the jury to make its findings upon each issue. If the court omits any issue of fact raised by the pleadings or evidence, each party waives his right to a trial by jury of the issue so omitted unless before the jury retires he demands its submission to the jury. As to an issue omitted without demand, the court may make an express finding or shall be deemed to have made a finding in accordance with the judgment.

(c) **General verdict accompanied by answers to interrogatories.** When the court requires the jury to return a general verdict, it may also require written answers to written interrogatories submitted to the jury upon one or more issues of fact. The court shall give sufficient instruction to enable the jury to render a general verdict and to answer the interrogatories. When the answers are consistent with each other but one or more is inconsistent with the general verdict, the court shall direct the entry of judgment in accordance with the answers, notwithstanding the general verdict, or it shall require the jury to further consider its answers and verdict or it shall order a new trial. When the answers are inconsistent with each other and one or more is inconsistent with the general verdict, the court shall require the jury to further consider its answers and verdict or it shall order a new trial.

Rule 4112. Entry of verdict

When the jury renders a verdict, the clerk shall make an entry in his minutes specifying the time and place of the trial, the names of the jurors and witnesses, the general verdict and any answers to written interrogatories, or the questions and answers or other written findings constituting the special verdict and the direction, if any, which the court gives with respect to subsequent proceedings.

4113. Disagreement by jury

(a) Unanimous verdict not required. A verdict may be rendered by not less than five-sixths of the jurors constituting a jury.

(b) Procedure where jurors disagree. Where five-sixths of the jurors constituting a jury cannot agree after being kept together for as long as is deemed reasonable by the court, the court shall discharge the jury and direct a new trial before another jury.

Criminal Procedure Law

PART ONE—GENERAL PROVISIONS

TITLE A—SHORT TITLE, APPLICABILITY AND DEFINITIONS

TITLE B—THE CRIMINAL COURTS

TITLE C—GENERAL PRINCIPLES TO REQUIREMENTS FOR AND EXEMPTIONS FROM CRIMINAL PROSECUTION

TITLE D—RULES OF EVIDENCE, STANDARDS OF PROOF, AND RELATED MATTERS

PART TWO—THE PRINCIPAL PROCEEDINGS

TITLE H—PRELIMINARY PROCEEDINGS IN LOCAL CRIMINAL COURT

TITLE I—PRELIMINARY PROCEEDINGS IN SUPERIOR COURT

TITLE J—PROSECUTION OF INDICTMENTS IN
SUPERIOR COURTS—PLEA TO SENTENCE

TITLE K—PROSECUTION OF INFORMATIONS IN LOCAL CRIMINAL COURTS—
PLEA TO SENTENCE

TITLE L—SENTENCE

TITLE M—PROCEEDINGS AFTER JUDGMENT

PART THREE—SPECIAL PROCEEDINGS AND
MISCELLANEOUS PROCEDURES

TITLE P—PROCEDURES FOR SECURING ATTENDANCE AT CRIMINAL ACTIONS AND
PROCEEDINGS OF DEFENDANTS AND WITNESSES UNDER CONTROL OF COURT—
RECOGNIZANCE, BAIL, AND COMMITMENT

TITLE Q—PROCEDURES FOR SECURING ATTENDANCE AT CRIMINAL ACTIONS AND PROCEEDINGS OF DEFENDANTS NOT SECURABLE BY CONVENTIONAL MEANS—AND RELATED MATTERS

TITLE R—PROCEDURES FOR SECURING ATTENDANCE OF WITNESSES IN CRIMINAL ACTIONS

TITLE S—PROCEDURES FOR SECURING TESTIMONY FOR FUTURE USE, AND FOR USING TESTIMONY GIVEN IN A PRIOR PROCEEDING

TITLE T—PROCEDURES FOR SECURING EVIDENCE BY MEANS OF COURT ORDER AND FOR SUPPRESSING EVIDENCE UNLAWFULLY OR IMPROPERLY OBTAINED

TITLE U—SPECIAL PROCEEDINGS WHICH REPLACE, SUSPEND, OR ABATE CRIMINAL ACTIONS

Selected Articles and Sections of the
Criminal Procedure Law

(Full text of the CPL along with notes, commentaries and amendments may be found in Volume 11A of McKinney's *Consolidated Laws of New York State*)

1.20 Definitions of terms of general use in this chapter

Except where different meanings are expressly specified in subsequent provisions of this chapter, the term definitions contained in section 10.00 of the penal law are applicable to this chapter, and, in addition, the following terms have the following meanings:

1. "Accusatory instrument" means an indictment, an information, a simplified information, a prosecutor's information, a superior court information, a misdemeanor complaint or a felony complaint. Every accusatory instrument, regardless of the person designated therein as accuser, constitutes an accusation on behalf of the state as plaintiff and must be entitled "the people of the state of New York" against a designated person, known as the defendant.

2. "Local criminal court accusatory instrument" means any accusatory instrument other than an indictment or a superior court information.

3. "Indictment" means a written accusation by a grand jury, more fully defined and described in article two hundred, filed with a superior court, which charges one or more defendants with the commission of one or more offenses, at least one of which is a crime, and which serves as a basis for prosecution thereof.

3-a. "Superior court information" means a written accusation by a district attorney more fully defined and described in articles one hundred ninety-five and two hundred, filed with a superior court pursuant to article one hundred ninety-five, which charges one or more defendants with the commission of one or more offenses, at least one of which is a crime, and which serves as a basis for prosecution thereof.

4. "Information" means a verified written accusation by a person, more fully defined and described in article one hundred, filed with a local criminal court, which charges one or more defendants with the commission of one or more offenses, none of which is a felony, and which may serve both to commence a criminal action and as a basis for prosecution thereof.

5. [See, also, subd. 5 below.] "Simplified traffic information" means a written accusation, more fully defined and described in article one hundred, by a police officer or other public servant authorized by law to issue same, filed with a local criminal court, which, being in a brief or simplified form prescribed by the commissioner of motor vehicles, charges a person with one or more traffic infractions or misdemeanors relating to traffic, and which may serve both to commence a criminal action for such offense and as a basis for prosecution thereof.

5. [See, also, subd. 5 above.]

(a) "Simplified information" means a simplified traffic information, a simplified parks information, or a simplified environmental conservation information.

(b) "Simplified traffic information" means a written accusation by a police officer, or other public servant authorized by law to issue same, more fully defined and described in article one hundred, filed with a local criminal court, which, being in a brief or simplified form prescribed by the commissioner of motor vehicles, charges a person with one or more traffic infractions or misdemeanors relating to traffic, and which may serve both to commence a criminal action for such offense and as a basis for prosecution thereof.

(c) "Simplified parks information" means a written accusation by a police officer, or other public servant authorized by law to issue same, filed with a local criminal court, which, being in a brief or simplified form prescribed by the commissioner of parks and recreation, charges a person with one or more offenses, other than a felony, for which a uniform simplified parks information may be issued pursuant to the parks and recreation law and the navigation law, and which may serve both to commence a criminal action for such offense and as a basis for prosecution thereof.

(d) "Simplified environmental conservation information" means a written accusation by a police officer, or other public servant authorized by law to issue same, filed with a local criminal court, which being in a brief or simplified form prescribed by the commissioner of environmental conservation, charges a person with one or more offenses, other than a felony, for which a uniform simplified environmental conservation simplified information may be issued pursuant to the environmental conservation law, and which may serve both to commence a criminal action for such offense and as a basis for prosecution thereof.

6. "Prosecutor's information" means a written accusation by a district attorney, more fully defined and described in article one hundred, filed with a local criminal court, which charges one or more defendants with the commission of one or more offenses, none of which is a felony, and which serves as a basis for prosecution thereof.

7. "Misdemeanor complaint" means a verified written accusation by a person, more fully defined and described in article one hundred, filed with a local criminal court, which charges one or more defendants with the commission of one or more offenses, at least one of which is a misdemeanor and none of which is a felony, and which serves to commence a criminal action but which may not, except upon the defendant's consent, serve as a basis for prosecution of the offenses charged therein.

8. "Felony complaint" means a verified written accusation by a person, more fully defined and described in article one hundred, filed with a local criminal court, which charges one or more defendants with the commission of one or more felonies and which serves to commence a criminal action but not as a basis for prosecution thereof.

9. "Arraignment" means the occasion upon which a defendant against whom an accusatory instrument has been filed appears before the court in which the criminal action is pending for the purpose of having such court acquire and exercise control over his person with respect to such accusatory instrument and of setting the course of further proceedings in the action.

10. "Plea," in addition to its ordinary meaning as prescribed in sections 220.10 and 340.20, means, where appropriate, the occasion upon which a defendant enters such a plea to an accusatory instrument.

11. "Trial." A jury trial commences with the selection of the jury and includes all further proceedings through the rendition of a verdict. A non-jury trial commences with the first opening address, if there be any, and, if not, when the first witness is sworn, and includes all further proceedings through the rendition of a verdict.

12. "Verdict" means the announcement by a jury in the case of a jury trial, or by the court in the case of a non-jury trial, of its decision upon the defendant's guilt or innocence of the charges submitted to or considered by it.

13. "Conviction" means the entry of a plea of guilty to, or a verdict of guilty upon, an accusatory instrument other than a felony complaint, or to one or more counts of such instrument.

14. "Sentence" means the imposition and entry of sentence upon a conviction.

15. "Judgment." A judgment is comprised of a conviction and the sentence imposed thereon and is completed by imposition and entry of the sentence.

16. "Criminal action." A criminal action (a) commences with the filing of an accusatory instrument against a defendant in a criminal court, as specified in subdivision seventeen; (b) includes the filing of all further accusatory instruments directly derived from the initial one, and all proceedings, orders and motions conducted or made by a criminal court

in the course of disposing of any such accusatory instrument, or which, regardless of the court in which they occurred or were made, could properly be considered as a part of the record of the case by an appellate court upon an appeal from a judgment of conviction; and (c) terminates with the imposition of sentence or some other final disposition in a criminal court of the last accusatory instrument filed in the case.

17. "Commencement of criminal action." A criminal action is commenced by the filing of an accusatory instrument against a defendant in a criminal court, and, if more than one accusatory instrument is filed in the course of the action, it commences when the first of such instruments is filed.

18. "Criminal proceeding" means any proceeding which (a) constitutes a part of a criminal action or (b) occurs in a criminal court and is related to a prospective, pending or completed criminal action, either of this state or of any other jurisdiction, or involves a criminal investigation.

19. "Criminal court" means any court defined as such by section 10.10.

20. "Superior court" means any court defined as such by subdivision two of section 10.10.

21. "Local criminal court" means any court defined as such by subdivision three of section 10.10.

22. "Intermediate appellate court" means any court possessing appellate jurisdiction, other than the court of appeals.

23. "Judge" means any judicial officer who is a member of or constitutes a court, whether referred to in another provision of law as a justice or by any other title.

24. "Trial jurisdiction." A criminal court has "trial jurisdiction" of an offense when an indictment or an information charging such offense may properly be filed with such court, and when such court has authority to accept a plea to, to try or otherwise finally to dispose of such accusatory instrument.

25. "Preliminary jurisdiction." A criminal court has "preliminary jurisdiction" of an offense when, regardless of whether it has trial jurisdiction thereof, a criminal action for such offense may be commenced therein, and when such court may conduct proceedings with respect thereto which lead or may lead to prosecution and final disposition of the action in a court having trial jurisdiction thereof.

26. "Appearance ticket" means a written notice issued by a public servant, more fully defined in section 150.10, requiring a person to appear before a local criminal court in connection with an accusatory instrument to be filed against him therein.

27. "Summons" means a process of a local criminal court, more fully defined in section 130.10, requiring a defendant to appear before such court for the purpose of arraignment upon an accusatory instrument filed therewith by which a criminal action against him has been commenced.

28. "Warrant of arrest" means a process of a local criminal court, more fully defined in section 120.10, directing a police officer to arrest a defendant and to bring him before such court for the purpose of arraignment upon an accusatory instrument filed therewith by which a criminal action against him has been commenced.

29. "Superior court warrant of arrest" means a process of a superior court directing a police officer to arrest a defendant and to bring him before such court for the purpose of arraignment upon an indictment filed therewith by which a criminal action against him has been commenced.

30. "Bench warrant" means a process of a criminal court in which a criminal action is pending, directing a police officer, or a uniformed court officer, pursuant to paragraph b of subdivision two of section 530.70 of this chapter, to take into custody a defendant in such action who has previously been arraigned upon the accusatory instrument by which the action was commenced, and to bring him before such court. The function of a bench war-

rant is to achieve the court appearance of a defendant in a pending criminal action for some purpose other than his initial arraignment in the action.

31. "Prosecutor" means a district attorney or any other public servant who represents the people in a criminal action.

32. "District attorney" means a district attorney, an assistant district attorney or a special district attorney, and, where appropriate, the attorney general, an assistant attorney general, a deputy attorney general or a special deputy attorney general.

33. "Peace officer" means a person listed in section 2.10 of this chapter.

34. "Police officer." The following persons are police officers:

   (a) A sworn officer of the division of state police;

   (b) Sheriffs, under-sheriffs and deputy sheriffs of counties outside of New York City;

   (c) A sworn officer of an authorized county or county parkway police department;

   (d) A sworn officer of an authorized police department or force of a city, town, village or police district;

   (e) A sworn officer of an authorized police department of an authority or a sworn officer of the state regional park police in the office of parks and recreation;

   (f) A sworn officer of the capital police force of the office of general services;

   (g) An investigator employed in the office of a district attorney;

   (h) An investigator employed by a commission created by an interstate compact who is, to a substantial extent, engaged in the enforcement of the criminal laws of this state;

   (i) The chief and deputy fire marshals, the supervising fire marshals and the fire marshals of the bureau of fire investigation of the New York City fire department;

   (j) A sworn officer of the division of law enforcement in the department of environmental conservation;

   (k) A sworn officer of a police force of a public authority created by an interstate compact;

   (l) [See, also, par. (l) below] Long Island railroad police.

   (l) [See, also, par. (l) above] An employee of the department of taxation and finance assigned to enforcement of the tax on cigarettes imposed by article twenty of the tax law by the commissioner of taxation and finance for the purpose of applying for and executing search warrants under article six hundred ninety of this chapter in connection with the enforcement of such tax on cigarettes.

   (m) A special investigator employed in the statewide organized crime task force, while performing his assigned duties pursuant to section seventy-a of the executive law.

34-a. "Geographical area of employment." The "geographical area of employment" of certain police officers is as follows:

   (a) New York state constitutes the "geographical area of employment" of any police officer employed as such by an agency of the state or by an authority which functions throughout the state;

   (b) A county, city, town or village, as the case may be, constitutes the "geographical area of employment" of any police officer employed as such by an agency of such political subdivision or by an authority which functions only in such political subdivision; and

   (c) Where an authority functions in more than one county, the "geographical area of employment" of a police officer employed thereby extends through all of such counties.

35. "Commitment to the custody of the sheriff," when referring to an order of a court located in a county or city which has established a department of correction, means commitment to the commissioner of correction of such county or city.

36. "County" ordinarily means (a) any county outside of New York City or (b) New York City in its entirety. Unless the context requires a different construction, New York City, despite its five counties, is deemed a single county within the meaning of the provisions of this chapter in which that term appears.

37. "Lesser included offense." When it is impossible to commit a particular crime without concomitantly committing, by the same conduct, another offense of lesser grade or degree, the latter is, with respect to the former, a "lesser included offense." In any case in which it is legally possible to attempt to commit a crime, an attempt to commit such crime constitutes a lesser included offense with respect thereto.

38. "Oath" includes an affirmation and every other mode authorized by law of attesting to the truth of that which is stated.

39. "Petty offense" means a violation or a traffic infraction.

40. Evidence in chief" means evidence, received at a trial or other criminal proceeding in which a defendant's guilt or innocence of an offense is in issue, which may be considered as a part of the quantum of substantive proof establishing or tending to establish the commission of such offense or an element thereof or the defendant's connection therewith.

41. "Armed felony" means any violent felony offense defined in section 70.02 of the penal law that includes as an element either:

(a) possession, being armed with or causing serious physical injury by means of a deadly weapon, if the weaepon is a loaded weapon from which a shot, readily capable of producing death or other serious physical injury may be discharged; or

(b) Display of what appears to be a pistol, revolver, rifle, shotgun, machine gun or other firearm.

42. "Juvenile offender" means (1) a person, 13 years old, who is criminally responsible for acts constituting murder in the second degree as defined in subdivisions one and two of section 125.25 of the penal law and (2) a person fourteen or fifteen years old who is criminally responsible for acts constituting the crimes defined in subdivisions one and two of section 125.25 (murder in the second degree) and in subdivision three of such section provided that the underlying crime for the murder charge is one for which such person is criminally responsible; section 135.25 (kidnapping in the first degree); 150.20 (arson in the first degree); subdivisions one and two of section 120.10 (assault in the first degree); 125.20 (manslaughter in the first degree); subdivisions one and two of section 130.35 (rape in the first degree); subdivisions one and two of section 130.50 (sodomy in the first degree); 130.70 (aggravated sexual abuse); 140.30 (burglary in the first degree); subdivision one of section 140.25 (burglary in the second degree); 150.15 (arson in the second degree); 160.15 (robbery in the first degree) or subdivision two of section 160.10 (robbery in the second degree) of the penal law; or defined in the penal law as an attempt to commit murder in the second degree or kidnapping in the first degree.

2.10 Persons designated as peace officers

Notwithstanding the provisions of any general, special or local law or charter to the contrary, only the following persons shall have the powers of, and shall be peace officers:

1. Constables or police constables of a town or village, provided such designation is not inconsistent with local law.

2. The sheriff, undersheriff and deputy sheriffs of New York city.

3. Investigators of the office of the state commission of investigation.

4. Employees of the department of taxation and finance assigned to enforcement of the tax on cigarettes imposed by article twenty of the tax law by the commissioner of taxation and finance.

5. Employees of the New York city department of finance assigned to enforcement of the tax on cigarettes imposed by title D of chapter forty-six of the administrative code of the city of New York by the commissioner of finance.

6. Confidential investigators and inspectors, as designated by the commissioner of the department of agriculture and markets, pursuant to rules of the department.

7. Officers or agents of a duly incorporated society for the prevention of cruelty to animals or children.

8. Inspectors and officers of the New York city department of health when acting pursuant to their special duties as set forth in section 564—11.0 of the administrative code of the city of New York; provided, however, that nothing in this subdivision shall be deemed to authorize such officer to carry, possess, repair or dispose of a firearm unless the appropriate license therefor has been issued pursuant to section 400.00 of the penal law.

9. Park rangers in Suffolk county, who shall be authorized to issue apearance tickets, simplified traffic informations, simplified parks informations and simplified environmental conservation informations.

10. Broome county park rangers who shall be authorized to issue appearance tickets, simplified traffic informations, simplified parks informations, and simplified environmental conservation informations; provided, however, that nothing in this subdivision shall be deemed to authorize such officer to carry, possess, repair or dispose of a firearm unless the appropriate license therefor has been issued pursuant to section 400.00 of the penal law.

11. Park rangers in Onondaga county, who shall be authorized to issue appearance tickets, simplified traffic informations, simplified parks informations and simplified environmental conservation informations, within the county of Onondaga.

12. Special policemen designated by the commissioner and the directors of in-patient facilities in the office of mental health pursuant to section 7.25 of the mental hygiene law, and special policemen designated by the commissioner and the directors of facilities under his jurisdiction in the office of mental retardation and developmental disabilities pursuant to section 13.25 of the mental hygiene law; provided, however, that nothing in this subdivision shall be deemed to authorize such officers to carry, possess, repair or dispose of a firearm unless the appropriate license therefor has been issued pursuant to section 400.00 of the penal law.

13. Persons designated as special policemen by the director of a hospital in the department of health pursuant to section four hundred fifty-five of the public health law; provided, however, that nothing in this subdivision shall be deemed to authorize such officer to carry, possess, repair or dispose of a firearm unless the appropriate license therefor has been issued pursuant to section 400.00 of the penal law.

14. Peace officers appointed by the state university pursuant to paragraph m of subdivision two of section three hundred fifty-five of the education law; provided, however, that nothing in this subdivision shall be deemed to authorize such officer to carry, possess, repair or dispose of a firearm unless the appropriate license therefor has been issued pursuant to section 400.00 of the penal law.

15. Uniformed enforcement forces of the New York state thruway authority, when acting pursuant to subdivision two of section three hundred sixty-one of the public authorities law; provided, however, that nothing in this subdivision shall be deemed to authorize such officer to carry, possess, repair or dispose of a firearm unless the appropriate license therefor has been issued pursuant to section 400.00 of the penal law.

16. Employees of the department of health designated pursuant to section thirty-three hundred eighty-five of the public health law; provided, however, that nothing in this subdivision shall be deemed to authorize such officer to carry, possess, repair or dispose of a

firearm unless the appropriate license therefor has been issued pursuant to section 400.00 of the penal law.

17. Uniformed housing guards of the Buffalo municipal housing authority.

18. Bay constable of the city of Rye and bay constables of the towns of East Hampton, Hempstead, Oyster Bay, Southampton, Southold, Islip, Shelter Island, Brookhaven, Babylon and North Hempstead; provided, however, that nothing in this subdivision shall be deemed to authorize the bay constables in the city of Rye or the towns of Brookhaven, Babylon, East Hampton, Southold, Islip and Shelter Island to carry, possess, repair or dispose of a firearm unless the appropriate license therefor has been issued pursuant to section 400.00 of the penal law.

19. Harbor masters appointed by a county, city, town or village.

20. Bridge and tunnel officers, sergeants and lieutenants of the Triborough bridge and tunnel authority.

21. (a) Uniformed court officers of the unified court system.

(b) Court clerks of the unified court system in the first and second departments.

(c) Marshall, depty marshall, clerk or uniformed court officer of a district court.

(d)[1] Marshalls or deputy marshalls of a city court, provided, however, that nothing in this subdivision shall be deemed to authorize such officer to carry, possess, repair or dispose of a firearm unless the appropriate license therefor has been issued pursuant to section 400.00 of the penal law.

22. Persons appointed as railroad policemen pursuant to section eighty-eight of the railroad law.

23. Parole officers or warrant officers in the division of parole.

24. Probation officers.

25. Officials, as designated by the commissioner of the department of correctional services pursuant to rules of the department, and correction officers of any state correctional facility or of any penal correctional institution.

26. Peace officers designated pursuant to the provisions of the New York state defense emergency act, as set forth in chapter seven hundred eighty-four of the laws of nineteen hundred fifty-one,[2] as amended, when acting pursuant to their special duties during a period of attack by enemy forces, or during official drills in preparation for an attack by enemy forces; provided, however, that nothing in this subdivision shall be deemed to authorize such officer to carry, possess, repair or dispose of a firearm unless the approprirate license therefor has been issued pursuant to section 400.00 of the penal law; and provided further, that such officer shall have the powers set forth in section 2.20 of this article only during a period of attack by enemy forces.

27. New York city special patrolmen appointed by the police commissioner pursuant to subdivision (c) or (e) of section 434a–7.0 of the administrative code of the city of New York; provided, however, that nothing in this subdivision shall be deemed to authorize such officer to carry, possess, repair or dispose of a firearm unless the appropriate license therefor has been issued pursuant to section 400.00 of the penal law and the employer has authorized such officer to possess a firearm during any phase of the officers on-duty employment. Special patrolmen shall have the powers set forth in section 2.20 of this article only when they are acting pursuant to their special duties.

28. All officers and members of the uniformed force of the New York city fire department as set forth and subject to the limitations contained in section 487a–15.0 of the administrative code of the city of New York; provided, however, that nothing in this subdivision shall be deemed to authorize such officer to carry, possess, repair or dispose of a firearm unless the appropriate license therefor has been issued pursuant to section 400.00 of the penal law.

29. Special policemen for horse racing, appointed pursuant to the provisions of the pari-mutuel revenue law as set forth in chapter two hundred fifty-four of the laws of nineteen hundred forty, as amended; provided, however, that nothing in this subdivision shall be deemed to authorize such officer to carry, possess, repair or dispose of a firearm unless the appropriate license therefor has been issued pursuant to section 400.00 of the penal law.

30. Supervising fire inspectors, fire inspectors, the fire marshall and assistant fire marshalls, all full-time employees of the county of Nassau fire marshall's office, when acting pursuant to their special duties in matters arising under the laws relating to fires, the extinguishment thereof and fire perils.

31. A district ranger, assistant district ranger or a forest ranger employed by the state department of environmental conservation.

32. Investigators of the department of motor vehicles, pursuant to section three hundred ninety-two-b of the vehicle and traffic law; provided, however, that nothing in this subdivision shall be deemed to authorize such officer to carry, possess, repair or dispose of a firearm unless the appropriate license therefor has been issued pursuant to section 400.00 of the penal law.

33. A city marshall of the city of New York who has received training in firearms handling from the federal bureau of investigation or in the New York city police academy, or in the absence of the available training programs from the federal bureau of investigation and the New York city police academy, from another law enforcement agency located in the state of New York, and who has received a firearms permit from the license division of the New York city police department.

34. Waterfront and airport investigators, pursuant to subdivision four of section ninety-nine hundred six of the unconsolidated laws; provided, however, that nothing in this subdivision shall be deemed to authorize such officer to carry, possess, repair or dispose of a firearm unless the appropriate license therefor has been issued pursuant to section 400.00 of the penal law.

35. Special investigators appointed by the state board of elections, pursuant to section 3–107 of the election law.

36. Investigators appointed by the state liquor authority, pursuant to section fifteen of the alcoholic beverage control law; provided, however, that nothing in this subdivision shall be deemed to authorize such officer to carry, possess, repair or dispose of a firearm unless the appropriate license therefor has been issued pursuant to section 400.00 of the penal law.

37. Special patrolmen of a political subdivision, appointed pursuant to section two hundred nine-v of the general municipal law; provided, however, that nothing in this subdivision shall be deemed to authorize such officer to carry, possess, repair or dispose of a firearm unless the appropriate license therefor has been issued pursuant to section 400.00 of the penal law.

38. A special investigator of the New York city department of investigation who has received training in firearms handling in the New York police academy and has received a firearms permit from the license division of the New York city police department.

39. Broome county special patrolman, appointed by the Broome county attorney; provided, however, that nothing in this subdivision shall be deemed to authorize such officer to carry, possess, repair or dispose of a firearm unless the appropriate license therefor has been issued pursuant to section 400.00 of the penal law.

40. Special officers employed by the city of New York or by the New York city health and hospitals corporation; provided, however, that nothing in this subdivision shall be deemed to authorize such officer to carry, possess, repair or dispose of a firearm unless the appropriate license therefor has been issued pursuant to section 400.00 of the penal law.

41. Fire police squads organized pursuant to section two hundred nine-c of the general municipal law, at such times as the fire department, fire company or an emergency rescue and first aid squad of the fire department or fire company are on duty, or when, on orders of the chief of the fire department or fire company of which they are members, they are separately engaged in response to a call for assistance pursuant to the provisions of section two hundred nine of the general municipal law; provided, however, that nothing in this subdivision shall be deemed to authorize such officer to carry, possess, repair or dispose of a firearm unless the appropriate license therefor has been issued pursuant to section 400.00 of the penal law.

42. Special deputy sheriffs appointed by the sheriff of a county within which any part of the grounds of Cornell University or the grounds of any state institution constituting a part of the educational and research plants owned or under the supervision, administration or control of said university are located pursuant to section fifty-seven hundred nine of the education law; provided, however, that nothing in this subdivision shall be deemed to authorize such officer to carry, possess, repair or dispose of a firearm unless the appropriate license therefor has been issued pursuant to section 400.00 of the penal law.

43. Housing patrolmen of the Mount Vernon housing authority, acting pursuant to rules of the Mount Vernon housing authority; provided, however, that nothing in this subdivision shall be deemed to authorize such officer to carry, possess, repair or dispose of a firearm unless the appropriate license therefor has been issued pursuant to section 400.00 of the penal law.

44. The officers, employees and members of the New York city division of fire prevention, in the bureau of fire, as set forth and subject to the limitations contained in subdivision one of section 487a—1.0 of the administrative code of the city of New York; provided, however, that nothing in this subdivision shall be deemed to authorize such officer to carry, possess, repair or dispose of a firearm unless the appropriate license therefor has been issued pursuant to section 400.00 of the penal law.

45. Persons appointed and designated as peace officers by the Niagara frontier transportation authority, pursuant to subdivision thirteen of section twelve hundred ninety-nine-e of the public authorities law.

46. Persons appointed as peace officers by the Sea Gate Association pursuant to the provisions of chapter three hundred ninety-one of the laws of nineteen hundred forty, provided, however, that nothing in this subdivision shall be deemed to authorize such officer to carry, possess, repair or dispose of a firearm unless the appropriate license therefor has been issued pursuant to section 400.00 of the penal law.

47. Employees of the insurance frauds bureau of the state department of insurance when designated as peace officers by the superintendent of insurance and acting pursuant to their special duties; provided, however, that nothing in this subdivision shall be deemed to authorize such officer to carry, possess, repair or dispose of a firearm unless the appropriate license therefor has been issued pursuant to section 400.00 of the penal law.

10.10 The criminal courts; enumeration and definitions

1. The "criminal courts" of this state are comprised of the superior courts and the local criminal courts.

2. "Superior court" means:

  (a) The supreme court; or

  (b) A county court.

3. "Local criminal court" means:

  (a) A district court; or

  (b) The New York City criminal court; or

  (c) A city court; or

(d) A town court; or

(e) A village court; or

(f) A supreme court justice sitting as a local criminal court; or

(g) A county judge sitting as a local criminal court.

4. "City court" means any court for a city, other than New York City, having trial jurisdiction of offenses of less than felony grade only committed within such city, whether such court is entitled a city court, a municipal court, a police court, a recorder's court or is known by any other name or title.

5. "Town court." A "town court" is comprised of all the town justices of a town.

6. "Village court." A "village court" is comprised of the justice of a village, or all the justices thereof if there be more than one, or, at a time when he or they are absent, an acting justice of a village who is authorized to perform the functions of a village justice during his absence.

7. Notwithstanding any other provision of this section, a court specified herein which possesses civil as well as criminal jurisdiction does not act as a criminal court when acting solely in the exercise of its civil jurisdiction, and an order or determination made by such court in its civil capacity is not an order or determination of a criminal court even though it may terminate or otherwise control or affect a criminal action or proceeding.

10.20 Superior courts; jurisdiction

1. Superior courts have trial jurisdiction of all offenses. They have:

(a) Exclusive trial jurisdiction of felonies; and

(b) Trial jurisdiction of misdemeanors concurrent with that of the local criminal courts; and

(c) Trial jurisdiction of petty offenses, but only when such an offense is charged in an indictment which also charges a crime.

2. Superior courts have preliminary jurisdiction of all offenses, but they exercise such jurisdiction only by reason of and through the agency of their grand juries.

10.30 Local criminal courts; jurisdiction

1. Local criminal courts have trial jurisdiction of all offenses other than felonies. They have:

(a) Exclusive trial jurisdiction of petty offenses except for the superior court jurisdiction thereof prescribed in paragraph (c) of subdivision one of section 10.20; and

(b) Trial jurisdiction of misdemeanors concurrent with that of the superior courts but subject to divestiture thereof by the latter in any particular case.

2. Local criminal courts have preliminary jurisdiction of all offenses subject to divestiture thereof in any particular case by the superior courts and their grand juries.

3. Notwithstanding the provisions of subdivision one, a superior court judge sitting as a local criminal court does not have trial jurisdiction of any offense, but has preliminary jurisdiction only, as provided in subdivision two.

30.10 Timeliness of prosecutions; periods of limitation

1. A criminal action must be commenced within the period of limitation prescribed in the ensuing subdivisions of this section.

2. Except as otherwise provided in subdivision three:

(a) A prosecution for a class A felony may be commenced at any time;

(b) A prosecution for any other felony must be commenced within five years after the commission thereof;

(c) A prosecution for a misdemeanor must be commenced within two years after the commission thereof;

(d) A prosecution for a petty offense must be commenced within one year after the commission thereof.

3. Notwithstanding the provisions of subdivision two, the periods of limitation for the commencement of criminal actions are extended as follows in the indicated circumstances:

(a) A prosecution for larceny committed by a person in violation of a fiduciary duty may be commenced within one year after the facts constituting such offense are discovered or, in the exercise of reasonable diligence, should have been discovered by the aggrieved party or by a person under a legal duty to represent him who is not himself implicated in the commission of the offense.

(b) A prosecution for any offense involving misconduct in public office by a public servant may be commenced at any time during the defendant's service in such office or within five years after the termination of such service; provided however, that in no event shall the period of limitation be extended by more than five years beyond the period otherwise applicable under subdivision two.

(c) A prosecution for any crime set forth in section 27-0914 of the environmental conservation law may be commenced within two years after the facts constituting such crime are discovered or, in the exercise of reasonable diligence, should have been discovered by a public servant who has the responsibility to enforce the provisions of said section.

4. In calculating the time limitation applicable to commencement of a criminal action, the following periods shall not be included:

(a) Any period following the commission of the offense during which (i) the defendant was continuously outside this state, or (ii) the whereabouts of the defendant were continuously unknown and continuously unascertainable by the exercise of reasonable diligence. However, in no event shall the period of limitation be extended by more than five years beyond the period otherwise applicable under subdivision two.

(b) When a prosecution for an offense is lawfully commenced within the prescribed period of limitation therefor, and when an accusatory instrument upon which such prosecution is based is subsequently dismissed by an authorized court under directions or circumstances permitting the lodging of another charge for the same offense or an ofense based on the same conduct, the period extending from the commencement of the thus defeated prosecution to the dismissal of the accusatory instrument does not constitute a part of the period of limitation applicable to commencement of prosecution by a new charge.

30.30 Speedy trial; time limitations

1. Except as otherwise provided in subdivision three, a motion made pursuant to paragraph (e) of subdivision one of section 170.30 or paragraph (g) of subdivision one of section 210.20 must be granted where the people are not ready for trial within:

(a) six months of the commencement of a criminal action wherein a defendant is accused of one or more offenses, at least one of which is a felony;

(b) ninety days of the commencement of a criminal action wherein a defendant is accused of one or more offenses, at least one of which is a misdemeanor punishable by a sentence of imprisonment of more than three months and none of which is a felony;

(c) sixty days of the commencement of a criminal action wherein the defendant is accused of one or more offenses, at least one of which is a misdemeanor punishable by a sentence of imprisonment of not more than three months and none of which is a crime punishable by a sentence of imprisonment of more than three months;

(d) thirty days of the commencement of a criminal action wherein the defendant is accused of one or more offenses, at least one of which is a violation and none of which is a crime.

2. Except as provided in subdivision three, where a defendant has been committed to the custody of the sheriff in a criminal action he must be released on bail or on his own recognizance, upon such conditions as may be just and reasonable, if the people are not ready for trial in that criminal action within:

(a) ninety days from the commencement of his commitment to the custody of the sheriff in a criminal action wherein the defendant is accused of one or more offenses, at least one of which is a felony;

(b) thirty days from the commencement of his commitment to the custody of the sheriff in a criminal action wherein the defendant is accused of one or more offenses, at least one of which is a misdemeanor punishable by a sentence of imprisonment of more than three months and none of which is a felony;

(c) fifteen days from the commencement of his commitment to the custody of the sheriff in a criminal action wherein the defendant is accused of one or more offenses, at least one of which is a misdemeanor punishable by a sentence of imprisonment of not more than three months and none of which is a crime punishable by a sentence of imprisonment of more than three months;

(d) five days from the commencement of his commitment to the custody of the sheriff in a criminal action wherein the defendant is accused of one or more offenses, at least one of which is a violation and none of which is a crime.

3. (a) Subdivisions one and two do not apply to a criminal action wherein the defendant is accused of an offense defined in sections 125.10, 125.15, 125.20, 125.25 and 125.27 of the penal law.

(b) A motion made pursuant to subdivisions one or two upon expiration of the specified period may be denied where the people are not ready for trial if the people were ready for trial prior to the expiration of the specified period and their present unreadiness is due to some exceptional fact or circumstance, including, but not limited to, the sudden unavailability of evidence material to the people's case, when the district attorney has exercised due diligence to obtain such evidence and there are reasonable grounds to believe that such evidence will become available in a reasonable period.

(c) A motion made pursuant to subdivision two shall not:

(i) apply to any defendant who is serving a term of imprisonment for another offense;

(ii) require the release from custody of any defendant who is also being held in custody pending trial of another criminal charge as to which the applicable period has not yet elapsed;

(iii) prevent the redetention of or otherwise apply to any defendant who, after being released from custody pursuant to this section or otherwise, is charged with another crime or violates the conditions on which he has been released, by failing to appear at a judicial proceeding at which his presence is required or otherwise.

4. In computing the time within which the people must be ready for trial pursuant to subdivisions one and two, the following periods must be excluded:

(a) a reasonable period of delay resulting from other proceedings concerning the defendant, including but not limited to proceedings for the determination of competency and the period during which defendant is incompetent to stand trial; demand to produce; pre-trial motions; appeals; trial of other charges; and the period during which such matters are under consideration by the court; or

(b) the period of delay resulting from a continuance granted by the court at the request of, or with the consent of, the defendant or his counsel. The court must grant such a continuance only if it is satisfied that postponement is in the interest of justice, taking into account the public interest in the prompt dispositions of criminal charges. A defendant without counsel must not be deemed to have consented to a continuance unless he has been advised by the court of his rights under these rules and the effect of his consent; or

(c) the period of delay resulting from the absence or unavailability of the defendant. A defendant must be considered absent whenever his location is unknown and he is attempting to avoid apprehension or prosecution, or his location cannot be determined by due diligence. A defendant must be considered unavailable whenever his location is known but his presence for trial cannot be obtained by due diligence; or

(d) a reasonable period of delay when the defendant is joined for trial with a co-defendant as to whom the time for trial pursuant to this section has not run and good cause is not shown for granting a severance; or

(e) the period of delay resulting from detention of the defendant in another jurisdiction provided the district attorney is aware of such detention and has been diligent and has made reasonable efforts to obtain the presence of the defendant for trial; or

(f) the period during which the defendant is without counsel through no fault of the court; except when the defendant is proceeding as his own attorney with the permission of the court; or

(g) other periods of delay occasioned by exceptional circumstances, including but not limited to, the period of delay resulting from a continuance granted at the request of a district attorney if (i) the continuance is granted because of the unavailibility of evidence material to the people's case, when the district attorney has exercised due diligence to obtain such evidence and there are reasonable grounds to believe that such evidence will become available in a reasonable period; or (ii) the continuance is granted to allow the district attorney additional time to prepare the people's case and additional time is justified by the exceptional circumstances of the case.

5. For purposes of this section,

(a) where the defendant is to be tried following the withdrawal of the plea of guilty or is to be retried following a mistrial, an order for a new trial or an appeal or collateral attack, the criminal action and the commitment to the custody of the sheriff, if any, must be deemed to have commenced on the date the withdrawal of the plea of guilty or the date the order occasioning a retrial becomes final;

(b) where a defendant has been served with an appearance ticket, the criminal action must be deemed to have commenced on the date such appearance ticket is returnable in a local criminal court;

(c) where a criminal action is commenced by the filing of a felony complaint, and thereafter, in the course of the same criminal action either the felony complaint is replaced with or converted to an information, prosecutor's information or misdemeanor complaint pursuant to article 180 or a prosecutor's information is filed pursuant to section 190.70, the period applicable for the purposes of subdivision one must be the period applicable to the charges in the new accusatory instrument, calculated from the date of the filing of such new accusatory instrument; provided, however, that when the aggregate of such period and the period of time, excluding the periods provided in subdivision four, already elapsed from the date of the filing of the felony complaint to the date of the filing of the new accusatory instrument exceeds six months, the period applicable to the charges in the felony complaint must remain applicable and continue as if the new accusatory instrument had not been filed;

(d) where a criminal action is commenced by the filing of a felony complaint, and thereafter, in the course of the same criminal action either the felony complaint is replaced with or converted to an information, prosecutor's information or misdemeanor complaint pursuant to article 180 or a prosecutor's information is filed pursuant to section 190.70, the period applicable for the purposes of subdivision two must be the period applicable to the charges in the new accusatory instrument, calculated from the date of the filing of such new accusatory instrument; provided, however, that when the aggregate of such period and the period of time, excluding the periods provided in subdivision four, already elapsed from the date of the filing of the felony complaint to the date of the filing of the new accusatory instrument exceeds ninety days, the period applicable to the charges in the felony complaint must remain applicable and continue as if the new accusatory instrument had not been filed.

6. The procedural rules prescribed in subdivisions one through seven of section 210.45 with respect to a motion to dismiss an indictment are also applicable to a motion made pursuant to subdivision two.

190.05   Grand jury; definition and general functions

A grand jury is a body consisting of not less than sixteen nor more than twenty-three persons, impaneled by a superior court and constituting a part of such court, the functions of which are to hear and examine evidence concerning offenses and concerning misconduct, nonfeasance and neglect in public office, whether criminal or otherwise, and to take action with respect to such evidence as provided in section 190.60.

190.10   Grand jury; for what courts drawn

The appellate division of each judicial department shall adopt rules govening the number and the terms for which grand juries shall be drawn and impaneled by the superior courts within its department; provided, however, that a grand jury may be drawn and impaneled for any extraordinary term of the supreme court upon the order of a justice assigned to hold such term.

190.15   Grand jury; duration of term and discharge

1. A term of a superior court for which a grand jury has been impaneled remains in existence at least until and including the opening date of the next term of such court for which a grand jury has been designated. Upon such date, or within five days preceding it, the court may, upon declaration of both the grand jury and the district attorney that such grand jury has not yet completed or will be unable to complete certain business before it, extend the term of court and the existence of such grand jury to a specified future date, and may subsequently order further extensions for such purpose.

2. At any time when a grand jury is in recess and no other appropriate grand jury is in existence in the county, the court may, upon application of the district attorney or of a defendant held by a local criminal court for the action of a grand jury, order such grand jury reconvened for the purpose of dealing with a matter requiring grand jury action.

190.20   Grand jury; formation, organization and other matters preliminary to assumption of duties

1. The mode of selecting grand jurors and of drawing and impaneling grand juries is governed by the judiciary law.

2. Neither the grand jury panel nor any individual grand juror may be challenged, but the court may:

(a) At any time before a grand jury is sworn, discharge the panel and summon another panel if it finds that the original panel does not substantially conform to the requirements of the judiciary law; or

(b) At any time after a grand juror is drawn, refuse to swear him, or discharge him after he has been sworn, upon a finding that he is disqualified from service pursuant to the judiciary law, or incapable of performing his duties because of bias or prejudice, or guilty of misconduct in the performance of his duties such as to impair the proper functioning of the grand jury.

3. After a grand jury has been impaneled, the court must appoint one of the grand jurors as foreman and another to act as foreman during any absence or disability of the foreman. At some time before commencement of their duties, the grand jurors must appoint one of their number as secretary to keep records material to the conduct of the grand jury's business.

4. The grand jurors must be sworn by the court. The oath may be in any form or language which requires the grand jurors to perform their duties faithfully.

5. After a grand jury has been sworn, the court must deliver or cause to be delivered to each grand juror a printed copy of all the provisions of this article, and the court may, in addition, give the grand jurors any oral instructions relating to the proper performance of their duties as it deems necessary or appropriate.

6. If two or more grand juries are impaneled at the same court term, the court may thereafter, for good cause, transfer grand jurors from one panel to another, and any grand juror so transferred is deemed to have been sworn as a member of the panel to which he has been transferred.

190.25   Grand jury; proceedings and operation in general

1. Proceedings of a grand jury are not valid unless at least sixteen of its members are present. The finding of an indictment, a direction to file a prosecutor's information, a decision to submit a grand jury report and every other affirmative official action or decision requires the concurrence of at least twelve members thereof.

2. The foreman or any other grand juror may administer an oath to any witness appearing before the grand jury.

3. During the deliberations and voting of a grand jury, only the grand jurors may be present in the grand jury room. During its other proceedings, the following persons, in addition to witnesses, may, as the occasion requires, also be present:

(a) The district attorney;

(b) A clerk or other public servant authorized to assist the grand jury in the administrative conduct of its proceedings;

(c) A stenographer authorized to record the proceedings of the grand jury;

(d) An interpreter. Upon request of the grand jury, the prosecutor must provide an interpreter to interpret the testimony of any witness who does not speak the English language well enough to be readily understood. Such interpreter must, if he has not previously taken the constitutional oath of office, first take an oath before the grand jury that he will faithfully interpret the testimony of the witness and that he will keep secret all matters before such grand jury within his knowledge;

(e) A public servant holding a witness in custody. When a person held in official custody is a witness before a grand jury, a public servant assigned to guard him during his grand jury appearance may accompany him in the grand jury room. Such public servant must, if he has not previously taken the constitutional oath of office, first take an oath before the grand jury that he will keep secret all matters before it within his knowledge.

(f) An attorney representing a witness pursuant to section 190.52 of this chapter while that witness is present.

4. (a) Grand jury proceedings are secret, and no grand juror, or other person specified in subdivision three of this section or section 215.70 of the penal law, may, except in the lawful discharge of his duties or upon written order of the court, disclose the nature or substance of any grand jury testimony, evidence, or any decision, result or other matter attending a grand jury proceeding. For the purpose of assisting the grand jury in con-

ducting its investigation, evidence obtained by a grand jury may be independently examined by the district attorney, members of his staff, police officers specifically assigned to the investigation, and such other persons as the court may specifically authorize. Such evidence may not be disclosed to other persons without a court order. Nothing contained herein shall prohibit a witness from disclosing his own testimony.

(b) When a district attorney obtains evidence during a grand jury proceeding which provides reasonable cause to suspect that a child has been abused or maltreated, as those terms are defined by section ten hundred twelve of the family court act, he must apply to the court supervising the grand jury for an order permitting disclosure of such evidence to the state central register of child abuse and maltreatment. A district attorney need not apply to the court for such order if he has previously made or caused a report to be made to the state central register of child abuse and maltreatment pursuant to section four hundred thirteen of the social services law and the evidence obtained during the grand jury proceeding, or substantially similar information, was included in such report. The district attorney's application to the court shall be made ex parte and in camera. The court must grant the application and permit the district attorney to disclose the evidence to the state central register of child abuse and maltreatment unless the court finds that such disclosure would jeopardize the life or safety of any person or interfere with a continuing grand jury proceeding.

5. The grand jury is the exclusive judge of the facts with respect to any matter before it.

6. The legal advisors of the grand jury are the court and the district attorney, and the grand jury may not seek or receive legal advice from any other source. Where necessary or appropriate, the court or the district attorney, or both, must instruct the grand jury concerning the law with respect to its duties or any matter before it, and such instructions must be recorded in the minutes.

190.71 Grand jury; direction to file request for removal to family court

(a) Except as provided in subdivision six of section 200.20 of this chapter, a grand jury may not indict (i) a person thirteen years of age for any conduct or crime other than conduct constituting a crime defined in subdivisions one and two of section 125.25 (murder in the second degree); (ii) a person fourteen or fifteen years of age for any conduct or crime other than conduct constituting a crime defined in subdivisions one and two of section 125.25 (murder in the second degree) and in subdivision three of such section provided that the underlying crime for the murder charge is one for which such person is criminally responsible; 135.25 (kidnapping in the first degree); 150.20 (arson in the first degree); subdivisions one and two of section 120.10 (assault in the first degree); 125.20 (manslaughter in the first degree); subdivisions one and two of section 130.35 (rape in the first degree); subdivisions one and two of section 130.50 (sodomy in the first degree); 130.70 (aggravated sexual abuse); 140.30 (burglary in the first degree); subdivision one of section 140.25 (burglary in the second degree); 150.15 (arson in the second degree); 160.15 (robbery in the first degree); or subdivision two of section 160.10 (robbery in the second degree) of the penal law; or defined in the penal law as an attempt to commit murder in the second degree or kidnapping in the first degree.

(b) A grand jury may vote to file a request to remove a charge to the family court if it finds that a person thirteen, fourteen or fifteen years of age did an act which, if done by a person over the age of sixteen, would constitute a crime provided (1) such act is one for which it may not indict; (2) it does not indict such person for a crime; and (3) the evidence before it is legally sufficient to establish that such person did such act and competent and admissible evidence before it provides reasonable cause to believe that such person did such act.

(c) Upon voting to remove a charge to the family court pursuant to subdivision (b) of this section, the grand jury must through its foreman or acting foreman, file a request to transfer such charge to the family court. Such request shall be filed with the court by which it was impaneled. It must (1) allege that a person named therein did any act which, if done by a person over the age of sixteen, would constitute a crime; (2) specify the act and the time and place of its commission; and (3) be signed by the foreman or the acting foreman.

(d) Upon the filing of such grand jury request, the court must, unless such request is improper or insufficient on its face, issue an order approving such request and direct that the charge be removed to the family court in accordance with the provisions of article seven hundred twenty-five of this chapter.

190.85 Grand jury; grand jury reports

1. The grand jury may submit to the court by which it was impaneled, a report:

(a) Concerning misconduct, non-feasance or neglect in public office by a public servant as the basis for a recommendation of removal or disciplinary action; or

(b) Stating that after investigation of a public servant it finds no misconduct, non-feasance or neglect in office by him provided that such public servant has requested the submission of such report; or

(c) Proposing recommendations for legislative, executive or administrative action in the public interest based upon stated findings.

2. The court to which such report is submitted shall examine it and the minutes of the grand jury and, except as otherwise provided in subdivision four, shall make an order accepting and filing such report as a public record only if the court is satisfied that it complies with the provisions of subdivision one and that:

(a) The report is based upon facts revealed in the course of an investigation authorized by section 190.55 and is supported by the preponderance of the credible and legally admissible evidence; and

(b) When the report is submitted pursuant to paragraph (a) of subdivision one, that each person named therein was afforded an opportunity to testify before the grand jury prior to the filing of such report, and when the report is submitted pursuant to paragraph (b) or (c) of subdivision one, it is not critical of an identified or identifiable person.

3. The order accepting a report pursuant to pagraph (a) of subdivision one, and the report itself, must be sealed by the court and may not be filed as a public record, or be subject to subpoena or otherwise be made public until at least thirty-one days after a copy of the order and the report are served upon each public servant named therein, or if an appeal is taken pursuant to section 190.90, until the affirmance of the order accepting the report, or until reversal of the order sealing the report, or until dismissal of the appeal of the named public servant by the appellate division, whichever occurs later. Such public servant may file with the clerk of the court an answer to such report, not later than twenty days after service of the order and report upon him. Such an answer shall plainly and concisely state the facts and law constituting the defense of the public servant to the charges in said report, and, except for those parts of the answer which the court may determine to be scandalously or prejudicially and unnecessarily inserted therein, shall become an appendix to the report. Upon the expiration of the time set forth in this subdivision, the district attorney shall deliver a true copy of such report, and the appendix if any, for appropriate action, to each public servant or body having removal or disciplinary authority over each public servant named therein.

4. Upon the submission of a report pursuant to subdivision one, if the court finds that the filing of such report as a public record, may prejudice fair consideration of a pending criminal matter, it must order such report sealed and such report may not be subject to subpoena or public inspection during the pendency of such criminal matter, except upon order of the court.

5. Whenever the court to which a report is submitted pursuant to paragraph (a) of subdivision one is not satisfied that the report complies with the provisions of subdivision

two, it may direct that additional testimony be taken before the same grand jury, or it must make an order sealing such report, and the report may not be filed as a public record, or be subject to subpoena or otherwise be made public.

Prosecution of Indictments

260.10   Jury trial; requirement thereof

Except as otherwise provided in section 320.10, every trial of an indictment must be a jury trial.

260.20   Jury trial; defendant's presence at trial

A defendant must be personally present during the trial of an indictment; provided, however, that a defendant who conducts himself in so disorderly and disruptive a manner that his trial cannot be carried on with him in the courtroom may be removed from the courtroom if, after he has been warned by the court that he will be removed if he continues such conduct, he continues to engage in such conduct.

260.30   Jury trial; in what order to proceed

The order of a jury trial, in general, is as follows:

1.   The jury must be selected and sworn.

2.   The court must deliver preliminary instructions to the jury.

3.   The people must deliver an opening address to the jury.

4.   The defendant may deliver an opening address to the jury.

5.   The people must offer evidence in support of the indictment.

6.   The defendant may offer evidence in his defense.

7.   The people may offer evidence in rebuttal of the defense evidence, and the defendant may then offer evidence in rebuttal of the people's rebuttal evidence. The court may in its discretion permit the parties to offer further rebuttal or surrebuttal evidence in this pattern. In the interest of justice, the court may permit either party to offer evidence upon rebuttal which is not technically of a rebuttal nature but more properly a part of the offering party's original case.

8.   At the conclusion of the evidence, the defendant may deliver a summation to the jury.

9.   The people may then deliver a summation to the jury.

10.   The court must then deliver a charge to the jury.

11.   The jury must then retire to deliberate and, if possible, render a verdict.

270.05   Trial jury; formation in general

1.   A trial jury consists of twelve jurors, but "alternate jurors" may be selected and sworn pursuant to section 270.30.

2.   The panel from which the jury is drawn is formed and selected as prescribed in the judiciary law. The first twelve members of the panel returned for the term who appear as their names are drawn and called, and who are not excluded as prescribed by this article, must be sworn and thereupon constitute the trial jury.

270.50   Trial jury; viewing of premises

1.   When the court is of the opinion that a viewing or observation by the jury of the premises or place where an offense on trial was allegedly committed, or of any other premises or place involved in the case, will be helpful to the jury in determining any material factual issue, it may in its discretion, at any time before the commencement of the summations, order that the jury be conducted to such premises or place for such purpose in accordance with the provisions of this section.

2.   In such case, the jury must be kept together throughout under the supervision of an appropriate public servant or servants appointed by the court, and the court itself must be present throughout. The prosecutor, the defendant and counsel for the defendant may as a matter of right be present throughout, but such right may be waived.

3.   The purpose of such an inspection is solely to permit visual observation by the jury of the premises or place in question, and neither the court, the parties, counsel nor the jurors may engage in discussion or argumentation concerning the significance or implications of anything under observation or concerning any issue in the case.

310.10   Jury deliberation; requirement of; where conducted

Following the court's charge, the jury must retire to deliberate upon its verdict in a place outside the courtroom. It must be provided with suitable accommodations therefor and must be continuously kept together under the supervision of a court officer or court officers. In the event such court officer or court officers are not available, the jury shall be under the supervision of an appropriate public servant or public servants. Except when so authorized by the court or when performing administerial duties with respect to the jurors, such court officers or public servants, as the case may be, may not speak to or communicate with them or permit any other person to do so.

310.20   Jury deliberation; use of exhibits and other material

Upon retiring to deliberate, the jurors may take with them:

1.   Any exhibits received in evidence at the trial which the court, after according the parties an opportunity to be heard upon the matter, in its discretion permits them to take; and

2.   A written list prepared by the court containing the offenses submitted to the jury by the court in its charge and the possible verdicts thereon.

310.30   Jury deliberation; request for information

At any time during its deliberation, the jury may request the court for further instruction or information with respect to the law, with respect to the content or substance of any trial evidence, or with respect to any other matter pertinent to the jury's consideration of the case. Upon such a request, the court must direct that the jury be returned to the courtroom and, after notice to both the people and counsel for the defendant, and in the presence of the defendant, must give such requested information or instruction as the court deems proper. With the consent of the parties and upon the request of the jury for further instruction with respect to a statute, the court may also give to the jury copies of the text of any statute which, in its discretion, the court deems proper.

Prosecutions of Informations

Article 350—Non-Jury Trials

350.10 Conduct of single judge trial

1. A single judge trial of an information in a local criminal court must be conducted pursuant to this section.

2. The court, in addition to determining all questions of law, is the exclusive trier of all issues of fact and must render a verdict.

3. The order of the trial must be as follows:

(a) The court may in its discretion permit the parties to deliver opening addresses. If the court grants such permission to one party, it must grant it to the other also. If both parties deliver opening addresses, the people's address must be delivered first.

(b) The order in which evidence must or may be offered by the respective parties is the same as that applicable to a jury trial of an indictment as prescribed in subdivisions five, six and seven of section 260.30.

(c) The court may in its discretion permit the parties to deliver summations. If the court grants such permission to one party, it must grant permission to the other also. If both parties deliver summations, the defendant's summation must be delivered first.

(d) The court must then consider the case and render a verdict.

4. The provisions governing motion practice and general procedure with respect to a jury trial of an indictment are, wherever appropriate, applicable to a non-jury trial of an information.

5. If the information contains more than one count, the court must render a verdict upon each count not previously dismissed or must otherwise state upon the record its disposition of each such count. A verdict which does not so dispose of each count constitutes a verdict of not guilty with respect to each undisposed of count.

6. In rendering a verdict of guilty upon a count charging a misdemeanor, the court may find the defendant guilty of such misdemeanor, if it is established by legally sufficient trial evidence, or guilty of any lesser included offense which is established by legally sufficient trial evidence.

350.20 Trial by judicial hearing officer

1. Notwithstanding any provision of section 350.10 of this article, in any case where a single judge trial of an information in a local criminal court is authorized or required, the court may, upon agreement of the parties, assign a judicial hearing officer to conduct the trial. Where such assignment is made, the judicial hearing officer shall entertain the case in the same manner as a court and shall:

(a) determine all questions of law;

(b) act as the exclusive trier of all issues of fact; and

(c) render a verdict.

2. In the discharge of this responsibility, the judicial hearing officer shall have the same powers as a judge of the court in which the proceeding is pending. The rules of evidence shall be applicable at a trial conducted by a judicial hearing officer.

3. Any action taken by a judicial hearing officer in the conduct of a trial shall be deemed the action of the court in which the proceeding is pending.

4. This section shall not apply where the single judge trial is of an information at least one count of which charges a class A misdemeanor.

360.10 Trial jury; formation in general

1. A trial jury consists of six jurors, but "alternate jurors" may be selected and sworn pursuant to section 360.35.

2. The panel from which the jury is drawn is formed and selected as prescribed in the uniform district court act, uniform city court act, and uniform justice court act. In the New York City criminal court the panel from which the jury is drawn is formed and selected in the same manner as is prescribed for the formation and selection of a panel in the supreme court in counties within cities having a population of one million or more.

360.40 Trial jury; conduct of jury trial in general

A jury trial of an information must be conducted generally in the same manner as a jury trial of an indictment, and the rules governing preliminary instructions by the court, supervision of the jury, motion practice and other procedural matters involved in the conduct of a jury trial of an indictment are, where appropriate, applicable to the conduct of a jury trial of an information.

360.55 Deliberation and verdict of jury

The provisions of article three hundred ten, governing the deliberation and verdict of a jury upon a jury trial of an indictment in a superior court, are applicable to a jury trial of an information in a local criminal court.

380.20 Sentence required

The court must pronounce sentence in every case where a conviction is entered. If an accusatory instrument contains multiple counts and a conviction is entered on more than one count the court must pronounce sentence on each count.

380.30 Time for pronouncing sentence

1. **In general.** Sentence must be pronounced without unreasonable delay.

2. **Court to fix time.** Upon entering a conviction the court must:

   (a) Fix a date for pronouncing sentence; or

   (b) Fix a date for one of the pre-sentence proceedings specified in article four hundred; or

   (c) Pronounce sentence on the date the conviction is entered in accordance with the provisions of subdivision three.

3. **Sentence on date of conviction.** The court may sentence the defendant at the time the conviction is entered if:

   (a) A pre-sentence report or a fingerprint report is not required; or

   (b) Where any such report is required, the report has been received.

Provided, however, that the court may not pronounce sentence at such time without inquiring as to whether an adjournment is desired by the defendant. Where an adjournment is requested, the defendant must state the purpose thereof and the court may, in its discretion, allow a reasonable time.

4. **Time for pre-sentence proceedings.** The court may conduct one or more of the pre-sentence proceedings specified in article four hundred at any time before sentence is pronounced. Notice of any such proceeding issued after the date for pronouncing sentence has been fixed automatically adjourns the date for pronouncing sentence. In such case the court must fix a date for pronouncing sentence at the conclusion of such proceeding.

380.40   Defendant's presence at sentencing

1. **In general.** The defendant must be personally present at the time sentence is pronounced.

2. **Exception.** Where sentence is to be pronounced for a misdemeanor or for a petty offense, the court may, on motion of the defendant, dispense with the requirement that the defendant be personally present. Any such motion must be accompanied by a waiver, signed and acknowledged by the defendant, reciting the maximum sentence that may be imposed for the offense and stating that the defendant waives the right to be personally present at the time sentence is pronounced.

3. **Corporations.** Sentence may be pronounced against a corporation in the absence of counsel if counsel fails to appear on the date of sentence after reasonable notice thereof.

380.50   Statements at time of sentence

At the time of pronouncing sentence, the court must accord the prosecutor an opportunity to make a statement with respect to any matter relevant to the question of sentence. The court must then accord counsel for the defendant an opportunity to speak on behalf of the defendant. The defendant also has the right to make a statement personally in his own behalf, and before pronouncing sentence the court must ask him whether he wishes to make such a statement.

The court may, either before or after receiving such statements, summarize the factors it considers relevant for the purpose of sentence and afford an opportunity to the defendant or his counsel to comment thereon.

380.60   Authority for the execution of sentence

Except where a sentence of death is pronounced, a certificate of conviction showing the sentence pronounced by the court, or a certified copy thereof, constitutes the authority for execution of the sentence and serves as the order of commitment, and no other warrant, order of commitment or authority is necessary to justify or to require execution of the sentence.

380.70   Minutes of sentence

In any case where a person receives an indeterminate sentence of imprisonment or a reformatory or alternative local reformatory sentence of imprisonment, a certified copy of the stenographic minutes of the sentencing proceeding must be delivered to the person in charge of the institution to which the defendant has been delivered within thirty days from the date such sentence was imposed; provided, however, that a sentence or commitment is not defective by reason of a failure to comply with the provisions of this section.

Judiciary — Court Acts

FAMILY COURT ACT

Selected Articles and Sections of the Family Court Articles of the Judiciary Court Acts

(Full text of the Family Court Act along with notes, commentaries, and amendments may be found in Volume 29A–Part 1 of McKinney's *Consolidated Laws of New York State*)

117. Parts of court

(a) There is hereby established in the family court a "child abuse part." Such part shall be held separate from all other proceedings of the court, and shall have jurisdiction over all proceedings in the family court involving abused children, and shall be charged with the immediate protection of these children. All cases involving abuse shall be originated in or be transferred to this part from other parts as they are made known to the court unless there is or was before the court a proceeding involving any members of the same family or household, in which event the judge who heard said proceeding may hear the case involving abuse. Consistent with its primary purpose, nothing in this section is intended to prevent the child abuse part from hearing other cases.

(b) For every juvenile delinquency proceeding under article three involving an allegation of an act committed by a person which, if done by an adult, would be a crime (i) defined in sections 125.27 (murder in the first degree); 125.25 (murder in the second degree); 135.25 (kidnapping in the first degree); or 150.20 (arson in the first degree) of the penal law committed by a person thirteen, fourteen or fifteen years of age; (ii) defined in sections 120.10 (assault in the first degree); 125.20 (manslaughter in the first degree); 130.25 (rape in the first degree); 130.50 (sodomy in the first degree); 135.20 (kidnapping in the second degree), but only where the abduction involved the use or threat of use of deadly physical force; 150.15 (arson in the second degree); or 160.15 (robbery in the first degree) of the penal law committed by a person thirteen, fourteen, or fifteen years of age; (iii) defined in the penal law as an attempt to commit murder in the first or second degree or kidnapping in the first degree committed by a person thirteen, fourteen or fifteen years of age; (iv) defined in section 140.30 (burglary in the first degree); subdivision one of section 140.25 (burglary in the second degree); or subdivision two of section 160.10 (robbery in the second degree) of the penal law committed by a person fourteen or fifteen years of age; (v) defined in section 120.05 (assault in the second degree) or 160.10 (robbery in the second degree) of the penal law committed by a person fourteen or fifteen years of age but only where there has been a prior finding by a court that such person has previously committed an act which, if committed by an adult, would be the crime of assault in the second degree, robbery in the second degree or any designated felony act specified in clause (i), (ii), or (iii) of this subdivision regardless of the age of such person at the time of the commission of the prior act; or (vi) other than a misdemeanor, committed by a person at least seven but less than sixteen years of age, but only where there has been two prior findings by the court that such person has committed a prior act which, if committed by an adult would be a felony:

(i) There is hereby established in the family court in the city of New York at least one "designated felony act part." Such part or parts shall be held separate from all other proceedings of the court, and shall have jurisdiction over all proceedings involving such an allegation. All such proceedings shall be originated in or be transferred to this part from other parts as they are made known to the court.

(ii) Outside the city of New York, all proceedings involving such an allegation shall have a hearing preference over every other proceeding in the court, except proceedings under article ten.

(c) The appellate division of the supreme court in each department may provide, in accordance with the standards and policies established by the administrative board of the judicial conference, that the family court in counties within its department shall or may be organized into such other parts, if any, as may be appropriate.

153. Subpoena, warrant and other process to compel attendance

The family court may issue a subpoena or in a proper case a warrant or other process to secure or compel the attendance of an adult respondent or child or any other person whose testimony or presence at a hearing or proceeding is deemed by the court to be necessary, and to admit to, fix or accept bail, or parole him pending the completion of the hearing or proceeding. The court is also authorized to issue a subpoena duces tecum in accordance with the applicable provisions of the civil practice act and, upon its effective date, in accordance with the applicable provisions of the CPLR.

153 – a. Warrant of arrest; when and how executed

(a) A warrant of arrest may be executed on any day of the week, and at any hour of the day or night.

(b) Unless encountering physical resistance, flight or other factors rendering normal procedure impractical, the arresting police officer must inform the subject named therein that a warrant for his arrest for attendance at the proceeding designated therein has been issued. Upon request of such subject, the police officer must show him the warrant if he has it in his possession. The officer need not have the warrant in his possession, and, if he has not, he must show it to the subject upon request as soon after the arrest as possible.

(c) In order to effect the arrest, the police officer may use such physical force as is justifiable pursuant to section 35.30 of the penal law.

(d) In order to effect the arrest, the police officer may enter any premises in which he reasonably believes the subject named therein to be present. Before such entry, he must give, or make reasonable effort to give, notice of his authority and purpose to an occupant thereof.

(e) If the officer, after giving such notice, is not admitted, he may enter such premises, and by a breaking if necessary.

153 – b. Service of process request for order of protection

Whenever a petitioner requests an order of protection or temporary order of protection under any article of this act:

(a) the summons and the petition and, if one has been issued, the temporary order of protection, or a copy or copies thereof, may be served on any day of the week, and at any hour of the day or night;

(b) a peace officer, acting pursuant to his special duties, or a police officer may serve the summons and the petition and, if one has been issued, the temporary order of protection.

153 – c. Temporary order of protection

Any person appearing at family court when the court is open requesting a temporary order of protection under any article of this act shall be entitled to file a petition without delay on the same day such person first appears at the family court, and a hearing on that request shall be held on the same day or the next day that the family court is open following the filing of such petition.

154. State-wide process

(a) The family court may send process or other mandates in any matter in which it has jurisdiction into any county of the state for service or execution in like manner and with the same force and effect as similar process or mandates of county courts as provided by law.

(b) In a proceeding to establish paternity or to seek support, the court may send process without the state in the same manner and with the same effect as process sent within the state in the exercise of personal jurisdiction over any person, subject to the jurisdiction of the court under section three hundred one or three hundred two of the civil practice law and rules, notwithstanding that such person is not a resident or domiciliary of the state where:

(1) the child was conceived in this state and the person over whom jurisdiction is sought is a parent or an alleged or probable parent of the child; or

(2) the child resides in the state as a result of the acts or directives of the person over whom jurisdiction is sought; or

(3) the person over whom jurisdiction is sought has resided with the child in this state; or

(4) the person has acknowledged paternity, in writing, or has furnished support for the child while either such person or the child resided in the state; or

(5) the person has filed with the putative father registry maintained by the state department of social services; or

(6) there is any basis consistent with the constitutions of this state or the United States for the exercise of personal jurisdiction.

154 – a.   Service of petition

In every proceeding in family court, a copy of the petition filed therein shall be served upon the respondent at the time of service of process or, if that is not practicable, at the first court appearance by respondent.

155.   Arrested adult

1. If an adult respondent is arrested under this act when the family court is not in session, he shall be taken to the most accessible magistrate and arraigned before him. The production of a warrant issued by the family court, a certificate of warrant, a copy or a certificate of order of protection or an order of protection or of temporary order of protection shall be evidence of the filing of a proper information or petition, and the magistrate shall thereupon hold such respondent, admit to, fix or accept bail, or parole him for hearing before the family court. Subject to the complainant's right of election under section eight hundred twelve or eight hundred forty-seven of this chapter to initiate a proceeding in criminal court, all subsequent proceedings shall be held in the family court.

2. If no warrant, order of protection or temporary order of protection has been issued by the family court, whether or not an information or petition has been filed, and an act alleged to be a family offense as defined in section eight hundred twelve of this act is the basis of an arrest, the magistrate shall permit the complainant to file a petition, information or accusatory instrument and for good cause shown, shall thereupon hold such respondent, admit to, fix or accept bail, or parole such respondent for hearing before the family court or appropriate criminal court as the complainant shall choose in accordance with the provisions of section eight hundred twelve of this act.

155 – a.   Admission to bail

A desk officer in charge at a police station, county jail or police headquarters, or any of his superior officers, may, in such place, take cash bail for his appearance before the family court the next morning from any person arrested pursuant to a warrant issued by the family court; provided that such arrest occurs between eleven o'clock in the morning and eight o'clock the next morning, except that in the city of New York bail shall be taken between two o'clock in the afternoon and eight o'clock the next morning. The amount of such cash bail shall be the amount fixed in the warrant of arrest.

Article 3 — Juvenile Delinquency

301.2 Definitions

As used in this article, the following terms shall have the following meanings:

1. "Juvenile delinquent" means a person over seven and less than sixteen years of age, who, having committed an act that would constitute a crime if committed by an adult, (a) is not criminally responsible for such conduct by reason of infancy, or (b) is the defendant in an action ordered removed from a criminal court to the family court pursuant to article seven hundred twenty-five of the criminal procedure law.

2. "Respondent" means the person against whom a juvenile delinquency petition is filed pursuant to section 310.1 Provided, however, that any act of the respondent required or authorized under this article may be performed by his attorney or law guardian unless expressly provided otherwise.

3. "Detention" means the temporary care and maintenance away from their own homes of children held pursuant to this article, or held pending a hearing for alleged violation of the conditions of release from a school or center of the division for youth, or held pending return to a jurisdiction other than the one in which the child is held, or held pursuant to a securing order of a criminal court if the person named therein as principal is under sixteen years of age.

4. "Secure detention facility" means a facility characterized by physically restricting construction, hardware and procedures.

5. "Non-secure detention facility" means a facility characterized by the absence of physically restricting construction, hardware and procedures.

6. "Fact-finding hearing" means a hearing to determine whether the respondent or respondents committed the crime or crimes alleged in the petition or petitions.

7. "Dispositional hearing" means a hearing to determine whether the respondent requires supervision, treatment or confinement.

8. "Designated felony act" means an act which, if done by an adult, would be a crime: (i) defined in sections 125.27 (murder in the first degree); 125.25 (murder in the second degree); 135.25 (kidnapping in the first degree); or 150.20 (arson in the first degree) of the penal law committed by a person thirteen, fourteen, or fifteen years of age; (ii) defined in sections 120.10 (assault in the first degree); 125.20 (manslaughter in the first degree); 130.35 (rape in the first degree); 130.50 (sodomy in the first degree); 130.70 (aggregated sexual abuse)[1]; 135.20 (kidnapping in the second degree) but only where the abduction involved the use or threat of use of deadly physical force; 150.15 (arson in the second degree) or 160.15 (robbery in the first degree) of the penal law committed by a person thirteen, fourteen or fifteen years of age; (iii) defined in the penal law as an attempt to commit murder in the first or second degree or kidnapping in the first degree committed by a person thirteen, fourteen or fifteen years of age; (iv) defined in section 140.30 (burglary in the first degree); subdivision one of section 140.25 (burglary in the second degree); or subdivision two of section 160.10 (robbery in the second degree) of the penal law committed by a person fourteen or fifteen years of age: (v) defined in section 120.05 (assault in the second degree) or 160.10 (robbery in the second degree) of the penal law committed by a person fourteen or fifteen years of age but only where there has been a prior finding by a court that such person has previously committed an act which, if committed by an adult, would be the crime of assault in the second degree, robbery in the second degree or any designated felony act specified in paragraph (i), (ii), or (iii) of this subdivision regardless of the age of such person at the time of the commission of the prior act; or (vi) other than a misdemeanor committed by a person at least seven but less than sixteen years of age, but only where there has been two prior findings by the court that such person has committed a prior felony.

9. "Designated Class A felony act" means a designated felony act defined in paragraph (i) of subdivision eight.

10. "Secure facility" means a residential facility in which the respondent may be placed under this article, which is characterized by physically restricting construction, hardware and procedures, and is designated as a secure facility by the division for youth.

11. "Restrictive placement" means a placement pursuant to section 353.5.

12. "Presentment agency" means the agency or authority which pursuant to section two hundred fifty-four or two hundred fifty-four-a is responsible for presenting a juvenile delinquency petition.

13. "Incapacitated person" means a respondent who, as a result of mental illness, mental retardation or developmental disability as defined in subdivisions twenty, twenty-one and twenty-two of section 1.03 of the mental hygiene law, lacks capacity to understand the proceedings against him or to assist in his own defense.

14. Any reference in this article to the commission of a crime includes any act which, if done by an adult, would constitute a crime.

301.4. Separability clause

If any clause, sentence, paragraph, section or part of this article shall be adjudged by any court of competent jurisdiction to be invalid, such judgment shall not affect, impair, or invalidate the remainder thereof, but shall be confined in its operation to the clause, sentence, paragraph, section or part thereof directly involved in the controversy in which such judgment shall have been rendered.

302.1. Jurisdiction

1. The family court has exclusive original jurisdiction over any proceeding to determine whether a person is a juvenile delinquent.

2. In determining the jurisdiction of the court the age of such person at the time the delinquent act allegedly was committed is controlling.

302.2. Statute of limitations

A juvenile delinquency proceeding must be commenced within the period of limitation prescribed in section 30.10 of the criminal procedure law or, unless the alleged act is a designated felony as defined in subdivision eight of section 301.2, commenced before the respondent's eighteenth birthday, whichever occurs earlier. When the alleged act constitutes a designated felony as defined in subdivision eight of section 301.2 such proceeding must be commenced within such period of limitation or before the respondent's twentieth birthday, whichever occurs earlier.

302.3. Venue

1. Juvenile delinquency proceedings shall be originated in the county in which the act or acts referred to in the petition allegedly occurred. For purposes of determining venue, article twenty of the criminal procedure law shall apply.

2. Upon motion of the respondent or the appropriate presentment agency the family court in which the proceedings have been originated may order, for good cause shown, that the proceeding be transferred to another county. If the order is issued after motion by the presentment agency, the court may impose such conditions as it deems equitable and appropriate to ensure that the transfer does not subject the respondent to an unreasonable burden in making his defense.

3. Any motion made pursuant to subdivision two by the respondent shall be made within the time prescribed by section 332.2. Any such motion by a presentment agency

must be based upon papers stating the ground therefor and must be made within thirty days from the date that the action was originated unless such time is extended for good cause shown.

4. In cases heard outside of the city of New York, and except for designated felony act petitions, after entering a finding pursuant to subdivision one of section 345.1, and prior to the commencement of the dispositional hearing the court may, in its discretion and for good cause shown, order that the proceeding be transferred to the county in which the respondent resides. The court shall not order such a transfer, however, unless it grants the respondent and the presentment agency an opportunity to state on the record whether each approves or disapproves of such a transfer and the reasons therefor. The court shall take into consideration the provisions of subdivisions two and three of section 340.2 in determining such transfer.

305.2.   Custody by a peace officer or a police officer without a warrant

1. For purposes of this section, the word "officer" means a peace officer or a police officer.

2. An officer may take a child under the age of sixteen into custody without a warrant in cases in which he may arrest a person for a crime under article one hundred forty of the criminal procedure law.

3. If an officer takes such child into custody or if a child is delivered to him under section 305.1, he shall immediately notify the parent or other person legally responsible for the child's care, or if such legally responsible person is unavailable the person with whom the child resides, that the child has been taken into custody.

4. After making every reasonable effort to give notice under subdivision three, the officer shall:

(a) release the child to the custody of his parents or other person legally responsible for his care upon the issuance in accordance with section 307.1 of a family court appearance ticket to the child and the person to whose custody the child is released; or

(b) forthwith and with all reasonable speed take the child directly, and without his first being taken to the police station house, to the family court located in the county in which the act occasioning the taking into custody allegedly was committed, unless the officer determines that it is necessary to question the child, in which case he may take the child to a facility designated by the state court administrator as a suitable place for the questioning of children and there question him for a reasonable period of time; or

(c) take the child to a place certified by the state division for youth as a juvenile detention facility for the reception of children.

5. If such child has allegedly committed a designated felony act as defined in subdivision eight of section 301.2, and the family court in the county is in session, the officer shall forthwith take the child directly to such family court, unless the officer takes the child to a facility for questioning in accordance with paragraph (b) of subdivision four. If such child has not allegedly committed a designated felony act and such family court is in session, the officer shall either forthwith take the child directly to such family court, unless the officer takes the child to a facility for questioning in accordance with paragraph (b) of subdivision four or release the child in accordance with paragraph (a) of subdivision four.

6. In all other cases, and in the absence of special circumstances, the officer shall release the child in accordance with paragraph (a) of subdivision four.

7. A child shall not be questioned pursuant to this section unless he and a person required to be notified pursuant to subdivision three if present, have been advised:

(a) of the child's right to remain silent;

(b) that the statements made by the child may be used in a court of law;

(c) of the child's right to have an attorney present at such questioning; and

(d) of the child's right to have an attorney provided for him without charge if he is indigent.

8. In determining the suitability of questioning and determining the reasonable period of time for questioning such a child, the child's age, the presence or absence of his parents or other persons legally responsible for his care and notification pursuant to subdivision three shall be included among relevant considerations.

307.1. Family court appearance ticket

1. A family court appearance ticket is a written notice issued and subscribed by a peace officer or police officer, a probation service director or his designee or the administrator responsible for operating a detention facility or his designee, directing a child and his parent or other person legally responsible for his care to appear, without security, at a designated probation service on a specified return date in connection with the child's alleged commission of the crime or crimes specified on such appearance ticket. The form of a family court appearance ticket shall be prescribed by rules of the chief administrator of the courts.

2. If the crime alleged to have been committed by the child is a designated felony as defined by subdivision eight of section 301.2, the return date shall be no later than seventy-two hours excluding Saturdays, Sundays and public holidays after issuance of such family court appearance ticket. If the crime alleged to have been committed by such child is not a designated felony, the return date shall be no later than fourteen days after the issuance of such appearance ticket.

3. A copy of the family court appearance ticket shall be forwarded by the issuing person or agency to the complainant, respondent, respondent's parent, the appropriate probation service within twenty-four hours after its issuance.

311.1. The petition; definition and contents

1. A petition originating a juvenile delinquency proceeding is a written accusation by an authorized presentment agency.

2. A petition shall charge at least one crime and may, in addition, charge in separate counts one or more other crimes, provided that all such crimes are joinable in accord with section 311.6.

3. A petition must contain:

(a) the name of the family court in which it is filed;

(b) the title of the action;

(c) the fact that the respondent is a person under sixteen years of age at the time of the alleged act or acts;

(d) a separate accusation or count addressed to each crime charged, if there be more than one;

(e) the precise crime or crimes charged;

(f) a statement in each count that the crime charged was committed in a designated county;

(g) a statement in each count that the crime charged therein was committed on, or on or about, a designated date, or during a designated period of time;

(h) a plain and concise factual statement in each count which, without allegations of an evidentiary nature, asserts facts supporting every element of the crime charged and the respondent's commission thereof with sufficient precision to clearly apprise the respondent of the conduct which is the subject of the accusation;

(i) the name or names, if known, of other persons who are charged as co-respondents in the family court or as adults in a criminal court proceeding in the commission of the crime or crimes charged;

(j) a statement that the respondent requires supervision, treatment or confinement; and

(k) the signature of the appropriate presentment attorney.

4. A petition shall be verified in accordance with the civil practice law and rules and shall conform to the provisions of section 311.2.

5. If the petition alleges that the respondent committed a designated felony act, it shall so state, and the term "designated felony act petition" shall be prominently marked thereon. Certified copies of prior delinquency findings shall constitute sufficient proof of such findings for the purpose of filing a designated felony petition. If all the allegations of a designated felony act are dismissed or withdrawn or the respondent is found to have committed crimes which are not designated felony acts, the term "designated felony act petition" shall be stricken from the petition.

6. The form of petition shall be prescribed by the chief administrator of the courts. A petition shall be entitled "In the Matter of", followed by the name of the respondent.

When an order or removal pursuant to article seven hundred twenty-five of the criminal procedure law is filed with the clerk of the court, such order and those pleadings and proceedings, other than the minutes of any hearing inquiry or trial, grand jury proceeding, or of any plea accepted or entered, held in this action that has not yet been transcribed shall be transferred with it and shall be deemed to be a petition filed pursuant to subdivision one of section 310.1 containing all of the allegations required by this section notwithstanding that such allegations may not be set forth in the manner therein prescribed. Where the order or the grand jury request annexed to the order specifies an act that is a designated felony act, the clerk shall annex to the order a sufficient statement and marking to make it a designated felony act petition. The date such order is filed with the clerk of the court shall be deemed the date a petition was filed under this article. For purposes of service in accord with section 312.1, however, only the order of removal shall be deemed the petition. All minutes of any hearing inquiry or trial held in this action, the minutes of any grand jury proceeding and the minutes of any plea accepted and entered shall be transferred to the family court within thirty days.

311.6. Joinder, severance, and consolidation

1. Two crimes are joinable and may be included as separate counts in the same petition when:

(a) they are based upon the same act or upon the same criminal transaction, as that term is defined in subdivision two; or

(b) even though based upon different criminal transactions, such crimes, or the criminal transactions underlying them, are of such nature that either proof of the first crime would be material and admissible as evidence in chief upon a fact-finding hearing of the second, or proof of the second would be material and admissible as evidence in chief upon a fact-finding hearing of the first; or

(c) even though based upon different criminal transactions, and even though not joinable pursuant to paragraph (b), such crimes are defined by the same or similar statutory provisions and consequently are the same or similar in law.

2. "Criminal transaction" means conduct which establishes at least one crime, and which is comprised of two or more or a group of acts either:

(a) so closely related and connected in point of time and circumstance of commission as to constitute a single criminal incident; or

(b) so closely related in criminal purpose or objective as to constitute elements or integral parts of a single criminal venture.

3. In any case where two or more crimes or groups of crimes charged in a petition are based upon different criminal transactions, and where their joinability rests solely upon the fact that such crimes, or as the case may be at least one offense of each group, are the same or similar in law, as prescribed in paragraph (c) of subdivision one, the court, in the interest of justice and for good cause shown, may upon application of either the respondent or the presentment agency order than any one of such crimes or groups of crimes be tried separately from the other or others, or that two or more thereof be tried together but separately from two or more others thereof. Such application must be made within the period prescribed in section 332.2.

4. When two or more petitions against the same respondent charge different crimes of a kind that are joinable in a single petition pursuant to subdivision one, the court may, upon application of either the presentment agency or respondent order that such petitions be consolidated and treated as a single petition for trial purposes. Such application must be made within the period prescribed in section 332.2. If the respondent requests consolidation with respect to crimes which are, pursuant to paragraph (a) of subdivision one, of a kind that are joinable in a single petition by reason of being based upon the same act or criminal transaction, the court must order such consolidation unless good cause to the contrary be shown.

341.2. Presence of respondent and his parent

1. The respondent and his counsel or law guardian shall be personally present at any hearing under this article and at the initial appearance.

2. If a respondent conduct himself in so disorderly and disruptive a manner that the hearing cannot be carried on with him in the courtroom, the court may order a recess for the purpose of enabling his parent or other person responsible for his care and his law guardian or counsel to exercise full efforts to assist the respondent to conduct himself so as to permit the proceedings to resume in an orderly manner. If such efforts fail, the respondent may be removed from the courtroom if, after he is warned by the court that he will be removed, he continues such disorderly and disruptive conduct. Such time shall not extend beyond the minimum period necessary to restore order.

3. The respondent's parent or other person responsible for his care shall be present at any hearing under this article and at the initial appearance. However, the court shall not be prevented from proceeding by the absence of such parent or person if reasonable and substantial effort has been made to notify such parent or other person and if the respondent and his law guardian or counsel are present.

343.1. Rules of evidence; testimony given by children

1. Any person may be a witness in a delinquency proceeding unless the court finds that, by reason of infancy or mental disease or defect, he does not possess sufficient intelligence or capacity to justify reception of his evidence.

2. Every witness more than twelve years old may testify only under oath unless the court is satisfied that such witness cannot, as a result of mental disease or defect, understand the nature of an oath. A child less than twelve years old may not testify under oath unless the court is satisfied that he understands the nature of an oath. If the court is not so satisifed, such child or such witness over twelve years old who cannot, as a result of mental disease or defect, understand the nature of an oath may nevertheless be permitted to give unsworn evidence if the court is satisfied that the witness possesses sufficient intelligence and capacity to justify the reception thereof.

3. A respondent may not be found to be delinquent solely upon the unsworn evidence given pursuant to subdivision two.

343.2. Rules of evidence; corroboration of accomplice testimony

1. A respondent may not be found to be delinquent upon the testimony of an accomplice unsupported by corroborative evidence tending to connect the respondent with the commission of the crime or crimes charged in the petition.

2. An "accomplice" means a witness in a juvenile delinquency proceeding who, according to evidence adduced in such proceeding, may reasonably be considered to have participated in:

   (a) the crime charged; or

   (b) a crime based on the same or some of the same facts or conduct which constitutes the crime charged in the petition.

3. A witness who is an accomplice as defined in subdivision two is no less such because a proceeding, conviction or finding of delinquency against him would be barred or precluded by some defense or exemption such as infancy, immunity or previous prosecution amounting to a collateral impediment to such proceeding, conviction or finding, not affecting the conclusion that such witness engaged in the conduct constituting the crime with the mental state required for the commission thereof.

343.3. Rules of evidence; identification by means of previous recognition in absence of present identification

1. In any juvenile delinquency proceeding in which the respondent's commission of a crime is in issue, testimony as provided in subdivision two may be given by a witness when:

   (a) such witness testifies that:

   (i) he observed the person claimed by the presentment agency to be the respondent either at the time and place of the commission of the crime or upon some other occasion relevant to the case; and

   (ii) on a subsequent occasion he observed, under circumstances consistent with such rights as an accused person may derive under the constitution of this state or of the United States, a person whom he reconized as the same person whom he had observed on the first incriminating occasion; and

   (iii) he is unable at the proceeding to state, on the basis of present recollection, whether or not the respondent is the person in question; and

   (b) it is established that the respondent is in fact the person whom the witness observed and recognized on the second occasion. Such fact may be established by testimony of another person or persons to whom the witness promptly declared his recognition on such occasion.

2. Under circumstances prescribed in subdivision one, such witness may testify at the proceeding that the person whom he observed the recognized on the second occasion is the same person whom he observed on the first or incriminating occasion. Such testimony, together with the evidence that the respondent is in fact the person whom the witness observed and recognized on the second occasion, constitutes evidence in chief.

343.4. Rules of evidence; identification by means of previous recognition, in addition to present identification

In any juvenile delinquency proceeding in which the respondent's commission of a crime is in issue, a witness who testifies that: (a) he observed the person claimed by the presentment agency to be the respondent either at the time and place of the commission of the crime or upon some other occasion relevant to the case, and (b) on the basis of present recollection, the respondent is the person in question, and (c) on a subsequent occasion he observed the respondent, under circumstances consistent with such rights as an accused person may derive under the constitution of this state or of the United States, and then also recognized him as the same person whom he had observed on the first or incriminating occasion, may, in addition to making an identification of the respondent at the delinquency proceeding on the basis of present recollection as the person whom he observed on the first or incriminating occasion, also describe his previous recognition of the respondent and testify that the person whom he observed on such second occasion is the same person whom he had observed on the first or incriminating occasion. Such testimony constitutes evidence in chief.

343.5. Rules of evidence; impeachment of own witness by proof of prior contradictory statement

1. When, upon examination by the party who called him, a witness in a delinquency proceeding gives testimony upon a material issue of the case which tends to disprove the position of such party, such party may introduce evidence that such witness has previously made either a written statement signed by him or an oral statement under oath contradictory to such testimony.

2. Evidence concerning a prior contradictory statement introduced pursuant to subdivision one may be received only for the purpose of impeaching the credibility of the witness with respect to his testimony upon the subject, and does not constitute evidence in chief.

3. When a witness has made a prior signed or sworn statement contradictory to his testimony in a delinquency proceeding upon a material issue of the case, but his testimony does not tend to disprove the position of the party who called him and elicited such testimony, evidence that the witness made such prior statement is not admissible, and such party may not use such prior statement for the purpose of refreshing the recollection of the witness in a manner that discloses its contents to the court.

344.2. Rules of evidence; statements of respondent; corroboration

1. Evidence of a written or oral confession, admission, or other statement made by a respondent with respect to his participation or lack of participation in the crime charged, may not be received in evidence against him in a juvenile delinquency proceeding if such statement was involuntarily made.

2. A confession, admission or other statement is "involuntarily made" by a respondent when it is obtained from him:

(a) by any person by the use or threatened use of physical force upon the respondent or another person, or by means of any other improper conduct or undue pressure which impaired the respondent's physical or mental condition to the extent of undermining his ability to make a choice whether or not to make a statement; or

(b) by a public servant engaged in law enforcement activity or by a person then acting under his direction or in cooperation with him:

(i) by means of any promise or statement of fact, which promise or statement creates a substantial risk that the respondent might falsely incriminate himself; or

(ii) in violation of such rights as the respondent may derive from the constitution of this state or of the United States; or

(iii) in violation of section 305.2.

3. A child may not be found to be delinquent based on the commission of any crime solely upon evidence of a confession or admission made by him without additional proof that the crime charged has been committed.

Penal Law

PART ONE—GENERAL PROVISIONS

TITLE A—GENERAL PURPOSES, RULES OF CONSTRUCTION, AND DEFINITIONS

TITLE B—PRINCIPLES OF CRIMINAL LIABILITY

TITLE C—DEFENSES

PART TWO—SENTENCES

TITLE E—SENTENCES

PART THREE—SPECIFIC OFFENSES

TITLE G—ANTICIPATORY OFFENSES

TITLE H—OFFENSES AGAINST THE PERSON INVOLVING PHYSICAL INJURY, SEXUAL CONDUCT, RESTRAINT, AND INTIMIDATION

PART FOUR—ADMINISTRATIVE PROVISIONS

TITLE W—PROVISIONS RELATING TO FIREARMS, FIREWORKS, PORNOGRAPHY EQUIPMENT AND VEHICLES USED IN THE TRANSPORTATION OF GAMBLING RECORDS

TITLE X—ORGANIZED CRIME CONTROL ACT

TITLE Z—LAWS REPEALED; TIME OF TAKING EFFECT

Selected Articles and Sections of the Penal Law

(Full text of the Penal Law along with notes, commentaries, and amendments may be found in Volume 39 of McKinney's *Consolidated Laws of New York State*)

10.00 Definitions of terms of general use in this chapter

Except where different meanings are expressly specified in subsequent provisions of this chapter, the following terms have the following meanings:

1. "Offense" means conduct for which a sentence to a term of imprisonment or to a fine is provided by any law of this state or by any law, local law or ordinance of a political subdivision of this state, or by any order, rule or regulation of any governmental instrumentality authorized by law to adopt the same.

2. "Traffic infraction" means any offense defined as "traffic infraction" by section one hundred fifty-five of the vehicle and traffic law.

3. "Violation" means an offense, other than a "traffic infraction," for which a sentence to a term of imprisonment in excess of fifteen days cannot be imposed.

4. "Misdemeanor" means an offense, other than a "traffic infraction," for which a sentence to a term of imprisonment in excess of fifteen days may be imposed, but for which a sentence to a term of imprisonment in excess of one year cannot be imposed.

5. "Felony" means an offense for which a sentence to a term of imprisonment in excess of one year may be imposed.

6. "Crime" means a misdemeanor or a felony.

7. "Person" means a human being, and where appropriate, a public or private corporation, an unincorporated association, a partnership, a government or a governmental instrumentality.

8. "Possess" means to have physical possession or otherwise to exercise dominion or control over tangible property.

9. "Physical injury" means impairment of physical condition or substantial pain.

10. "Serious physical injury" means physical injury which creates a substantial risk of death, or which causes death or serious and protracted disfigurement, protracted impairment of health or protracted loss of impairment of the function of any bodily organ.

11. "Deadly physical force" means physical force which, under the circumstances in which it is used, is readily capable of causing death or other serious physical injury.

12. "Deadly weapon" means any loaded weapon from which a shot, readily capable of producing death or other serious physical injury, may be discharged, or a switchblade knife, gravity knife, pilum ballistic knife, dagger, billy, blackjack, or metal knuckles.

13. "Dangerous instrument" means any instrument, article or substance, including a "vehicle" as that term is defined in this section, which, under the circumstances in which it is used, attempted to be used or threatened to be used, is readily capable of causing death or other serious physical injury.

14. "Vehicle" means a "motor vehicle", "trailer" or "semi-trailer," as defined in the vehicle and traffic law, any snowmobile as defined in the parks and recreation law, any aircraft, or any vessel equipped for propulsion by mechanical means or by sail.

15. "Public servant" means (a) any public officer or employee of the state or of any political subdivision thereof or of any governmental instrumentality within the state, or (b) any person exercising the functions of any such public officer or employee. The term public servant includes a person who has been elected or designated to become a public servant.

16. "Juror" means any person who is a member of any jury, including a grand jury, impaneled by any court in this state or by any public servant authorized by law to impanel

a jury. The term juror also includes a person who has been drawn or summoned to attend as a prospective juror.

17. "Benefit" means any gain or advantage to the beneficiary and includes any gain or advantage to a third person pursuant to the desire or consent of the beneficiary.

18. "Juvenile offender" means (1) a person thirteen years old who is criminally responsible for acts constituting murder in the second degree as defined in subdivisions one and two of this section 125.25 of this chapter and (2) a person fourteen or fifteen years old who is criminally responsible for acts constituting the crimes defined in subdivisions one and two of section 125.25 (murder in the second degree) and in subdivision three of such section provided that the underlying crime for the murder charge is one for which such person is criminally responsible; section 135.25 (kidnapping in the first degree); 150.20 (arson in the first degree); subdivisions one and two of section 120.10 (assault in the first degree); 125.20 (manslaughter in the first degree); subdivisions one and two of section 130.35 (rape in the first degree); subdivisions one and two of section 130.50 (sodomy in the first degree); 130.70 (aggravated sexual abuse); 140.30 (burglary in the first degree); subdivision one of section 140.25 (burglary in the second degree); 150.15 (arson in the second degree); 160.15 (robbery in the first degree); or subdivision two of section 160.10 (robbery in the second degree) of this chapter; or defined in this chapter as an attempt to commit murder in the second degree or kidnapping in the first degree.

15.00 Culpability; definitions of terms

The following definitions are applicable to this chapter:

1. "Act" means a bodily movement.

2. "Voluntary act" means a bodily movement performed consciously as a result of effort or determination, and includes the possession of property if the actor was aware of his physical possession or control thereof for a sufficient period to have been able to terminate it.

3. "Omission" means a failure to perform an act as to which a duty of performance is imposed by law.

4. "Conduct" means an act or omission and its accompanying mental state.

5. "To act" means either to perform an act or to omit to perform an act.

6. "Culpable mental state" means "intentionally" or "knowingly" or "recklessly" or with "criminal negligence," as these terms are defined in section 15.05.

15.05 Culpability; definitions of culpable mental states

The following definitions are applicable to this chapter:

1. "Intentionally." A person acts intentionally with respect to a result or to conduct described by a statute defining an offense when his conscious objective it to cause such result or to engage in such conduct.

2. "Knowingly." A person acts knowingly with respect to conduct or to a circumstance described by a statute defining an offense when he is aware that his conduct is of such nature or that such circumstance exists.

3. "Recklessly." A person acts recklessly with respect to a result or to a circumstance described by a statute defining an offense when he is aware of and consciously disregards a substantial and unjustifiable risk that such result will occur or that such circumstance exists. The risk must be of such nature and degree that disregard thereof constitutes a gross deviation from the standard of conduct that a reasonable person would observe in the situation. A person who creates such a risk but is unaware thereof solely by reason of voluntary intoxication also acts recklessly with respect thereto.

4. "Criminal negligence." A person acts with criminal negligence with respect to a result or to a circumstance described by a statute defining an offense when he fails to perceive a substantial and unjustifiable risk that such result will occur or that such circumstance exists. The risk must be of such nature and degree that the failure to perceive it constitutes a gross deviation from the standard of care that a reasonable person would observe in the situation.

15.10 Requirements for criminal liability in general and for offenses of strict liability and mental culpability

The minimal requirement for criminal liability is the performance by a person of conduct which includes a voluntary act or the omission to perform an act which he is physically capable of performing. If such conduct is all that is required for commission of a particular offense, or if an offense or some material element thereof does not require a culpable mental state on the part of the actor, such offense is one of "strict liability." If a culpable mental state on the part of the actor is required with respect to every material element of an offense, such offense is one of "mental culpability."

15.20 Effect of ignorance or mistake upon liability

1. A person is not relieved of criminal liability for conduct because he engages in such conduct under a mistaken belief of fact, unless:

(a) Such factual mistake negatives the culpable mental state required for the commission of an offense; or

(b) The statute defining the offense or a statute related thereto expressly provides that such factual mistake constitutes a defense or exception; or

(c) Such factual mistake is a kind that supports a defense of justification as defined in article thirty-five of this chapter.

2. A person is not relieved of criminal liability for conduct because he engages in such conduct under a mistaken belief that it does not, as a matter of law, constitute an offense, unless such mistaken belief is founded upon an official statement of the law contained in (a) a statute or other enactment, or (b) an administrative order or grant of permission, or (c) a judicial decision of a state or federal court, or (d) an interpretation of the statute or law relating to the offense, officially made or issued by a public servant, agency or body legally charged or empowered with the responsibility or privilege of administering, enforcing or interpreting such statute or law.

3. Notwithstanding the use of the term "knowingly" in any provision of this chapter defining an offense in which the age of a child is an element thereof, knowledge by the defendant of the age of such child is not an element of any such offense and it is not, unless expressly so provided, a defense to a prosecution therefor that the defendant did not know the age of the child or believed such age to be the same as or greater than that specified in the statute.

15.25 Effects of intoxication upon liability

Intoxication is not, as such, a defense to a criminal charge; but in any prosecution for an offense, evidence of intoxication of the defendant may be offered by the defendant whenever it is relevant to negative an element of the crime charged.

400.00 Licenses to carry, possess, repair, and dispose of firearms

1. Eligibility. No license shall be issued or renewed pursuant to this section except by the licensing officer, and then only after investigation and finding that all statements in a proper application for a license are true. No license shall be issued or renewed except for an applicant (a) of good moral character; (b) who has not been convicted anywhere of a

felony or a serious offense; (c) who has stated whether he has ever suffered any mental illness or been confined to any hospital or institution, public or private, for mental illness; and (d) concerning whom no good cause exists for the denial of the license. No person shall engage in the business of gunsmith or dealer in firearms unless licensed pursuant to this section. An applicant to engage in such business shall also be a citizen of the United States, more than twenty-one years of age and maintain a place of business in the city or county where the license is issued. For such business, if the applicant is a firm or partnership, each member thereof shall comply with all of the requirements set forth in this subdivision and if the applicant is a corporation, each officer thereof shall so comply.

2. Types of licenses. A license for gunsmith or dealer in firearms shall be issued to engage in such business. A license for a pistol or revolver shall be issued to (a) have and possess in his dwelling by a householder; (b) have and possess in his place of business by a merchant or storekeeper; (c) have and carry concealed while so employed by a messenger employed by a banking institution or express company; (d) have and carry concealed while so employed by a regular employee of an institution of the state, or of any county, city, town or village, under control of a commissioner of correction of the city or any warden, superintendent or head keeper of any state prison, penitentiary, workhouse, county jail or other institution for the detention of persons convicted or accused of crime or held as witnesses in criminal cases, provided that application is made therefor by such commissioner, warden, superintendent or head keeper; (e) have and carry concealed, without regard to employment or place of possession, by any person when proper cause exists for the issuance thereof; and (f) have, possess, collect and carry antique pistols which are defined as follows: (i) any single shot, muzzle loading pistol with a matchlock, flintlock, percussion cap, or similar type of ignition system manufactured in or before 1898, which is not designed for using rimfire or conventional centerfire fixed ammunition; and (ii) any replica of any pistol described in clause (i) hereof if such replica—

(1) is not designed or redesigned for using rimfire or conventional centerfire fixed ammunition, or

(2) uses rimfire or conventional centerfire fixed ammunition which is no longer manufactured in the United States and which is not readily available in the ordinary channels of commercial trade.

3. Applications. Applications shall be made and renewed, in the case of a license to carry or possess a pistol or revolver, to the licensing officer in the city or county, as the case may be, where the applicant resides, is principally employed or has his principal place of business as merchant or storekeeper; and, in the case of a license as gunsmith or dealer in firearms, to the licensing officer where such place of business is located. Blank applications shall, except in the city of New York, be approved as to form by the superintendent of state police. An application shall state the full name, date of birth, residence, present occupation of each person or individual signing the same, whether or not he is a citizen of the United States, whether or not he complies with each requirement for eligibility specified in subdivision one of this section and such other facts as may be required to show the good character, competency and integrity of each person or individual signing the application. An application shall be signed and verified by the applicant. Each individual signing an application shall submit one photograph of himself and a duplicate for each required copy of the application. Such photographs shall have been taken within thirty days prior to filing the application. In case of a license as gunsmith or dealer in firearms, the photographs submitted shall be two inches square, and the application shall also state the previous occupation of each individual signing the same and the location of the place of such business, or of the bureau, agency, subagency, office or branch office for which the license is sought, specifying the name of the city, town or village, indicating the street and number and otherwise giving such apt description as to point out reasonably the location thereof. In such case, if the applicant is a firm, partnership or corporation, its name, date and place of formation, and principal place of business shall be stated. For such firm or partnership,

the application shall be signed and verified by each individual composing or intending to compose the same, and for such corporation, by each officer thereof.

4. Investigation. Before a license is issued or renewed, there shall be an investigation of all statements required in the application by the duly constituted police authorities of the locality where such application is made. For that purpose, the records of the department of mental hygiene concerning previous or present mental illness of the applicant shall be available for inspection by the investigating officer of the police authority. In order to ascertain any previous criminal record, the investigating officer shall take the fingerprints and physical descriptive data in quadruplicate of each individual by whom the application is signed and verified. Two copies of such fingerprints shall be taken on standard fingerprint cards eight inches square, and one copy may be taken on a card supplied for that purpose by the federal bureau of investigation. When completed, one standard card shall be forwarded to and retained by the division of criminal identification, department of correction, at Albany. A search of the files of such division and written notification of the results of the search to the investigating officer shall be made without unnecessary delay. Thereafter, such division shall notify the licensing officer and the executive department, division of state police, Albany, of any criminal record of the applicant filed therein subsequent to the search of its files. A second standard card, or the one supplied by the federal bureau of investigation, as the case may be, shall be forwarded to that bureau at Washington with a request that the files of the bureau be searched and notification of the results of the search be made to the investigating police authority. The failure or refusal of the federal bureau of investigation to make the fingerprint check provided for in this section shall not constitute the sole basis for refusal to issue a permit pursuant to the provisions of this section. Of the remaining two fingerprint cards, one shall be filed with the executive department, division of state police, Albany, within ten days after issuance of the license, and the other remain on file with the investigating police authority. No such fingerprints may be inspected by any person other than a peace officer, except on order of a judge or justice of a court of record either upon notice to the licensee or without notice, as the judge or justice may deem appropriate. Upon completion of the investigation, the police authority shall report the results to the licensing officer without unnecessary delay.

4-a. Processing of license applications. Applications for licenses shall be accepted for processing by the licensing officer at the time of presentment. Except upon written notice to the applicant specifically stating the reasons for any delay, in each case the licensing officer shall act upon any application for a license pursuant to this section within six months of the date of presentment of such an application to the appropriate authority. Such delay may only be for good cause and with respect to the applicant. In acting upon an application, the licensing officer shall either deny the application for reasons specifically and concisely stated in writing or grant the application and issue the license applied for.

5. Filing of approved applications. The application for any license, if granted, shall be a public record. Such application shall be filed by the licensing officer with the clerk of the county of issuance, except that in the city of New York and, in the counties of Nassau and Suffolk, the licensing officer shall designate the place of filing in the appropriate division, bureau or unit of the police department thereof, and in the county of Suffolk the county clerk is hereby authorized to transfer all records or applications relating to firearms to the licensing authority of that county. Upon application by a licensee who has changed his place of residence, such records or applications shall be transferred to the appropriate officer at the licensee's new place of residence. A duplicate copy of such application shall be filed by the licensing officer in the executive department, division of state police, Albany, within ten days after issuance of the license. Nothing in this subdivision shall be constructed to change the expiration date or term of such licenses if otherwise provided for in law.

6. License: validity. Any license issued pursuant to this section shall be valid notwithstanding the provisions of any local law or ordinance. No license shall be transferable to

any other person or premises. A license to carry or possess a pistol or revolver, not otherwise limited as to place or time of possession, shall be effective throughout the state, except that the same shall not be valid within the city of New York unless a special permit granting validity is issued by the police commissioner of that city. Such license to carry or possess shall be valid within the city of New York in the absence of a permit issued by the police commissioner of that city, provided that (a) the firearms covered by such license are being transported by the licensee in a locked container; and (b) the trip through the city of New York is continuous and uninterrupted. A license as gunsmith or dealer in firearms shall not be valid outside the city or county, as the case may be, where issued.

7. License: form. Any license issued pursuant to this section shall, except in the city of New York, be approved as to form by the superintendent of state police. A license to carry or possess a pistol or revolver shall have attached the licensee's photograph, and a coupon which shall be removed and retained by any person disposing of a firearm to the licensee. Such license shall specify the weapon covered by calibre, make, model, manufacturer's name and serial number, or if none, by any other distinguishing number or identification mark, and shall indicate whether issued to carry on the person or possess on the premises, and if on the premises shall also specify the place where the licensee shall possess the same. If such license is issued to an alien, or to a person not a citizen of and usually a resident in the state, the licensing officer shall state in the license the particular reason for the issuance and the names of the persons certifying to the good character of the applicant. Any license as gunsmith or dealer in firearms shall mention and describe the premises for which it is issued and shall be valid only for such premises.

8. License: exhibition and display. Every licensee while carrying a pistol or revolver shall have on his person a license to carry the same. Every person licensed to possess a pistol or revolver on particular premises shall have the license for the same on such premises. Upon demand, the license shall be exhibited for inspection to any peace officer. A license as gunsmith or dealer in firearms shall be prominently displayed on the licensed premises. Failure of any licensee to so exhibit or display his license, as the case may be, shall be presumptive evidence that he is not duly licensed.

9. License: amendment. Elsewhere than in the city of New York, a person licensed to carry or possess a pistol or revolver may apply at any time to his licensing officer for amendment of his license to include one or more such weapons or to cancel weapons held under license. If granted, a record of the amendment describing the weapons involved shall be filed by the licensing officer in the executive department, division of state police, Albany. Notification of any change of residence shall be made in writing by any licensee within ten days after such change occurs, and a record of such change shall be inscribed by such licensee on the reverse side of his license. Elsewhere than in the city of New York, and in the counties of Nassau and Suffolk, such notification shall be made to the executive department, division of state police, Albany, and in the city of New York to the police commissioner of that city, and in the county of Nassau to the police commissioner of that county, and in the county of Suffolk to the licensing officer of that county, who shall, within ten days after such notification shall be received by him, give notice in writing of such change to the executive department, division of state police, at Albany.

10. License: expiration and renewal. Any license for gunsmith or dealer in firearms and, in the city of New York and the counties of Nassau and Suffolk, any license to carry or possess a pistol or revolver, issued at any time pursuant to this section or prior to the first day of July, nineteen hundred sixty-three and not limited to expire on an earlier date fixed in the license, shall expire not more than three years after the date of issuance. Elsewhere than in the city of New York and the counties of Nassau and Suffolk, any license to carry or possess a pistol or revolver, issued at any time pursuant to this section or prior to the first day of July, nineteen hundred sixty-three and not previously revoked or cancelled, shall be in force and effect until revoked as herein provided. Any application to renew a license that has not previously expired, been revoked or cancelled shall thereby extend the

term of the license until disposition of the application by the licensing officer. In the case of a license for gunsmith or dealer in firearms, in counties having a population of less than two hundred thousand inhabitants, photographs and fingerprints shall be submitted on original applications and upon renewal thereafter only at six year intervals. Upon satisfactory proof that a currently valid original license has been despoiled, lost or otherwise removed from the possession of the licensee and upon application containing an additional photograph of the licensee, the licensing officer shall issue a duplicate license.

11. License: revocation. The conviction of a licensee anywhere of a felony or serious offense shall operate as a revocation of the license.

A license may be revoked and cancelled at any time in the city of New York, and in the counties of Nassau and Suffolk, by the licensing officer, and elsewhere than in the city of New York by any judge or justice of a court of record. The official revoking a license shall give written notice thereof without unnecessary delay to the executive department, division of state police, Albany, and shall also notify immediately the duly constituted police authorities of the locality.

12. Records required of gunsmiths and dealers in firearms. Any person licensed as gunsmith or dealer in firearms shall keep a record book approved as to form, except in the city of New York, by the superintendent of state police. In the record book shall be entered at the time of every transaction involving a firearm the date, name, age, occupation and residence of any person from whom a firearm is received or to whom a firearm is delivered, and the calibre, make, model, manufacturer's name and serial number, of if none, any other distinguishing number or identification mark on such firearm. Before delivering a firearm to any person, the licensee shall require him to produce either a license valid under this section to carry or possess the same, or proof of lawful authority as a peace officer or other exempt person pursuant to section 265.20. In addition, before delivering a firearm to a peace officer, the licensee shall verify that person's status as a peace officer with the division of state police. After completing the foregoing, the licensee shall remove and retain the attached coupon and enter in the record book the date of such license, number, if any, and name of the licensing officer, in the case of the holder of a license to carry or possess, or the shield or other number, if any, assignment and department or unit, in the case of an exempt person. The original transaction report shall be forwarded to the division of state police within ten days of delivering a firearm to any peace officer, and a duplicate copy shall be kept by the licensee. The record book shall be maintained on the premises mentioned and described in the license and shall be open at all reasonable hours for inspection by any peace officer, acting pursuant to his special duties, or police officer. In the event of cancellation or revocation of the license for gunsmith or dealer in firearms, or discontinuance of business by a licensee, such record book shall be immediately surrendered to the licensing officer in the city of New York, and in the counties of Nassau and Suffolk, and elsewhere in the state to the executive department, division of state police.

12-a. State police regulations applicable to licensed gunsmiths engaged in the business of assembling or manufacturing firearms. The superintendent of state police is hereby authorized to issue such rules and regulations as he deems reasonably necessary to prevent the manufacture and assembly of unsafe firearms in the state. Such rules and regulations shall establish safety standards in regard to the manufacture and assembly of firearms in the state, including specifications as to materials and parts used, the proper storage and shipment of firearms, and minimum standards of quality control. Regulations issued by the state police pursuant to this subdivision shall apply to any person licensed as a gunsmith under this section engaged in the business of manufacturing or assembling firearms, and any violation thereof shall subject the licensee to revocation of license pursuant to subdivision eleven of this section.

13. Expenses. The expense of providing a licensing officer with blank applications, licenses and record books for carrying out the provisions of this section shall be a charge against the county, and in the city of New York against the city.

14. Fees. In the city of New York and the county of Nassau, the annual license fee shall be twenty-five dollars for gunsmiths and fifty dollars for dealers in firearms. In such city, the city council and in the county of Nassau the Board of Supervisors shall fix the fee to be charged for a license to carry or possess a pistol or revolver and provide for the disposition of such fees. Elsewhere in the state, the licensing officer shall collect and pay into the county treasury the following fees: for each license to carry or possess a pistol or revolver, not less than three dollars nor more than ten dollars as may be determined by the legislative body of the county; for each amendment thereto, three dollars, and five dollars in the county of Suffolk:[2] and for each license issued to a gunsmith or dealer in firearms, ten dollars. The fee for a duplicate license shall be five dollars. The fee for processing a license transfer between counties shall be five dollars. The fee for processing a license for a qualified retired police officer as defined under subdivision thirty-four of section 1.20 of the criminal procedure law shall be waived in all counties throughout the state.

15. Any violation by any person of any provision of this section is a class A misdemeanor.

16. Unlawful disposal. No person shall except as otherwise authorized pursuant to law dispose of any firearm unless he is licensed as gunsmith or dealer in firearms.

PROMOTION EXAM QUESTIONS

1. A directed verdict is made by a court when

   (A) the facts are not disputed
   (B) the defendant's motion for a directed verdict has been denied
   (C) there is no question of the law involved
   (D) neither party has moved for a directed verdict

2. A pleading titled "Smith vs Jones et al." indicates

   (A) two plaintiffs
   (B) two defendants
   (C) more than two defendants
   (D) unknown defendants

3. A District Attorney makes out a "prima facie" case when

   (A) there is proof of guilt beyond a reasonable doubt
   (B) the evidence is sufficient to convict in the absence of rebutting evidence
   (C) the prosecution presents more evidence than the defense
   (D) the defendant fails to take the stand

4. A proper or legal attestation is called a (an)

   (A) verification
   (B) authentication
   (C) oath
   (D) jurat

5. Insolent and contemptuous behavior to a judge during a court of record proceeding is punishable as

   (A) civil contempt
   (B) criminal contempt
   (C) disorderly conduct
   (D) disorderly person

6. When a judge asks the court attendant for a copy of "McKinney's, " he wants

   (A) federal laws
   (B) Consolidated Laws of N.Y. State
   (C) local ordinances
   (D) rules of evidence

7. A writing authorizing one to act for another is known as

   (A) verification
   (B) Power of Attorney
   (C) a Certification
   (D) substituted service

8. Statutes which fix the time within which particular actions must be instituted or otherwise be barred, are known as

   (A) Statutes of Frauds
   (B) Exclusionary Acts
   (C) Statutes of Limitation
   (D) Unconsolidated Laws

9. When a jury has reached a verdict, the presence of the defendant is required in

   (A) all cases
   (B) all criminal cases
   (C) civil cases only
   (D) felony cases

10. The basic distinction between an affidavit and a deposition is that

    (A) one is sworn
    (B) the latter is sworn written testimony
    (C) the former is sworn written testimony
    (D) the latter is unsigned

11. Arraignment is best defined as the

    (A) placing of the accused in custody
    (B) opportunity of giving bail
    (C) calling of the accused before the court to answer a charge
    (D) justification for an arrest

12. The subject matter or property with which the action is concerned is known as the

   (A) fee simple
   (B) freehold
   (C) res
   (D) abstract of title

13. An *ex parte* motion is one which

   (A) requires the adversary to appear and be heard
   (B) is made by the court in the absence of either party to the litigation
   (C) is made without notice to an adversary
   (D) is made by a person not a party to a litigation

14. When counsel in a trial takes "exception" to a court ruling, it means that

   (A) an adjournment is required before additional evidence is introduced
   (B) he or she formally objects to the court ruling
   (C) he or she withdraws his or her original objection
   (D) he or she wishes to give reasons for original objections

15. Direct appeals from the lower courts are taken to the Court of Appeals when

   (A) actions involve constitutional questions
   (B) the rights of children are involved
   (C) exceptions to court rulings have been formally recorded
   (D) nonresidents are involved

16. The right of the state to take private property for public use is known as

   (A) ejectment
   (B) easement
   (C) eminent domain
   (D) franchise

17. The purpose of the "Affidavit of Service" on the back of a summons is to

   (A) verify the personal service of summons on an individual or a corporation
   (B) validate the nature of the action
   (C) make effective the date of the commencement of the action
   (D) stop the running of the statute of limitations.

18. Prosecution of all felonies in County Courts must be by

   (A) petition
   (B) information
   (C) summons
   (D) indictment

19. A jury verdict in a criminal case must be returned by

   (A) at least $5/6$ of the jurors
   (B) at least 10 out of 12 jurors
   (C) the majority of the jurors
   (D) all the jurors

20. "Polling the jury" means

   (A) challenging the jury because of bias
   (B) requiring each juror to declare his or her individual verdict before it is legally recorded
   (C) selecting the jury
   (D) waive of trial by jury

21. Rules of procedure as to selection, drawing, and empaneling of jurors are made by the

   (A) Appellate Division of 1st and 2nd Departments
   (B) County Clerks
   (C) County Jury Board
   (D) Court of Judiciary

22. Subject to certain conditions, the one of the following persons who may be permitted to testify in a criminal case without being sworn, is a (an)

   (A) adult over 70 years of age
   (B) justice of a court of record
   (C) court attendant who witnessed a criminal contempt in court
   (D) child under 12 years of age

23. The distinction between a criminal contempt and a civil contempt is

   (A) one occurs in a court of record
   (B) one is punishable by jail
   (C) one is remedial in nature
   (D) one occurs in a criminal court

24. A witness who has conscientious scruples against taking an oath

    (A) shall not be permitted to testify
    (B) may solemnly affirm to tell the truth instead of taking an oath
    (C) may testify if the testimony is corroborated by further evidence
    (D) may testify only in special proceedings

25. The venue in an action refers to the

    (A) place of trial
    (B) amount of money damages sought
    (C) nature of the action
    (D) probable duration of the trial

26. A statute is best defined as

    (A) a legislative enactment
    (B) a legal prosecution
    (C) adjective law
    (D) a codification of principles and procedure

27. In the case of a disagreement in a jury

    (A) the opinion of the jury foreman shall be the jury's verdict
    (B) a quotient verdict is obtained
    (C) court may order a partial retrial if the jury's disagreement was on a separate phase of the litigation
    (D) the court dismisses the jury and a retrial is ordered without a jury

28. When the judge enters the courtroom

    (A) everyone is directed to rise
    (B) only the litigants are directed to rise
    (C) all except court employees are directed to rise
    (D) all court employees are directed to rise

29. A statute of limitations places a restriction on the

    (A) maximum penalty that may be imposed
    (B) time within which an action should be commenced
    (C) number of causes of action that may be pleaded at one time
    (D) amount and quality of evidence that may be introduced

30. According to the Criminal Procedure Law, the one of the following who is not a peace officer is a

    (A) court officer
    (B) criminal investigator attached to District Attorney's office in Westchester County
    (C) State parole officer
    (D) civilian employee of State Prison

31. A summons is usually attached to a (an)

    (A) complaint
    (B) answer
    (C) reply
    (D) counterclaim

32. A case which has been adjourned is

    (A) stricken from the calendar
    (B) postponed for a time
    (C) dismissed without prejudice
    (D) tried without a jury

33. An objection to a juror for which no reason is given is called

    (A) an exception
    (B) peremptory challenge
    (C) challenge for cause
    (D) challenge to the favor

34. A trial jury consisting of 12 persons is called a

    (A) struck jury
    (B) special jury
    (C) grand jury
    (D) petit jury

35. A fictitious name used by a person is called a (an)

    (A) alibi
    (B) alias
    (C) facsimile
    (D) alienist

36. A "recidivist" is

    (A) mentally incompetent
    (B) incapable of committing crime
    (C) a psychopath
    (D) an habitual offender

37. A "writ of certiorari" is a legal process for the purpose of

    (A) reviewing the decision or ruling of an administrative board
    (B) reviewing the denial of bail
    (C) compelling a public officer to perform a duty imposed by law
    (D) correcting an error or amending the allegations in a pleading

38. The "Statute of Frauds"

    (A) defines the several degrees of larceny
    (B) requires certain contracts to be written
    (C) requires written instruments to be witnessed and signed
    (D) makes contracts made by minors voidable

39. The Criminal Procedure Law is

    (A) contained in the Civil Practice Law and Rules of New York State
    (B) defines crimes and their punishments
    (C) a uniform and comprehensive system of criminal procedure
    (D) a law that regulates criminal procedures uniformly throughout the United States

40. In the trial of a felony action, the court charges the jury

    (A) before People's summation
    (B) before the defendant's summation
    (C) after the summation by both parties
    (D) before the summation of either party

41. In legal parlance, an "alienist" is one who

    (A) has entered this country illegally
    (B) constantly changes his or her name
    (C) specializes in mental disorders
    (D) studies the causes of crime

42. The "polling of a jury" is exercised

    (A) before the jury is empaneled
    (B) after the jurors are sworn
    (C) after the verdict
    (D) after the judge's charge

43. In the trial of a felony action, the jurors must be warned by the court after each adjournment, that they shall not

    (A) be separated
    (B) converse among themselves
    (C) form any opinion as to the case until the cause is submitted to them
    (D) communicate with other persons

44. In a criminal action, "impeaching a witness" means

    (A) compelling a witness to testify
    (B) rejecting a witness as incompetent
    (C) attacking the credibility of a witness
    (D) holding a witness for perjury

45. A prosecution for murder must be commenced within

    (A) 5 years
    (B) 10 years
    (C) 20 years
    (D) any period of time after the act

46. The *least accurate* of the following statements, is

    (A) a panel is a group of jurors summoned to report for duty at a term of court
    (B) a criminal action is brought in the name of the People of New York
    (C) the term "veniremen" means place of trial
    (D) the term "res" means a thing

47. The final determination by a judge that a sum of money is owed to one of the parties in a law suit is called a

    (A) judgment
    (B) decision
    (C) verdict
    (D) report

48. A plaintiff is to a complaint as a defendant is to a (an)

    (A) rebuttal
    (B) reply
    (C) answer
    (D) demurrage

49. A person whose negligence has caused damage to another is called a

    (A) tortfeasor
    (B) decedent
    (C) testator
    (D) demurrer

50. A restraining order issued by a court is called a (an)

    (A) subpoena
    (B) injunction
    (C) mandamus
    (D) rescission

51. Appeals from convictions for murder in the first degree go in the first instance to the

    (A) Appellate Term of the Supreme Court
    (B) County Court
    (C) Court of Appeals
    (D) Appellate Division of the Supreme Court

52. A person who dies in New York leaving a will disposing of real property in New Jersey is said to have died

    (A) interstate
    (B) intestate
    (C) testate
    (D) intrastate

53. The memorandum of a judge explaining the reasons for a decision in a case is called the

    (A) judgment
    (B) opinion
    (C) verdict
    (D) sentence

54. If an attempt is made to free the defendant at a murder trial by the use of automatic firearms, the court officer's primary obligation is to

    (A) handcuff the defendant to prevent escape
    (B) protect the spectators and court officials from possible harm
    (C) commit to memory a good description of those assisting in the delivery of the defendant
    (D) advise the spectators and court officials not to give way to panic

55. The best attitude for a court officer to assume toward the public is to

    (A) be kind and pleasant, ready to assist, but never argumentative
    (B) be very friendly and cultivate all the acquaintances possible as they may prove useful in the future
    (C) hold himself or herself apart and assume a superior manner as the public should be taught to look up to and respect a representative of the law
    (D) be understanding and sympathetic

56. The legal term used to describe all the means by which the truth regarding any alleged matter of fact is established or disproved in court is

    (A) testimony
    (B) exhibit
    (C) evidence
    (D) proof

57. A suspended sentence is a (an)

    (A) indeterminate sentence
    (B) postponed sentence
    (C) decreased sentence
    (D) cumulative sentence

58. A person who, when examined under oath, deliberately gives false information commits the crime of

    (A) barratry
    (B) forgery
    (C) perjury
    (D) slander

59. If a witness under a severe cross-examination becomes indignant and engages the attorney in a heated argument, a court officer should

    (A) await any action the judge may take
    (B) order the witness to be more respectful
    (C) try to attract the attention of the witness
    (D) call for assistance

60. If a spectator in a court room faints and falls to the floor, he or she should be

    (A) placed in a chair in a sitting position
    (B) laid on a flat surface with the head lower than the body
    (C) picked up and removed to a hospital
    (D) placed on the stomach with the head turned to the side

61. Several of the spectators in a courtroom get into a fight and one of them is seriously injured. As a court officer, the *first* thing you should do is to

    (A) get the facts and make a report
    (B) call an ambulance or a physician
    (C) hold the people who engaged in the fight and arrest them for creating a public nuisance
    (D) evacuate the courtroom

62. A true legal copy of an official court record is called a

    (A) facsimile
    (B) transcript
    (C) certificate
    (D) folio

63. When the doors of a court are closed and only the persons involved in a case are admitted, the proceeding is called

    (A) ex parte
    (B) in camera
    (C) coram nobis
    (D) extra judicial

64. A term sometimes used in medical jurisprudence to designate a mercy killing or painless death in the case of an incurable disease is

    (A) genocide
    (B) uxoricide
    (C) paranoia
    (D) euthanasia

65. An endorsement signed by the foreman of the grand jury that an indictment has been found on the concurrence of at least twelve grand jurors is known as a (an)

    (A) presentment
    (B) true bill
    (C) commission
    (D) ascertainment

66. An allegation made to a magistrate that a person has been guilty of some designated crime is known as a (an)

    (A) charge
    (B) inquest
    (C) incrimination
    (D) information

67. A person who, after the commission of a felony, aids the offender to escape arrest, knowing that such offender has committed a felony, is defined in the Penal Law as a (an)

    (A) principal
    (B) accomplice
    (C) accessory
    (D) conspirator

68. A term used in law to describe licentious art or literature is

    (A) pornography
    (B) amercement
    (C) masochism
    (D) didacticism

69. An agreement to conceal a crime or to abstain from prosecuting a crime for some consideration is known in the Penal Law as

    (A) compounding a crime
    (B) compromising a crime
    (C) obstruction of justice
    (D) misprision of crime

70. The one of the following words, which means a wrongdoer, is

    (A) litigant
    (B) complainant
    (C) tortfeasor
    (D) prosecutor

71. A paper served on the clerk of the court to have a civil case placed on the calendar for trial is a (an)

    (A) note of issue
    (B) lis pendens
    (C) order of trial
    (D) motion for trial

72. A Plaintiff is to a Defendant as an Appellant is to a (an)

    (A) Appellor
    (B) Petitioner
    (C) Relator
    (D) Respondent

73. A Felony is to an Indictment as a Misdemeanor is to a (an)

    (A) Presentment
    (B) Complaint
    (C) Information
    (D) Summons

74. Defendant is to Counterclaim as Plaintiff is to

    (A) Answer
    (B) Denial
    (C) Reply
    (D) Complaint

75. A judgment entered in consequence of the nonappearance of a party in a civil action is called

    (A) interlocutory
    (B) declaratory
    (C) nonsuit
    (D) default

76. The papers containing the names of the jurors who are being impaneled are called

    (A) exhibits
    (B) canons
    (C) ballots
    (D) drafts

77. Sentences imposed by a court on a defendant convicted of several crimes but with the provision that the sentences shall be served at the same time are

    (A) consecutive
    (B) cumulative
    (C) concurrent
    (D) intermittent

78. The science of fingerprint identification is called

    (A) ballistics
    (B) semantics
    (C) dactylography
    (D) anthropometry

79. A designation given to a crime punishable by imprisonment in a state prison is

    (A) malicious
    (B) lascivious
    (C) turpitude
    (D) infamous

80. The inducement that incites or stimulates a person to commit a criminal act is the

    (A) intent
    (B) deliberation
    (C) premeditation
    (D) motive

81. Where a New York statute requires 5 days notice of a hearing to be held at 10 A.M. on June 11, there is sufficient compliance if such notice is served prior to but not later than

    (A) the close of business on June 6
    (B) 10 A.M. on June 6
    (C) midnight on June 5
    (D) the close of business on June 5

82. In selecting a jury, the parties to the litigation have a certain number of peremptory challenges. The word "peremptory" means most nearly

    (A) discretionary
    (B) absolute
    (C) preliminary
    (D) inalienable

83. A guardian ad litem is a guardian for

    (A) the suit
    (B) all purposes
    (C) the purpose of conserving real property
    (D) the purpose of representing a corporation

84. The fundamental basis for allowing people to be free on bail is the

    (A) prevention of overcrowding in prisons
    (B) centralization of administrative responsibility in criminal cases
    (C) detection of violations of the law
    (D) prevention of punishment before trial

85. That system of law that does not rest for its authority on acts passed by the legislature is called

    (A) statutory law
    (B) civil law
    (C) common law
    (D) codified law

86. You are an officer assigned to guard the door in a criminal court where an important robbery case is on trial. A man whom you know not to be a police officer approaches and requests admission. In speaking with him you observe that he has a revolver in his overcoat pocket. You should

    (A) refuse to admit him
    (B) summon another court officer and search him
    (C) ask him to identify himself
    (D) refuse him admittance and call the matter to the attention of a detective who is nearby.

87. You are an officer in charge of a prison pen in which there are a large number of men awaiting trial for felony. One of them falls to the floor and cries out that he has been poisoned. You should

    (A) open the door of the pen and, with the assistance of another officer, remove him

    (B) summon other officers to guard the pen while you take him to the doctor's office
    (C) make him as comfortable as possible pending the arrival of a physician
    (D) summon a number of other court officers before opening the pen door

88. As a court officer in charge of a jury which is deliberating, you are approached by one of the attorneys in the case who asks you to inform him as to how the jury is voting. You should

    (A) tell him it is none of his business
    (B) tell him that the rules prohibit your giving him any information
    (C) call another officer and have the attorney arraigned before the court
    (D) procure his name and report him to the judge immediately

89. You are in charge of a jury that is deliberating on a case and one of the jurors becomes seriously ill, you should

    (A) permit the jurors to continue their discussion of the case
    (B) stop all discussion and notify the clerk of the court
    (C) send for an ambulance
    (D) render first aid and, when the juror recovers, return him or her to the jury room

90. An attorney in a case on trial in a court in which you are an officer requests that you refer to him any person who is in need of legal services. You should

    (A) tell him that it is against the rules
    (B) procure his name and address, give it to the judge, and tell the judge what the attorney has said
    (C) immediately arraign him before the court and explain what he has said to you
    (D) agree to do so only if you think he is a good attorney

91. You are assigned, as an officer, to the door of a criminal court while three desperate criminals are being sentenced for robbery.

Your instructions are to admit no one to the courtroom. The detective who made the arrest and who is late for the proceeding requests that he be admitted, as the judge may want to speak to him. You should

(A) admit him
(B) obey the orders given to the letter
(C) ask another officer to find out if the judge wants to see the detective
(D) tell the detective to wait until the sentencing is over

92. You are one of three officers assigned to guard a jury in a hotel where they are confined during the trial of a case. A hotel employee tells you that a physician is on the telephone and wants to speak to one of the jurors as his wife has had a serious accident. You should

(A) convey the message to the juror immediately
(B) permit the juror to talk to the physician
(C) speak to the juror and tell him that he will have to get in touch with the judge
(D) advise the employee to tell the doctor that you will convey the message as soon as you can get the judge's permission to do so

93. In legal parlance, an "execution" is

(A) a decree appointing an executor of a decedent's estate
(B) a summons
(C) a court process directing the satisfaction of a judgment
(D) the service of a warrant

94. Direct evidence is required in prosecutions of criminal homicides to prove the

(A) identity of the victim
(B) death of the victim
(C) killing by the accused
(D) intent

95. A person imprisoned or restrained in his or her liberty within the State of New York is entitled to a hearing to inquire into the cause of the imprisonment or restraint. Such hearing is brought on by a writ of

(A) attachment
(B) habeas corpus
(C) replevin
(D) arrest

96. A Magistrate is

(A) any judicial officer
(B) a judicial officer of any court, except those that are not courts of record
(C) any officer having power to issue a warrant for the arrest of a person charged with a crime
(D) any officer authorized by law to accept bail

97. Evidence that the accused was voluntarily intoxicated at the time of committing the crime for which he or she is on trial is admissible evidence

(A) as a defense based on excuse or lack of knowledge at time the crime was committed
(B) whenever a specific intent is a necessary element to constitute a particular degree of the crime charged
(C) only when total and not partial intoxication prevented the forming of a specific criminal intent
(D) solely for the purpose of mitigating the punishment upon conviction of the crime charged

98. An appeal from which of the following courts is *not* taken directly to the Appellate Division of the Supreme Court?

(A) Surrogate's Court
(B) Civil Court
(C) Appellate Term of the Supreme Court
(D) Supreme Court

99. To control bleeding from a cut artery, pressure may be applied at some point where the main artery to the injured part lies close to the bone. The one of the following which is not a recognized "pressure

point" where hand or finger pressure against a bone may stop bleeding is

(A) the body side of the upper arm half-way between the shoulder and elbow
(B) just in front of the ear
(C) behind the inner end of the collar bone
(D) about 1 inch below the kneecap

100. The degree of the crime of larceny is never affected by the

(A) intent of the perpetrator
(B) kind of property stolen
(C) place from which the property is stolen
(D) time when the property is taken

101. Every injured person is potentially a patient in shock and should be regarded and treated as such. The one of the following which is *not* a common symptom of shock is

(A) shallow, irregular breathing
(B) nausea
(C) weak pulse
(D) hot, dry skin

102. It would be most *incorrect* to state that

(A) an "alienist" is a physician or psychiatrist specializing in the mental disease or conditions of persons
(B) a "bill of attainder" is a law that fixes the guilt of a person without the benefit of a trial
(C) a "chattel" is an unoccupied house or other building
(D) a "defalcation" is an embezzlement

103. For the purposes of the statute of limitations, criminal prosecution is deemed to have been commenced when

(A) an information is laid before a magistrate
(B) the defendant is lawfully arrested
(C) an indictment, having been presented by the Grand Jury, is received and filed in court
(D) the crime in question becomes or is made known to the police

104. Never administer a liquid to an unconscious person. The basic reason for this admonition is most probably the fact that

(A) liquids will have a harmful effect on the heart under these circumstances
(B) the body of the person may already be overheated
(C) the liquids may cause the person to choke
(D) alcohol is an excessive stimulant

105. A break in a bone should be classified as a compound fracture if

(A) one or more parts of the bone protrude through the surface of the skin
(B) any portion of the bone is splintered
(C) the bone is broken in two or more places
(D) the break in the bone is vertical rather than horizontal

106. The essential distinction between a felony and a misdemeanor under the criminal laws of New York State depends primarily on the

(A) seriousness of the injury caused by the criminal act
(B) actual penalty imposed on the perpetrator after conviction
(C) inherent evil in the act itself that the community recognizes as socially and morally wrong
(D) maximum penalty that the court may legally impose upon the perpetrator after conviction of the crime charged

107. Smith says that Jones broke into a safe in a factory office at 2 A.M. Brown swears that he saw Jones walking out of the factory shortly after that time. The evidence of Brown is said to be

(A) hearsay
(B) demonstrative
(C) corroborative
(D) presumptive

108. Witnesses not actually testifying may be excluded from the courtroom while another witness is testifying. The most logical basis for such procedure is to

   (A) avoid the possibility of being prejudiced
   (B) permit the testifying witness to testify without fear of reprisal
   (C) prevent perjury
   (D) keep certain matters in confidence

109. The jury which has been chosen for a criminal trial may visit the place in which the crime is alleged to have been committed provided the

   (A) crime charged is a felony
   (B) court believes that such visit is proper
   (C) jury feels that such a visit might prove helpful
   (D) crime charged is murder

110. The law will allow a compulsory disclosure of

   (A) the deliberations of a grand jury
   (B) the deliberations of a trial jury
   (C) matters that transpired during a criminal trial
   (D) the deliberations of the court

111. If evidence is illegally seized, its use in the courts of New York State would be

   (A) illegal
   (B) compulsory self-incrimination
   (C) incompetent
   (D) legal

112. Lie detector machines are operated on the principle that

   (A) most persons are unable to tell a consistent story
   (B) emotional stress causes physiological changes in a person
   (C) many individuals are not afraid to lie
   (D) a guilty person will unconsciously associate ideas in an indicative manner

113. A single action that is divided into two or more separate actions, each of which terminates in a separate judgment, is known as

   (A) consolidation
   (B) severance
   (C) joinder
   (D) election of remedies

114. Of the following instances, the one in which the Court of Appeals has the power to review the questions of *fact*, is

   (A) contested divorce actions
   (B) any felony committed by a minor
   (C) death penalty case
   (D) personal injury case based on negligence

115. That a court is a court of record means that

   (A) its process is valid anywhere in the State
   (B) the justices are elected rather than appointed
   (C) it was created by the State Constitution
   (D) its records are perpetuated

116. Where a complaint is dismissed "without prejudice," it means that

   (A) it is a final determination of the merits
   (B) no costs will be charged against the plaintiff
   (C) the cause of action may be brought again
   (D) the defendant will hold no prejudice against the plaintiff

117. The best definition of a motion is

   (A) an application for an order
   (B) an application for a dismissal
   (C) the right to introduce evidence
   (D) an application to start a suit

118. A reply is served if

    (A) there are inconsistencies in the plaintiff's complaint
    (B) corrections in the plaintiff's complaint are to be made
    (C) the defendant sets up a counter claim in his answer
    (D) the plaintiff intends to set up counterclaims

119. The main distinction between a riot and an unlawful assembly is

    (A) the disturbance of peace
    (B) the power to make good the threats
    (C) the number of persons
    (D) existence of threats

120. In legal parlance, an "information" is

    (A) an informer's information to the District Attorney
    (B) an allegation to a magistrate that a person has committed a designated crime
    (C) in the nature of a bill of particulars
    (D) the report of a grand jury after an investigation of crime

121. A person accused of crime may be permitted to testify before a grand jury provided

    (A) he or she has not been arrested
    (B) it is a capital crime
    (C) he or she is a citizen
    (D) he or she files a request to be heard

122. If the court deems the evidence insufficient to warrant a conviction of one or more of the crimes in the indictment, it may advise the jury to acquit the defendant thereof. In this connection, the jury

    (A) need not follow the recommendation until evidence on both sides has been introduced
    (B) must follow the advice
    (C) may disregard the advice if it believes otherwise
    (D) may accept the advice on condition that a new trial be ordered

123. Legal proceedings concerning the property of a deceased person are ordinarily held in the

    (A) Supreme Court
    (B) Surrogate's Court
    (C) County Court
    (D) Court of Claims

124. "A wrong is not presumed" means most nearly

    (A) one cannot presume that a person has done wrong just because he or she has committed a crime
    (B) hard cases make bad law
    (C) one wrong does not excuse another
    (D) a person is innocent until found guilty

125. Generally, the plaintiff furnishes the court with copies of the summons and pleadings, noting in the margin which allegations are admitted and which are denied. These papers are known as

    (A) supplemental pleadings
    (B) marked pleadings
    (C) alternative pleadings
    (D) amended pleadings

Correct Answers

1. A	26. A	51. C	76. C	101. D
2. C	27. C	52. C	77. C	102. C
3. B	28. A	53. B	78. C	103. C
4. B	29. B	54. B	79. D	104. C
5. B	30. D	55. A	80. D	105. A
6. B	31. A	56. C	81. A	106. D
7. B	32. B	57. B	82. B	107. C
8. C	33. B	58. C	83. A	108. A
9. D	34. D	59. A	84. D	109. B
10. B	35. B	60. B	85. C	110. C
11. C	36. D	61. B	86. D	111. D
12. C	37. A	62. B	87. D	112. B
13. C	38. B	63. B	88. D	113. B
14. B	39. C	64. D	89. B	114. C
15. A	40. C	65. B	90. B	115. D
16. C	41. C	66. D	91. B	116. C
17. A	42. C	67. C	92. D	117. A
18. D	43. C	68. A	93. C	118. C
19. D	44. C	69. A	94. B	119. B
20. B	45. D	70. C	95. B	120. B
21. A	46. C	71. A	96. C	121. D
22. D	47. B	72. D	97. B	122. B
23. C	48. C	73. C	98. B	123. B
24. B	49. A	74. D	99. D	124. D
25. A	50. B	75. D	100. A	125. B

Explanatory Answers

1. **(A)** Where the facts are not disputed, the jury has nothing to find, and the matter becomes a question of law for the court. In such instance as the judge would set aside a contrary verdict as against the weight of evidence, he or she may direct a verdict.

2. **(C)** "Et al." means "and others." Since "others" is plural, "et al." indicates that there are two or more defendants in addition to Jones.

3. **(B)** "Prima facie" evidence is evidence so strong that it is sufficient to establish the fact unless rebutted.

4. **(B)** An *authentication* is an attestation by a proper officer that a record is in due form of law. A *verification* is a confirmation by affidavit of the truth of a statement. An *oath* is an attestation of the truth of a statement. The *jurat* is a certification by an officer that a writing was sworn to by the signer. *Attestation* is the act of witnessing the signing of a writing and subscribing it as such witness.

5. **(B)** Criminal contempt in a court of record consists of disorderly, contemptuous, or insolent behavior committed during the sitting of the court in its immediate view and presence and directly tending to disrupt its proceedings or to impair the respect due its authority. Criminal contempt proceedings are punitive in nature. Actions taken on civil contempt are remedial and coercive in nature.

6. **(B)** McKinney's Consolidated Laws of New York State includes all state laws with citations, notes, commentaries, and annotations from state and federal courts.

7. **(B)** A *Power of Attorney* is a written, sworn document authorizing one person to take legal action for another. *Verification* is an affidavit attached to a pleading, wherein the party swears that the contents of the pleading are true or that he believes them to be true. *Certification* is a statement signed by the clerk stating that he or she has compared a copy of a document with the original and has found the copy to be an exact copy of the original. *Substituted service* is a form of service of summons other than by personal service, such as affixing to the door.

8. **(C)** A *Statute of Limitations* states the time after which an action may not be commenced. The Statute of Limitations varies with the nature of the matter; action on a contract, for instance, must be instituted within 6 years. The *Statute of Frauds* states that certain agreements, such as agreements for sale of real property, must be in writing.

9. **(D)** In criminal cases, the presence of the defendant when the verdict is rendered is required only if the charge is a felony. In misdemeanor cases, the defendant need not be present as long as counsel is present. In civil cases, the presence of litigants is not required.

10. **(B)** Both are sworn, signed statements, but a *deposition* is specifically the testimony of the deponent, usually in the form of questions and answers, while an *affidavit* is any sworn statement.

11. **(C)** At *arraignment* the accused is brought before the court, the charge is read, and he or she is given an opportunity to answer it. Setting and posting of bail is incidental to the arraignment, and not an integral part of it.

12. **(C)** The Latin word *res* means "thing." The subject matter or property is the thing or res with which an action is concerned. *Fee Simple* is full, unencumbered ownership of real property. A *Freehold* is a fee simple absolute, ownership without time limitation. *Abstract of Title* is a document prepared by a title company presenting its findings after search of title records for liens, taxes, judgments, and so forth.

13. **(C)** An *ex parte* motion is made by a party without notice to an adversary, thereby giving the adversary no opportunity to oppose. It is made in those cases in which the applicant is entitled to relief as a matter of right upon the presentation of certain proof. Motions which require that the adversary be notified so as to rebut the motion are *contested motions*.

14. **(B)** An *exception* is an attorney's formal objection to the action of the court in denying a request or overruling an objection. Objections are taken to adverse rulings and to the court's instructions to a jury.

15. **(A)** Appeals are taken directly to the Court of Appeals from the lower courts only when actions involve constitutional questions and in capital cases. Otherwise, appeals come to the Court of Appeals from the Appellate Division.

16. **(C)** *Eminent Domain* is the right of sovereignty to seize any private property for the public good in exercise of the police power of the state. *Ejectment* is eviction. An *easement* is the right of the owner of one parcel of land to use the land of another for some special purposes not inconsistent with the general property rights of the owner, such as the right to cross another's property to gain access to one's own. A *franchise* is a privilege.

17. **(A)** After a summons has been served, the server fills out the *Affidavit of Service* on the back and has it notarized. The form states that the server was over 18 years of

age, that he or she served the summons on the defendant, and that he or she knew the person served to be the defendant.

18. **(D)** Prosecution of all felonies is by *indictment*. Misdemeanors may be prosecuted on the basis of an *information*.

19. **(D)** The decision of the jury in criminal cases must be unanimous. In a civil case, 5 out of 6 or 10 out of 12 jurors may decide the case.

20. **(B)** "Polling the jury" is done by the attorney for the losing party. The attorney calls each juror by name and asks each whether or not the verdict is a true verdict. If so, the verdict is recorded.

21. **(A)** In the first and second Departments, the Appellate Division makes the rules regulating the procedures as to jurors. The rules also regulate the duties of the County Clerk and County Jury Board.

22. **(D)** A child under 12 may testify without oath if, in the opinion of the court, the child does not understand the nature of an oath but that child is sufficiently intelligent to justify reception of the child's evidence. Such testimony must be corroborated.

23. **(C)** *Civil contempt* is remedial and coercive in nature. It involves a neglect or violation of duty or other misconduct by which a right or a remedy of a party to a civil action or proceeding pending in the court may be defeated, impaired or prejudiced. *Criminal contempt* may occur in any court. It is punitive in nature. The State and the People are interested in its prosecution. It does not involve any personal right or injury.

24. **(B)** "No person shall be rendered incompetent to be a witness on account of his opinions on matters of religious belief." (New York Constitution) The person may affirm to tell the truth, instead of taking an oath.

25. **(A)** The *venue* is the place of trial, generally the place where the legal cause of action arose.

26. **(A)** A *statute* is a legislative enactment. *Adjective law* is law governing procedures, such as the CPLR; *substantive law* is law defining rights, obligations, duties, and so forth, like the Penal Law.

27. **(C)** Disagreement in a civil action means that fewer than 5/6 of the jurors agree; in a criminal case disagreement occurs when only one juror is in disagreement. If the disagreement is on a separate phase of the litigation, rather than have the entire case retried, the court may order a partial retrial on the phase involved and accept the verdict of the jurors on the main phase. A *quotient verdict* is arrived at by striking an average of the jurors (in dollars) and dividing by 12. This is forbidden.

28. **(A)** Everyone, except those physically unable, is directed to rise. This is a symbol of respect and dignity, which attaches to the court.

29. **(B)** The *statute of limitations* prescribes the time periods within which various actions should be commenced. Felonies, for instance, must be prosecuted within five years.

30. **(D)** Article 2.10 of the Criminal Procedure Law enumerates who is designated a peace officer.

31. **(A)** A summons is usually attached to a complaint. However, in the Supreme Court a summons may be served without the complaint. If the summons is served with the complaint, the defendant has to file an answer. If the summons is served without the complaint, the defendant need not answer but must serve a notice of appearance on the attorney for the plaintiff.

32. **(B)** *Adjournment* means postponement.

33. **(B)** A *peremptory* challenge of a juror is a challenge for which no reason is given. A limited number of peremptory challenges is allowed. A challenge *for cause* is a challenge for a reason, such as bias. A challenge *to the favor* is a challenge for a reason such as that the juror is an interested party, perhaps an employee of one of the parties. An *exception* is an attorney's objection to a court ruling.

34. **(D)** A *petit jury* is a trial jury of 12 persons. A *struck jury* is a special or Blue Ribbon panel. A *grand jury* consisting of 16 to 23 persons is not a trial jury.

35. **(B)** An *alias* is a fictitious name. An *alibi* is a claim of being at another place at the time in question. A *facsimile* is an exact copy. An *alienist* is a psychiatrist.

36. **(D)** A *recidivist* is a backslider, a repeater or a habitual offender.

37. **(A)** A *writ of certiorari* is an order from a court to an administrative trial body to send the minutes of a trial or hearing to it so as to determine the legal procedure of the hearing. For instance, if a public employee has been dismissed, the court may determine by certiorari whether the dismissal was just and reasonable.

38. **(B)** The *statute of frauds* requires that certain contracts be written in order to be enforceable. It serves as protection for all parties concerned.

39. **(C)** The *Criminal Procedure Law* of the Consolidated Laws of New York State establishes the practice in all criminal cases and defines the authority for the orders and judgments of the courts. The law applies only within New York State.

40. **(C)** After all testimony has been given and after summation by both parties in the case, the court makes its charge to the jury. The *charge to the jury* states to the jury all matters of law that the judge considers necessary for their information as they consider and reach their verdict. The charge may also inform the jury that they are the exclusive judges of all questions of fact but that punishment should not enter their deliberations. Punishment rests with the judge.

41. **(C)** An *alienist* is a psychiatrist. An *alien* is a foreigner; an illegal alien has entered the country illegally. An *alias* is an assumed name. A *criminologist* studies causes of crime.

42. **(C)** *Polling of the jury* may occur after announcement but before recording of the verdict. The purpose is to ensure that the jurors concur.

43. **(C)** During the adjourned period, the jurors may not converse among themselves or with others on any subject connected with the trial, nor may they form or express any opinion on the matter before them until the cause is finally submitted by the court. Separation of the jury and communication on other topics are permitted.

44. **(C)** In a criminal case, *impeaching a witness* is attacking the credibility of the witness by demonstrating bad character, bias, or criminal record. A witness may also be impeached by his own actions in making contradictory statements.

45. **(D)** There is no statute of limitations for murder or for kidnapping. The statute of limitations for most other felonies is 5 years and, for most misdemeanors, 2 years.

46. **(C)** *Veniremen* are jurors. The term referring to place of trial is *venue*. All the other statements are correct.

47. **(B)** A judge reaches a *decision*; a jury renders a *verdict*. The *judgment*, the final determination of the rights of the parties in an action, is entered on the basis of either decision or verdict.

48. **(C)** A plaintiff files a complaint; a defendant files an answer to a complaint. *Complaint* is a plaintiff's pleading; *answer* is a defendant's pleading. *Demurrage* is the compensation payable to owners of a vessel for delays in loading or unloading.

49. **(A)** A *tortfeasor* is a wrongdoer or trespasser. A *decedent* is one who has died. A *testator* is one who has made a will. A *demurrer* is a legal objection by a defendant based on some irregularity.

50. **(B)** An *injunction* is a restraining order. It prohibits one party from committing any acts in violation of the other's rights. A *subpoena* is a request for the appearance of a witness in court. *Mandamus* is a court order to a public official demanding performance of a specified act. *Rescission* is the annulling of a contract by mutual agreement, by one of the parties, or by a court.

51. **(C)** Appeals from murder convictions go directly to the Court of Appeals. Appeals from other convictions ordinarily go to the Appellate Division of the Supreme Court.

52. **(C)** *Testate* means having a will. *Intestate* means without a will. *Interstate* means between states. *Intrastate* means within a state.

53. **(B)** The judge's *opinion* is the statement or memorandum usually accompanying his or her decision and explaining the reasons for the decision.

54. **(B)** In the case of an armed assailant, the first consideration on the part of the court officer is the safety of the persons in the courtroom. The officer should make every effort to subdue the armed person in order to prevent injury to others.

55. **(A)** The court officer must be ready to assist and must be friendly. He or she must never argue with parties to litigations nor with anyone else in the courtroom. The court officer must be firm in enforcement of courtroom rules.

56. **(C)** *Evidence* is the means used to prove or disprove a fact. *Proof* is the result of the evidence. An *exhibit* is a document or object introduced as evidence. *Testimony* is spoken or written evidence.

57. **(B)** A *suspended sentence* is a postponed sentence. A *cumulative sentence* is an accumulated sentence, that is, one sentence is to be served after the completion of another. An *indeterminate* sentence is not fixed, but has a minimum and maximum, as 15 to 20 years. Exact time of release is dependent upon behavior of the inmate.

58. **(C)** *Perjury* is lying under oath. *Slander* is making false statements about another so as to defame that person's character. *Forgery* is counterfeiting of documents or signature. *Barratry* is habitual bringing of groundless lawsuits.

59. **(A)** The court officer serves the bidding of the court. As long as the argument is verbal, the court officer should do nothing but await instructions from the bench. If the witness becomes physically violent, the court officer as peace officer must restrain the witness.

60. **(B)** In *fainting*, an inadequate flow of blood to the brain causes pallor and weakness. The person who has fainted should be laid flat with the head slightly lower than the trunk so that blood may flow to the head.

61. **(B)** Health and safety are first considerations. The court officer must render first aid and send for professional assistance, then consider arrest according to proper procedures.

62. **(B)** A *transcript* is a true legal copy of an official court record. A *facsimile* is a duplicate of anything.

63. **(B)** *In camera* means in chambers or in private. *Extra judicial* means outside the judicial proceedings. *Coram Nobis* is a writ of error on a judgment given by a previous court. *Ex parte* means on one side only, unilaterally.

64. **(D)** *Euthanasia* is mercy killing. *Genocide* is the extermination of an entire race or nationality. *Paranoia* is a persecution complex. *Uxoricide* is the killing of a wife by her husband.

65. **(B)** A *true bill* is an indictment on the concurrence of at least twelve grand jurors and signed by the foreman. A *presentment* is the report of a grand jury on an investigation conducted by them. A *commission* is an authority granted by a court to a person named to perform certain acts or to exercise certain jurisdiction.

66. **(D)** An *information* is a formal allegation before a magistrate, charging a named person with a specific crime and serving the same function as an indictment in a felony charge.

67. **(C)** An *accessory after the fact* is a person who, with full knowledge that a felony has been committed, aids the felon to avoid arrest, trial, and punishment by harboring and sheltering the person. Under most circumstances, such accessory after the fact is treated as a principal in the felony as are the *accomplice* who helps carry out the felony and the *conspirator* who helps plan it.

68. **(A)** *Pornography* constitutes obscene art or literature. *Amercement* is punishment by assessing and collecting a fine. *Didacticism* is boring instruction. *Masochism* is the gaining of sexual pleasure from physical pain.

69. **(A)** Taking a reward (in effect, accepting a bribe) to withhold evidence or to refrain from prosecuting a crime (in effect, to obstruct justice) is *compounding a crime*. *Compromising a crime* is adjusting of misdemeanors by mutual concession without resort to the law, a settling out of court in the criminal sphere. Compromise is legal if done according to law. *Misprision* is failure to reveal a crime.

70. **(C)** A *tortfeasor* is a wrongdoer. A *litigant* is one of the parties to a lawsuit.

71. **(A)** A *note of issue* is filed with the clerk of the court by either party in order to have the case placed on the calendar. The note of issue contains all the pertinent information: title of the case, names, and addresses of attorneys, time when the last pleading was served, whether the matter is triable by jury, and the specific nature of the action.

72. **(D)** A *respondent* answers an appellant's appeal as a defendant answers a plaintiff's charge.

73. **(C)** An *information* is the basis of jurisdiction over a misdemeanor as an indictment is the basis of jurisdiction over a felony.

74. **(D)** The *counterclaim* is in effect the defendant's "complaint" or "countercomplaint," just as the complaint is the plaintiff's claim.

75. **(D)** A *default judgment* is rendered in favor of the party that appears when the opposing party fails to appear on the trial date. A default judgment may be reopened if the court later deems that the default was excusable. An *interlocutory judgment* is a provisional, not final, judgment. A *declaratory judgment* declares the rights of the parties or expresses the opinion of the court on a question of law without ordering anything to be done. *Nonsuit* is the name of a judgment given against a plaintiff who is unable to prove a case.

76. **(C)** *Ballots* are the pieces of paper containing the names of the prospective jurors. *Canons* are laws or rules.

77. **(C)** *Concurrent sentences* are sentences for more than one crime all being served at the same time. For instance, a defendant serving 5 years for burglary and 2 years for breaking and entering need serve only the 5-year sentence, since the 2-year sentence is being served at the same time. *Consecutive* and *cumulative* sentences (the same thing) are served one after another.

78. **(C)** *Dactylography* is the science of fingerprinting. *Ballistics* is the science of projectiles that come from firearms. *Semantics* is the study of linguistics and deals with the meanings of words. *Anthropometry* is the measurement of body bones.

79. **(D)** An *infamous* crime is a felony punishable by imprisonment in a state prison. Infamous crime is a legal term. Malicious crimes, lascivious crimes, and crimes of moral turpitude (vileness) may all be felonies, but they are not legal terms.

80. **(D)** One's *motive* is one's reason for doing an act. One's *intent* is the decision to do or not to do. *Deliberation* is the act of considering in order to reach the decision. *Premeditation* is the planning of the act beforehand.

81. **(A)** The date of the hearing is June 11. Counting back 5 days, including June 11, we come to June 7. Notice must be served before June 7; the close of business June 6 is fine.

82. **(B)** *Peremptory* means absolute and without cause.

83. **(A)** A *guardian ad litem* is a guardian appointed by the court to represent the rights of a minor or incompetent in a particular civil suit. The guardianship is for this single purpose.

84. **(D)** The reason for allowing people to be free before trial is to avoid punishment without proof of guilt. The purpose of bail is to guarantee the appearance of the accused at the trial.

85. **(C)** The *common law*, the great body of unwritten law, is founded in precedent or on the decisions of courts in previous cases decided on the same or similar facts and circumstances. *Statutory law* is the written law, the laws passed by a legislature.

86. **(D)** The court officer guarding the door has the authority to refuse admittance. Noticing the revolver, but not knowing whether the person has a pistol permit, the court officer must not act hastily or belligerently, but must be wary and cautious. Since the answer choice has placed a detective nearby, the stage is set to call in the detective to do the questioning.

87. **(D)** Accused persons tend to be ingenious in devising escape methods. Poisoning of a prisoner in a holding pen seems unlikely, but it is possible that the man is truly ill. On the other hand, this may be a calculated ploy to have the gate opened and to create confusion, during which prisoners may escape. There should be a sufficient number of officers on hand before the door is opened, to check on the health of the man on the floor.

88. **(D)** This behavior constitutes contempt of court and, as such, should be reported to the judge presiding in the case.

89. **(B)** The deliberation should be stopped and the court clerk notified. If there are alternate jurors, the judge may select an alternate to take the place of the ailing juror. Deliberations may then resume.

90. **(B)** Soliciting business in this way is a violation of the Code of Ethics. This is not an emergency situation as in jury tampering or contempt of court, but the behavior should be reported to the judge for action.

91. **(B)** Your instructions are to admit no one, so admit no one. If the case has reached sentencing, the detective who made the arrest has had plenty of time to be heard.

92. **(D)** Judges are human beings, and undoubtedly the judge will act with compassion, suspend deliberation, and release the juror to go to his wife. However, only the judge has the power to suspend the deliberations. Get the message to the judge at once, so that he or she may grant this permission.

93. **(C)** In a civil case, the *execution* describes the judgment and directs the sheriff to enforce or satisfy the judgment. The judgment specifies if specific property is to be recovered, money is to be paid or performance is mandated. The decree appointing an executor of a decedent's estate is called *Letters Testamentary*.

94. **(B)** The death of the victim cannot be established by circumstantial evidence; there must be direct evidence.

95. **(B)** Habeas corpus is an order to produce a person before a court to determine the legality of detention. Its application is not limited to New York State. *Replevin* is an action to recover goods unlawfully taken or withheld.

96. **(C)** A *magistrate* is a civil officer who has the power to issue a warrant for the arrest of a person charged with a public offense. Examples include judges of Supreme Court, county courts, Court of General Sessions, Family Court, and also such nonjudicial officers, such as the Mayor or Recorder of a city.

97. **(B)** Evidence of intoxication cannot be used as a defense to the crime. However, should it be necessary to prove motive or intent as a necessary element of a crime, the jury may take into consideration the fact that the accused was intoxicated at the time.

98. **(B)** Appeals from the Civil Court go first to the Appellate Term of the Supreme Court, and only from there to the Appellate Division.

99. **(D)** In the portion of the leg just below the kneecap, the artery is not sufficiently close to the bone for application of pressure to stop the flow of blood.

100. **(A)** The intent of the perpetrator is important for the purpose of determining whether a larceny was committed but it has no role in affecting the degree of the larceny. The kind of property stolen, the dollar value of the property, the place from which the property was stolen and the time of day all help determine the degree of larceny.

101. **(D)** The symptoms of shock are pale, cold, clammy skin; weak pulse; and shallow breathing.

102. **(C)** *Chattel* is property that is not realty.

103. **(C)** Action in a criminal prosecution has commenced when an indictment has been rendered, received and filed in the proper court or when an information has been laid before a magistrate and a warrant has been issued. Either stops the running of the statute of limitations.

104. **(C)** An unconscious person is unable to swallow, so administering of a liquid may cause choking.

105. **(A)** The word "compound" of *compound fracture* means that more than one thing has happened. The bone has broken and the skin has been punctured by the bone. If the skin is not broken, the fracture is a simple fracture, no matter how many breaks there are or how serious a fracture it may be.

106. **(D)** The fundamental distinction between "felony" and "misdemeanor" rests on the maximum penalty that may be imposed. The character of the crime is not determined by the extent of the injuries caused nor by the vile nature of the crime itself. A felony

is a crime punishable by death or by imprisonment in a state prison; any other crime is a misdemeanor.

107. **(C)** *Corroborative evidence* confirms or substantiates the statement of another. In this question, Brown's corroborative evidence confirms the presence of Jones at the time of the crime but not that Jones committed the crime. *Presumptive* evidence is similar to circumstantial evidence. *Hearsay* evidence is testimony based upon the witness of another (not admissible). *Demonstrative* evidence is the same as real evidence—the thing itself.

108. **(A)** A witness who has been excluded from the courtroom will be protected from the contamination of his or her own recollection by the testimony of another witness. This is the most important reason to exclude one witness during the testimony of another. The other reasons are also plausible, although the effect of exclusion on perjury is questionable.

109. **(B)** The matter of a jury's visit to the scene of a crime is left to the discretion of the court. The nature or degree of the crime is irrelevant.

110. **(C)** Any person who comes within the category of being a party properly interested in a trial or its outcome may compel the disclosure of what occurred during such trial. However, a combination of statutory law and court decisions makes the deliberations of judges, grand jurors, and trial jurors privileged.

111. **(D)** Illegally seized evidence is admissible in New York State Courts. The aggrieved party, however, may bring criminal and civil actions against the officer or persons illegally seizing such evidence. Conversely, evidence illegally seized by agents of the federal government or by persons acting at their direction is inadmissible in any of the federal courts.

112. **(B)** A person who knows that he or she is guilty of lying will suffer fear and emotional stress. Emotional stress or apprehension leads to physiological changes in blood pressure, pulse, respiration, and perspiration. The lie detector technique, the polygraph (literally, "many measures") is designed to measure and record these changes.

113. **(B)** *Severance* means cutting apart or separating. It is the opposite of consolidation. An action may be severed if the court deems it desirable in the interests of justice and if it can be done without prejudice to a substantial right of any of the parties.

114. **(C)** The essential function of the Court of Appeals is to review questions of law. However, the Court of Appeals can review questions of fact in cases involving the death penalty and in civil cases where the Appellate Division has made new findings of fact and has rendered a final judgment or order.

115. **(D)** A court of record is a court in which the acts and judicial proceedings are recorded as a permanent record, thereby serving as precedent for future decisions.

116. **(C)** Dismissal of a case *without prejudice* is not a final determination on the merits of the case, but rather a dismissal because of some technicality that can be cured. Dismissal without prejudice means that the plaintiff has not lost the right to reinstitute the action.

117. **(A)** A *motion* is an application for an order. During the pendency of an action, numerous applications may be made to the court for various orders, such as an order to set aside service of a summons or an order to amend the complaint. The papers on which these applications are brought to the attention of the court are commonly called *motion papers.*

118. **(C)** A *reply* is a plaintiff's pleading that responds to the defendant's answer if the answer has set up a counterclaim. The reply consists of denials and defenses; it must not contain any counterclaims and must be consistent with allegations in the plaintiff's complaint. Both the complaint and the reply are pleadings of the plaintiff. If the defendant's answer sets up a counterclaim, the plaintiff must make a reply; otherwise the defendant may obtain a default judgment on the counterclaim.

119. **(B)** In a *riot*, three or more persons actually disturb the peace by force or violence or threaten to disturb the peace while they have the power of immediate execution. Riot is a felony. In the case of *unlawful assembly*, three or more persons assemble with intent to commit an unlawful act with force or threaten to commit breach of peace but do not actually do so, nor do they have the power to carry out such threat immediately. Unlawful assembly is a misdemeanor.

120. **(B)** An *information* is the alleging of facts that constitute a crime and is the basis of the magistrate's jurisdiction for the issuance of a warrant of arrest. The report of a grand jury after an investigation of corruption or crime is a *presentment*.

121. **(D)** The accused may file a request to appear in person before a grand jury. Such request must be filed with the foreman of the grand jury and with the District Attorney. The accused must also file a waiver of immunity with the county clerk in order to be heard.

122. **(B)** This is a directed verdict. If the court deems evidence insufficient to warrant a conviction on one or more of the counts of an indictment or information, it may advise the jury to acquit the defendant and the jury must follow the advice. The court cannot advise the jury to convict, only to acquit.

123. **(B)** The Surrogate's Court handles matters concerning decedents' estates, probate of wills, and such. The Court of Claims handles suits against the State of New York.

124. **(D)** The basic principle of all criminal prosecutions in the United States is the presumption by the law that the defendant is presumed innocent until proved guilty.

125. **(B)** *Marked pleadings* enable the court to determine the nature of the action, which facts are at issue, and the questions of law which will be presented. *Supplemental pleadings*, filed later, show additional causes of action and new facts which occurred after the commencement of the action. *Amended pleadings* are corrections to the original pleadings. *Alternative pleadings* are usually not permitted. All pleadings should be clear and unequivocal from the outset.